THE
EMPIRE OF BUSINESS

By

ANDREW CARNEGIE

GREENWOOD PRESS, PUBLISHERS
NEW YORK   1968

First Greenwood reprinting, 1968

LIBRARY OF CONGRESS catalogue card number: 68-23280

Publishers' Note

Several of the chapters of this book first appeared in various forms in several periodicals to which acknowledgments are due:

From THE NORTH AMERICAN REVIEW
The A B C of Money and *The Bugaboo of Trusts*

From THE FORUM
What Would I Do With the Tariff if I Were Czar?

From THE NEW YORK EVENING POST
Steel Manufacture in the United States

From THE NEW YORK TRIBUNE
How to Win Fortune

From THE IRON AGE
Iron and Steel at Home and Abroad

From THE NEW YORK JOURNAL
The Three-Legged Stool

From THE YOUTH'S COMPANION
Thrift as a Duty

From THE CONTEMPORARY REVIEW of Britain
The Cost of Living in Britain Compared with the United States

From THE NINETEENTH CENTURY of Britain
The Manchester School and To-day

From MACMILLAN'S MAGAZINE
The Natural Oil and Gas Wells of Western Pennsylvania

Contents

PAGE

THE ROAD TO BUSINESS SUCCESS   *I*

A Talk to Young Men

Lessons drawn from a long business career.

THE A B C OF MONEY   *17*

Barter—the direct exchange of commodities. The needs and uses of money. Comparison of the two standards—gold and silver. How the money standard affects the credit of a nation.

THE COMMON INTEREST OF LABOUR AND CAPITAL   *57*

Employer and employe interdependent. The advantages of mutual trust. The employer who helps his workmen through education, recreation and social uplift, helps himself.

THRIFT AS A DUTY   *77*

The Duties of Rich Men

Thrift an evidence of civilization. Saving one of the highest duties of citizenship. The accumulation of a competence a duty; the acquirement of vast wealth not a virtue but a great responsibility.

HOW TO WIN FORTUNE   *85*

The advantages of an early start. College education not necessary to business success. Poor boys the successful men of to-day. Men of business ability sure of recognition.

Contents

PAGE

WEALTH AND ITS USES   *105*

Poverty an incentive to great achievement. Surplus wealth allows merely an elaboration of the simple needs of life. Wealth helps consolidation and cheapens production.

THE BUGABOO OF TRUSTS   *129*

What is a Trust? Combinations the order of the day. Trusts that increase production and reduce prices.

ANGLO-AMERICAN TRADE RELATIONS   *145*

Contrasting the commercial methods of the two countries. The part the tariff plays in trade. Protective tariff in the United States; free trade in Britain, a comparison of results.

"BUSINESS"   *159*

Business is a large word and in its primary meanings covers the whole range of man's efforts. The same principles of thrift, energy, concentration and brains win success in any branch of business from medicine to dry goods.

STEEL MANUFACTURE IN THE UNITED STATES   *193*

Some reasons why the United States has become the greatest steel-producing country in the world. Comparative costs of raw material and manufacture of steel in this country and abroad.

THE COST OF LIVING IN BRITAIN   *207*

As compared with the United States. The costs of the necessities of life in England and America. Why the American can enjoy luxuries that are denied the Englishman.

PAGE

OIL AND GAS WELLS 223

A short history of the discovery of oil and gas. The
method of driving wells and the use of the product.
The fortunes won on a small capital. The possibilities
of its use in the future.

THE THREE-LEGGED STOOL 241

Scheme of the World's Work

The triple alliance of labour, capital and business
ability is necessary to produce successfully. Each dependent on the others—combined, invincible.

RAILROADS PAST AND PRESENT 247

Railroading in the seventies; rails, systems, speeds,
salaries and methods. Railroading in the future. The
needs of the railroad man and his responsibilities.

IRON AND STEEL AT HOME AND ABROAD 257

Conditions of the iron and steel trade in the United
States and abroad compared. The future of these
metals.

THE MANCHESTER SCHOOL AND TO-DAY 263

The British contention that each nation is specially
qualified for but one general branch of industry discussed and combatted.

WHAT WOULD I DO WITH THE TARIFF IF I WERE CZAR? 277

The advantage of taxing the imported luxuries heavily
and reducing the tax on raw materials and necessities.
A few striking examples of correct and misapplied
tariffs.

INDEX 293

Introduction

THIS volume was published in 1902—in the second year of the Roosevelt administration. Though many of the articles were written in the years preceding, practically all the public questions that made the Roosevelt era exciting and memorable are passed in view. The fact that the monetary situation was still unsatisfactory, having sustained the assaults of two Bryan campaigns, gave additional importance to Carnegie's calm setting forth of the principles underlying a sound banking system; there are probably those who think that his "A B C of Money" makes timely and profitable reading today. On the railroad problem, one of the most vexing matters of Roosevelt's time, Carnegie spoke with the voice of experience, both as an ex-railroad man himself and as the largest patron of railroads in the world, for the products of his steel mills in themselves "created" more freight than the total handled by railroads of considerable size. The great strike in the anthracite regions in 1902—to name only one industrial convulsion of the period—gave particular point to his ideas on capital and labor. The trusts, the tariff, Anglo-American trade relations—on these subjects Carnegie always had plenty to say, nor could he have found a more suitable time than the beginning of the twentieth century to say it.

At this time Carnegie was in retirement, having dis-

posed of his business interests to the United States Steel
Corporation in 1901. He was much in the public eye, for
now he began distributing his wealth on a great scale.
Though he had published several books previously, none
of them, characteristically enough, dealt with subjects
that had formed the economic substance of his life. This
volume consists of a selection, made by Mr. Russell
Doubleday, from magazine articles and speeches of the
preceding twenty years. It had an excellent public wel-
come and a liberal sale.

B. J. H.

THE ROAD TO BUSINESS SUCCESS

A Talk to Young Men

Lessons drawn from a long business career.

THE ROAD TO BUSINESS SUCCESS

A Talk to Young Men

IT IS well that young men should begin at the beginning and occupy the most subordinate positions. Many of the leading business men of Pittsburg had a serious responsibility thrust upon them at the very threshold of their career. They were introduced to the broom, and spent the first hours of their business lives sweeping out the office. I notice we have janitors and janitresses now in offices, and our young men unfortunately miss that salutary branch of a business education. But if by chance the professional sweeper is absent any morning the boy who has the genius of the future partner in him will not hesitate to try his hand at the broom. The other day a fond fashionable mother in Michigan asked a young man whether he had ever seen a young lady sweep in a room so grandly as her Priscilla. He said no, he never had, and the mother was gratified beyond measure, but then said he, after a pause, "What I should like to see her do is sweep out a room." It does not hurt the newest comer to sweep out the office if necessary. I was one of those sweepers myself, and who do you suppose were my fellow sweepers? David McCargo, now superintendent of the Alleghany Valley Railroad; Robert Pitcairn, Super-

From an address to Students of the Curry Commercial College, Pittsburg, June 23, 1885.

1

intendent of the Pennsylvania Railroad, and Mr. Moreland, City Attorney. We all took turns, two each morning
did the sweeping; and now I remember Davie was so
proud of his clean white shirt bosom that he used to
spread over it an old silk bandana handkerchief which he
kept for the purpose, and we other boys thought he was
putting on airs. So he was. None of us had a silk handkerchief.

Assuming that you have all obtained employment and
are fairly started, my advice to you is "aim high." I
would not give a fig for the young man who does not
already see himself the partner or the head of an important firm. Do not rest content for a moment in your
thoughts as head clerk, or foreman, or general manager
in any concern, no matter how extensive. Say each to yourself, "My place is at the top." *Be king in your dreams.*
Make your vow that you will reach that position, with
untarnished reputation, and make no other vow to dis-
tract your attention, except the very commendable one
that when you are a member of the firm or before that,
if you have been promoted two or three times, you will
form another partnership with the loveliest of her sex—
a partnership to which our new partnership act has no
application. The liability there is never limited.

Let me indicate two or three conditions essential to
success. Do not be afraid that I am going to moralize, or
inflict a homily upon you. I speak upon the subject only
from the view of a man of the world, desirous of aiding
you to become successful business men. You all know that
there is no genuine, praiseworthy success in life if you
are not honest, truthful, fair-dealing. I assume you are
and will remain all these, and also that you are determined to live pure, respectable lives, free from pernicious

or equivocal associations with one sex or the other. There is no creditable future for you else. Otherwise your learning and your advantages not only go for naught, but serve to accentuate your failure and your disgrace. I hope you will not take it amiss if I warn you against three of the gravest dangers which will beset you in your upward path.

The first and most seductive, and the destroyer of most young men, is the drinking of liquor. I am no temperance lecturer in disguise, but a man who knows and tells you what observation has proved to him; and I say to you that you are more likely to fail in your career from acquiring the habit of drinking liquor than from any, or all, the other temptations likely to assail you. You may yield to almost any other temptation and reform——may brace up, and if not recover lost ground, at least remain in the race and secure and maintain a respectable position. But from the insane thirst for liquor escape is almost impossible. I have known but few exceptions to this rule. First, then, you must not drink liquor to excess. Better if you do not touch it at all——much better; but if this be too hard a rule for you then take your stand firmly here:——Resolve never to touch it except at meals. A glass at dinner will not hinder your advance in life or lower your tone; but I implore you hold it inconsistent with the dignity and self-respect of gentlemen, with what is due from yourselves to yourselves, being the men you are, and especially the men you are determined to become, to drink a glass of liquor at a bar. Be far too much of the gentleman ever to enter a barroom. You do not pursue your careers in safety unless you stand firmly upon this ground. Adhere to it and you have escaped danger from the deadliest of your foes.

The next greatest danger to a young business man in this community I believe to be that of speculation. When I was a telegraph operator here we had no Exchanges in the City, but the men or firms who speculated upon the Eastern Exchanges were necessarily known to the operators. They could be counted on the fingers of one hand. These men were not our citizens of first repute: they were regarded with suspicion. I have lived to see all of these speculators irreparably ruined men, bankrupt in money and bankrupt in character. There is scarcely an instance of a man who has made a fortune by speculation and kept it. Gamesters die poor, and there is certainly not an instance of a speculator who has lived a life creditable to himself, or advantageous to the community. The man who grasps the morning paper to see first how his speculative ventures upon the Exchanges are likely to result, unfits himself for the calm consideration and proper solution of business problems, with which he has to deal later in the day, and saps the sources of that persistent and concentrated energy upon which depend the permanent success, and often the very safety, of his main business.

The speculator and the business man tread diverging lines. The former depends upon the sudden turn of fortune's wheel; he is a millionnaire to-day, a bankrupt to-morrow. But the man of business knows that only by years of patient, unremitting attention to affairs can he earn his reward, which is the result, not of chance, but of well-devised means for the attainment of ends. During all these years his is the cheering thought that by no possibility can he benefit himself without carrying prosperity to others. The speculator on the other hand had better never have lived so far as the good of others or the good of the community is concerned. Hundreds of young men were tempted in this city not long since to gamble in oil, and many were ruined; all were injured whether they lost or won. You may be, nay, you are certain to be similarly tempted; but when so tempted I hope you will remember this advice. Say to the tempter who asks you to risk your small savings, that if ever you decide to speculate you are determined to go to a regular and well-conducted house where they cheat fair. You can get fair play and about an equal chance upon the red and black in such a place; upon the Exchange you have neither. You might as well try your luck with the three-card-monte man. There is another point involved in speculation. Nothing is more essential to young business men than untarnished credit, credit begotten of confidence in their prudence, principles and stability of character. Well, believe me, nothing kills credit sooner in any Bank Board than the knowledge that either firms or men engage in speculation. It matters not a whit whether gains or losses be the temporary result of these operations. The moment a man is known to speculate, his credit is impaired, and soon thereafter it is gone. How can a man be credited whose resources may be swept away in one hour by a panic among gamesters? Who can tell how he stands among them? except that this is certain: he has given due notice that he may stand to lose all, so that those who credit him have themselves to blame. Resolve to be business men, but speculators never.

The third and last danger against which I shall warn you is one which has wrecked many a fair craft which started well and gave promise of a prosperous voyage. It is the perilous habit of indorsing—all the more dangerous, inasmuch as it assails one generally in the garb of friendship. It appeals to your generous instincts, and you say, "How can I refuse to lend my name only, to assist a friend?" It is because there is so much that is true and commendable in that view that the practice is so dangerous. Let me endeavour to put you upon safe honourable grounds in regard to it. I would say to you to make it a rule now, *never indorse:* but this is too much like never taste wine, or never smoke, or any other of the "nevers." They generally result in exceptions. You will as business men now and then probably become security for friends. Now, here is the line at which regard for the success of friends should cease and regard for your own honour begin.

If you owe anything, all your capital and all your effects are a solemn trust in your hands to be held inviolate for the security of those who have trusted you. Nothing can be done by you with honour which jeopardizes these first claims upon you. When a man in debt indorses for another, it is not his own credit or his own capital he risks, it is that of his own creditors. He violates a trust. Mark you then, never indorse until you have cash means not required for your own debts, and never indorse beyond those means.

Before you indorse at all, consider indorsements as gifts, and ask yourselves whether you wish to make the gift to your friend and whether the money is really yours to give and not a trust for your creditors.

You are not safe, gentlemen, unless you stand firmly upon this as the only ground which an honest business man can occupy.

I beseech you avoid liquor, speculation and indorsement. Do not fail in either, for liquor and speculation are the Scylla and Charybdis of the young man's business sea, and indorsement his rock ahead.

Assuming you are safe in regard to these your gravest dangers, the question now is how to rise from the subordinate position we have imagined you in, through the successive grades to the position for which you are, in my opinion, and, I trust, in your own, evidently intended. I can give you the secret. It lies mainly in this. Instead of the question, "What must I do for my employer?" substitute "What can I do?" Faithful and conscientious discharge of the duties assigned you is all very well, but the verdict in such cases generally is that you perform your present duties so well that you had better continue performing them. Now, young gentlemen, this will not do. It will not do for the coming partners. There must be something beyond this. We make Clerks, Bookkeepers, Treasurers, Bank Tellers of this class, and there they remain to the end of the chapter. The rising man must do something exceptional, and beyond the range of his special department. HE MUST ATTRACT ATTENTION. A shipping clerk, he may do so by discovering in an invoice an error with which he has nothing to do, and which has escaped the attention of the proper party. If a weighing clerk, he may save for the firm by doubting the adjustment of the scales and having them corrected, even if this be the province of the master mechanic. If a messenger boy, even he can lay the seed of promotion by going beyond the letter of his instructions in order to secure the desired reply. There is no service so low and simple, neither any so high, in which the young man of ability and willing disposition cannot readily and almost daily prove himself capable of greater trust and usefulness, and, what is equally important, show his invincible determination to rise. Some day, in your own department, you will be directed to do or say something which you know will prove disadvantageous to the interest of the firm. Here is your chance. Stand up like a man and say so. Say it boldly, and give your reasons, and thus prove to your employer that, while his thoughts have been engaged upon other matters, you have been studying during hours when perhaps he thought you asleep, how to advance his interests. You may be right or you may be wrong, but in either case you have gained the first condition of success. You have attracted attention. Your employer has found that he has not a mere hireling in his service, but a man; not one who is content to give so many hours of work for so many dollars in return, but one who devotes his spare hours and constant thoughts to the business. Such an employe must perforce be thought of, and thought of kindly and well. It will not be long before his advice is asked in his special branch, and if the advice given be sound, it will soon be asked and taken upon questions of broader bearing. This means partnership; if not with present employers then with others. Your foot, in such a case, is upon the ladder; the amount of climbing done depends entirely upon yourself.

One false axiom you will often hear, which I wish to guard you against: "Obey orders if you break owners." Don't you do it. This is no rule for you to follow. Always break orders to save owners. There never was a great character who did not sometimes smash the routine regulations and make new ones for himself. The rule is only suitable for such as have no aspirations, and you have not forgotten that you are destined to be owners and to make orders and break orders. Do not hesitate to do it whenever you are sure the interests of your employer will be thereby promoted and when you are so sure of the result that you are willing to take the responsibility. You will never be a partner unless you know the business of your department far better than the owners possibly can. When called to account for your independent action, show him the result of your genius, and tell him that you knew that it would be so; show him how mistaken the orders were. Boss your boss just as soon as you can; try it on early. There is nothing he will like so well if he is the right kind of boss; if he is not, he is not the man for you to remain with—leave him whenever you can, even at a present sacrifice, and find one capable of discerning genius. Our young partners in the Carnegie firm have won their spurs by showing that we did not know half as well what was wanted as they did. Some of them have acted upon occasion with me as if they owned the firm and I was but some airy New Yorker presuming to advise upon what I knew very little about. Well, they are not interfered with much now. They were the true bosses—the very men we were looking for.

There is one sure mark of the coming partner, the future millionnaire; his revenues always exceed his expenditures. He begins to save early, almost as soon as he begins to earn. No matter how little it may be possible to save, save that little. Invest it securely, not necessarily in bonds, but in anything which you have good reason to believe will be profitable, but no gambling with it, remember. A rare chance will soon present itself for investment. The little you have saved will prove the basis for an amount of credit utterly surprising to you. Capitalists trust the saving young man. For every hundred dollars you can produce as the result of hard-won savings, Midas, in search of a partner, will lend or credit a thousand; for every thousand, fifty thousand. It is not capital that your seniors require, it is the man who has proved that he has the business habits which create capital, and to create it in the best of all possible ways, as far as self-discipline is concerned, is, by adjusting his habits to his means. Gentlemen, it is the first hundred dollars saved which tells. Begin at once to lay up something. The bee predominates in the future millionnaire.

Of course there are better, higher aims than saving. As an end, the acquisition of wealth is ignoble in the extreme; I assume that you save and long for wealth only as a means of enabling you the better to do some good in your day and generation. Make a note of this essential rule: Expenditure always within income.

You may grow impatient, or become discouraged when year by year you float on in subordinate positions. There is no doubt that it is becoming harder and harder as business gravitates more and more to immense concerns, for a young man without capital to get a start for himself, and in this city especially, where large capital is essential, it is unusually difficult. Still, let me tell you for your encouragement that there is no country in the world where able and energetic young men can so readily rise as this, nor any city where there is more room at the top. It has been impossible to meet the demand for capable, first-class bookkeepers (mark the adjectives), the supply has *never* been equal to the demand. Young men give all kinds of reasons why in their cases failure was clearly attributable to exceptional circumstances which render success impossible. Some never had a chance, according to their own story. This is simply nonsense. No young man ever lived who had not a chance, and a splendid chance, too, if he ever was employed at all. He is assayed in the mind of his immediate superior, from the day he begins work, and, after a time, if he has merit, he is assayed in the council chamber of the firm. His ability, honesty, habits, associations, temper, disposition, all these are weighed and analysed. The young man who never had a chance is the same young man who has been canvassed over and over again by his superiors, and found destitute of necessary qualifications, or is deemed unworthy of closer relations with the firm, owing to some objectionable act, habit, or association, of which he thought his employers ignorant.

Another class of young men attribute their failure to employers having relations or favourites whom they advanced unfairly. They also insist that their employers disliked brighter intelligences than their own, and were disposed to discourage aspiring genius, and delighted in keeping young men down. There is nothing in this. On the contrary, there is no one suffering so much for lack of the right man in the right place, nor so anxious to find him as the owner. There is not a firm in Pittsburg to-day which is not in the constant search for business ability, and every one of them will tell you that there is no article in the market at all times so scarce. There is always a boom in brains, cultivate that crop, for if you grow any amount of that commodity, here is your best market and you cannot overstock it, and the more brains you have to sell, the higher price you can exact. They are not quite so sure a crop as wild oats, which never fail to produce a bountiful harvest, but they have the advantage over these in always finding a market. Do not hesitate to engage in any legitimate business, for there is no business in America, I do not care what, which will not yield a fair profit if it receive the unremitting, exclusive attention, and all the capital of capable and industrious men. Every business will have its season of depression—years always come during which the manufacturers and merchants of the city are severely tried—years when mills must be run, not for profit, but at a loss, that the organization and men may be kept together and employed, and the concern may keep its products in the market. But on the other hand, every legitimate business producing or dealing in an article which man requires is bound in time to be fairly profitable, if properly conducted.

And here is the prime condition of success, the great secret: concentrate your energy, thought, and capital exclusively upon the business in which you are engaged. Having begun in one line, resolve to fight it out on that line, to lead in it; adopt every improvement, have the best machinery, and know the most about it.

The concerns which fail are those which have scattered their capital, which means that they have scattered their brains also. They have investments in this, or that, or the other, here, there and everywhere. "Don't put all your eggs in one basket" is all wrong. I tell you "put all your eggs in one basket, and then watch that basket." Look round you and take notice; men who do that do not often fail. It is easy to watch and carry the one basket. It is trying to carry too many baskets that breaks most eggs in this country. He who carries three baskets must put one on his head, which is apt to tumble and trip him up. One fault of the American business man is lack of concentration.

To summarize what I have said: Aim for the highest; never enter a bar-room; do not touch liquor, or if at all only at meals; never speculate; never indorse beyond your surplus cash fund; make the firm's interest yours; break orders always to save owners; concentrate; put all your eggs in one basket, and watch that basket; expenditure always within revenue; lastly, be not impatient, for, as Emerson says, "no one can cheat you out of ultimate success but yourselves."

I congratulate poor young men upon being born to that ancient and honourable degree which renders it necessary that they should devote themselves to hard work. A basketful of bonds is the heaviest basket a young man ever had to carry. He generally gets to staggering under it. We have in this city creditable instances of such young men, who have pressed to the front rank of our best and most useful citizens. These deserve great credit. But the vast majority of the sons of rich men are unable to resist the temptations to which wealth subjects them, and sink to unworthy lives. I would almost as soon leave a young man a curse, as burden him with the almighty dollar. It is not from this class you have rivalry to fear. The partner's sons will not trouble you much, but look out that some boys poorer, much poorer than yourselves, whose parents cannot afford to give them the advantages of a course in this institute, advantages which should give you a decided lead in the race—look out that such boys do not challenge you at the post and pass you at the grand stand. Look out for the boy who has to plunge into work direct from the common school and who begins by sweeping out the office. He is the probable dark horse that you had better watch.

THE A B C OF MONEY

*Barter—the direct exchange of com-
modities. The needs and uses of money.
Comparison of the two standards—gold
and silver. How the money standard
affects the credit of a nation.*

THE A B C OF MONEY

I SUPPOSE every one who has spoken to or written for the public has wished at times that everybody would drop everything and just listen to him for a few minutes. I feel so this morning, for I believe that a grave injury threatens the people and the progress of our country simply because the masses—the farmers and the wage-earners—do not understand the question of money. I wish therefore to explain "money" in so simple a way that all can understand it.

Perhaps some one in the vast audience which I have imagined I am about to hold spellbound cries out: "Who are you—a gold-bug, a millionnaire, an iron-baron, a beneficiary of the McKinley Bill?" Before beginning my address, let me therefore reply to that imaginary gentleman that I have not seen a thousand dollars in gold for many a year. So far as the McKinley Bill is concerned, I am perhaps the one man in the United States who has the best right to complain under it, for it has cut and slashed the duties upon iron and steel, reducing them 20, 25, and 30 per cent.; and if it will recommend me to my supposed interrupter, I beg to inform him that I do not greatly disapprove of these reductions, that as an American manufacturer I intend to struggle still against the foreigner for the home market, even with the lower duties

From *The North American Review*, June, 1891.

fixed upon our product by that bill, and that I am not in favour of protection beyond the point necessary to allow Americans to retain their own market in a fair contest with the foreigner.

It does not matter who the man is, nor what he does, —be he worker in the mine, factory, or field, farmer, labourer, merchant, manufacturer, or millionnaire,—he is deeply interested in understanding this question of money, and in having the right policy adopted in regard to it. Therefore I ask all to hear what I have to say, because what is good for one worker must be good for all, and what injures one must injure all, poor or rich.

To get at the root of the subject, you must know, first, why money exists; secondly, what money really is. Let me try to tell you, taking a new district of our own modern country to illustrate how "money" comes. In times past, when the people only tilled the soil, and commerce and manufactures had not developed, men had few wants, and so they got along without "money" by exchanging the articles themselves when they needed something which they had not. The farmer who wanted a pair of shoes gave so many bushels of corn for them, and his wife bought her sun-bonnet by giving so many bushels of potatoes; thus all sales and purchases were made by exchanging articles —by barter.

As population grew and wants extended, this plan became very inconvenient. One man in the district then started a general store and kept on hand a great many of the things which were most wanted, and took for these any of the articles which the farmer had to give in exchange. This was a great step in advance, for the farmer who wanted half a dozen different things when he went to the village had then no longer to search for half a dozen different people who wanted one or more of the things he had to offer in exchange. He could now go directly to one man, the storekeeper, and for any of his agricultural products he could get most of the articles he desired. It did not matter to the storekeeper whether he gave the farmer tea or coffee, blankets or a hayrake; nor did it matter what articles he took from the farmer, wheat or corn or potatoes, so he could send them away to the city and get other articles for them which he wanted. The farmer could even pay the wages of his hired men by giving them orders for articles upon the store. No dollars appear here yet, you see; all is still barter—exchange of articles; very inconvenient and very costly, because the agricultural articles given in exchange had to be hauled about and were always changing their value.

One day the storekeeper would be willing to take, say, a bushel of wheat for so many pounds of sugar; but upon the next visit of the farmer it might be impossible for him to do so. He might require more wheat for the same amount of sugar. But if the market for wheat had risen and not fallen, you may be sure the storekeeper didn't take less wheat as promptly as he required more. Just the same with any of the articles which the farmer had to offer. These went up and down in value; so did the tea and the coffee, and the sugar and the clothing, and the boots and the shoes which the storekeeper had for exchange.

Now, it is needless to remark that in all these dealings the storekeeper had the advantage of the farmer. He knew the markets and their ups and downs long before the farmer did, and he knew the signs of the times better than the farmer or any of his customers could. The cute storekeeper had the inside track all the time. Just here I wish you to note particularly that the storekeeper liked to take one article from the farmer better than another; that article being always the one for which the storekeeper had the best customers—something that was most in demand. In Virginia that article came to be tobacco; over a great portion of our country it was wheat,—whence comes the saying, "As good as wheat." It was taken everywhere, because it could be most easily disposed of for anything else desired. A curious illustration about wheat I find in the life of my friend, Judge Mellon, of Pittsburg, who has written one of the best biographies in the world because it is done so naturally. When the Judge's father bought his farm near Pittsburg, he agreed to pay, not in "dollars," but in "sacks of wheat"—so many sacks every year. This was not so very long ago.

What we now call "money" was not much used then in the West or South, but you see that in its absence experience had driven the people to select some one article to use for exchanging other articles, and that this was wheat in Pennsylvania and tobacco in Virginia. This was done, not through any legislation, but simply because experience had proved the necessity for making the one thing serve as "money" which had proved itself best as a basis in paying for a farm or for effecting any exchange of things; and, further, different articles were found best for the purpose in different regions. Wheat was "as good as wheat" for using as "money," independent of any law. The people had voted for wheat and made it their "money"; and because tobacco was the principal crop in Virginia, the people there found it the best for using as "money" in that State.

Please observe that in all cases human society chooses for that basis-article we call "money" that which fluctuates least in price, is the most generally used or desired, is in the greatest, most general, and most constant demand, and has value in itself. "Money" is only a word meaning the article used as the basis-article for exchanging all other articles. An article is not first made valuable by law and then elected to be "money." The article first proves itself valuable and best suited for the purpose, and so becomes of itself and in itself the basis-article—money. It elects itself. Wheat and tobacco were just as clearly "money" when used as the basis-article as gold and silver are "money" now.

We take one step further. The country becomes more and more populous, the wants of the people more and more numerous. The use of bulky products like wheat and tobacco, changeable in value, liable to decay, and of different grades, is soon found troublesome and unsuited for the growing business of exchange of articles, and they are therefore unfit to be longer used as "money." You see at once that we could not get along to-day with grain as "money." Then metals proved their superiority. These do not decay, do not change in value so rapidly, and they share with wheat and tobacco the one essential quality of also having value in themselves for other purposes than for the mere basis of exchange. People want them for personal adornment or in manufactures and the arts —for a thousand uses; and it is this very fact that makes them suitable for use as "money." Just try to count how many purposes gold is needed for, because it is best suited for those purposes. It meets us everywhere. We cannot even get married without the ring of gold.

Now, because metals have a value in the open market,

being desired for other uses than for the one use as "money," and because the supply of these is limited and cannot be increased as easily as that of wheat or tobacco, these metals are less liable to fluctuate in value than any article previously used as "money." This is of vital importance, for the one essential quality that is needed in the article which we use as a basis for exchanging all other articles is fixity of value. The race has instinctively always sought for the one article in the world which most resembles the North Star among the other stars in the heavens, and used it as "money"—the article that changes least in value, as the North Star is the star which changes its position least in the heavens; and what the North Star is among stars the article people elect as "money" is among articles. All other articles revolve around it, as all other stars revolve around the North Star.

We have proceeded so far that we have now dropped all perishable articles and elected metals as our "money" or, rather, metals have proved themselves better than anything else for the standard of value, "money." But another great step had to be taken. When I was in China, I received as change shavings and chips cut off a bar of silver and weighed before my eyes in the scales of the merchant, for the Chinese have no "coined" money. In Siam "cowries" are used—pretty little shells which the natives use as ornaments. Twelve of these represent a cent in value. But you can well see how impossible it was for me to prevent the Chinese dealer from giving me less than the amount of silver to which I was entitled, or the Siam dealer from giving me poor shells, of the value of which I knew nothing. Civilized nations soon felt the necessity of having their governments take certain quan-

tities of the metals and stamp upon them the evidence
of their weight, purity, and real value. Thus came the
"coinage" of metals into "money"—a great advance.
People then knew at sight the exact value of each piece,
and could no longer be cheated, no weighing or testing
being necessary. Note that the government stamp did not
add any value to the coin. The government did not attempt to "make money" out of nothing; it only told
the people the market value of the metal in each coin,
just what the metal—the raw material—could be sold for
as metal and not as "money."

But even after this much swindling occurred. Rogues
cut the edges and then beat the coins out, so that many
of these became very light. A clever Frenchman invented
the "milling" of the edges of the coins, whereby this
robbery was stopped, and civilized nations had at last
the coinage which still remains with us, the most perfect
ever known, because it is of high value in itself and
changes least. An ideally-perfect article for use as
"money" is one that never changes. This is essential for
the protection of the workers—the farmers, mechanics,
and all who labour; for nothing tends to make every
exchange of articles a speculation so much as "money"
which changes in value, and in the game of speculation
the masses of the people are always sure to be beaten by
the few who deal in money and know most about it.

Nothing places the farmer, the wage-earner, and all
those not closely connected with financial affairs at so
great a disadvantage in disposing of their labour or
products as changeable "money." All such are exactly in
the position occupied by the farmer trading with the storekeeper as before described. You all know that fish will
not rise to the fly in calm weather. It is when the wind

blows and the surface is ruffled that the poor victim mistakes the lure for a genuine fly. So it is with the business affairs of the world. In stormy times, when prices are going up and down, when the value of the article used as money is dancing about—up to-day and down to-morrow—and the waters are troubled, the clever speculator catches the fish and fills his basket with the victims. Hence the farmer and the mechanic, and all people having crops to sell or receiving salaries or wages, are those most deeply interested in securing and maintaining fixity of value in the article they have to take as "money."

When the use of metals as money came, it was found that more than two metals were necessary to meet all requirements. It would not be wise to make a gold coin for any smaller sum than a dollar, for the coin would be too small; and we could not use a silver coin for more than one dollar, because the coin would be too large. So we had to use a less valuable metal for small sums, and we took silver; but it was soon found that we could not use silver for less than ten-cent coins, a dime being as small a coin as can be used in silver; and we were compelled to choose something else for smaller coins. We had to take a metal less valuable than silver, and we took a mixture of nickel and copper to make five-cent pieces; but even then we found that nickel was too valuable to make one- and two-cent pieces, and so we had to take copper alone for these—the effort in regard to every coin being to put metal in it as nearly as possible to the full amount of what the government stamp said the coin was worth.

Thus for one cent in copper we tried to put in a cent's worth of copper; in the "nickel" we tried to put in something like five cents' worth of nickel and copper; but because copper and nickel change in value from day to day, even more than silver, it is impossible to get in each coin the exact amount of value. If we put in what was one day the exact value, and copper and nickel rose in the market as metals, coins would be melted down by the dealers in these metals and a profit made by them, and we should have no coin left. Therefore we have to leave a margin and always put a little less metal in these coins than would sell for the full amount they represent. Hence all this small coinage is called in the history of money "token money." It is a "token" that it will bring so much in gold. Anybody who holds twenty "nickels" must be able to get as good as one gold dollar for them in order that these may safely serve their purpose as money. Nations generally fix a limit to the use of "token money," and make it legal tender to a small amount. For instance, in Britain no one can make another take "token money" for more than ten dollars, and all silver coins there are classed as "token money."

I cannot take you any more steps forward in the development of "money," because in the coined-milled metals we have the last step of all; but I have some things yet to tell you about it.

Although one would think that in coined metal pieces we had reached perfection, and that with these the masses of the people could not be cheated out of what is so essential to their well-being,—"honest money,"—yet one way was found to defraud the people even when such coin was used. The coins have sometimes been "debased" by needy governments after exhausting wars or pestilence, when countries were really too poor or too weak to recover from their misfortunes. A coin is called a "debased" coin when it does not possess metal enough to bring in the open market the sum stamped upon the coin by the government. There is nothing new about this practice, which always cheats the masses. It is very, very old. Five hundred and seventy-four years before Christ the Greeks debased their coinage. The Roman emperors debased theirs often when in desperate straits. England debased hers in the year 1300. The Scotch coin was once so debased that one dollar was worth only twelve cents. The Irish, the French, German, and Spanish governments have all tried debased coin when they could wring no more taxes directly out of their people, and had therefore to get more money from them indirectly. It was always the last resort to "debase" the coinage. These instances happened long ago. Nations of the first rank in our day do not fall so low. I must pause to make one exception to this statement. I bow my head in shame as I write it— the republic of the United States. Every one of its silver dollars is a "debased coin." When a government issues "debased coin," it takes leave of all that experience has proved to be sound in regard to money. Sound finance requires the government only to certify to the real value possessed by each coin issued from its mints, so that the people may not be cheated. Every time the government stamps the words "One Dollar" upon 371 1-4 grains of silver, it stamps a lie; disgraceful, but, alas! too true, for the silver in it is worth to-day not a dollar, but only seventy-eight cents.

Another delusion about money has often led nations into trouble—the idea that a government could "make money" simply by stamping certain words upon pieces of paper, just as any of you can "make money" by writing a note promising to pay one hundred dollars on demand. But you know that when you do that, you are not "mak-

ing money," but making "a debt": so is any government
that issues its promise to pay. And there is this about
both the individual and the government who take to issuing such notes upon a large scale: they seldom pay them.
The French did this during their Revolution, and more
recently the Confederate States "made money" at a great
pace, and issued bonds which are now scarcely worth the
paper they are printed upon. Every experiment of this
kind has proved that there can be no money "made"
where there is not value behind it. Our own country issued
bonds, and the people of other nations bought them for
forty cents upon the dollar, although they bore and paid
interest at 6 per cent. in *gold,* so great was the fear that
even the bonds of this country would not prove an exception to the usual fate of such securities issued during
trying times. Only because the government kept strict
faith and paid the interest and principal of these bonds in
gold, and never in silver or in any depreciated currency,
has the value of its bonds advanced, and the credit of the
United States become the highest in the world, exceeding
that even of Great Britain. There has never been a better
illustration of the truth that in dealing with "money,"
as in everything else, "honesty is the best policy." Our
government also issued some notes known as "greenbacks." But the wise men who did this took care to provide a fund of one hundred millions of dollars in gold
to redeem them, so that any man having a greenback
can march to the Treasury and receive for it one dollar
in gold.

But I am now to tell you another quality which this
basis-article of metal has proved itself to possess, which
you will find it very difficult to believe. The whole world
has such confidence in its fixity of value that there has

been built upon it, as upon a sure foundation, a tower of "credit" so high, so vast, that all the silver and gold in the United States, and all the greenbacks and notes issued by the government, only perform 8 per cent. of the exchanges of the country. Go into any bank, trust company, mill, factory, store, or place of business, and you will find that for every one hundred thousand dollars of business transacted, only about eight thousand dollars of "money" is used, and this only for petty purchases and payments. Ninety-two per cent. of the business is done with little bits of paper—cheques, drafts. Upon this basis also rests all the government bonds, all State, county, and city bonds, and the thousands of millions of bonds the sale of which has enabled our great railway systems to be built, and also the thousands of millions of the earnings of the masses deposited in savings-banks, which have been lent by these banks, to various parties, and which must be returned in "good money" or the poor depositor's savings will be partially or wholly lost.

The business and exchanges of the country, therefore, are not done now with "money"—with the article itself. Just as in former days the articles themselves ceased to be exchanged, and a metal called "money" was used to effect the exchanges, so to-day the metal itself—the "money"—is no longer used. The cheque or draft of the buyer of articles upon a store of gold deposited in a bank —a little bit of paper—is all that passes between the buyer and the seller. Why is this bit of paper taken by the seller or the one to whom there is a debt due? Because the taker is confident that if he really needed the article itself that it calls for—the gold—he could get it. He is confident also that he will not need the article itself, and why? Because for what he wishes to buy the seller or

any man whom he owes will take his cheque, a similar
little bit of paper, instead of gold itself; and then, most
vital of all, every one is confident that the basis-article
cannot change in value. For remember it would be almost
as bad if it rose in value as if it fell; steadiness of value
being one essential quality in "money" for the masses of
the people.

When, therefore, people clamour for more "money" to
be put in circulation,—that is, for more of the article
which we use to effect an exchange of articles,—you see
that more "money" is not so much what is needed. Nobody who has had wheat or tobacco or any article to
sell has ever found any trouble for want of "money" in
the hands of the buyer to effect the exchange. We had a
very severe financial disturbance in this country only three
months ago. "Money," it was said, could not be had for
business purposes; but it was not the metal itself that was
lacking, but "credit," confidence, for upon that, as you
have seen, all business is done except small purchases and
payments which can scarcely be called "business" at all.
To-day the business man cannot walk the street without
being approached by people begging him to take this
"credit" at very low rates of interest: at 2 per cent. per
annum "money" (credit) can be had day by day. There
has been no considerable difference in the amount of
"money" in existence during the ninety days. There was
about as much money in the country in January as there
is in March. It was not the want of money, then, that
caused the trouble. The foundation had been shaken upon
which stood the ninety-two thousand of every one hundred thousand dollars of business. The metal itself and
notes—real "money," as we have seen—only apply to the
eight thousand dollars. Here comes the gravest of all

dangers in tampering with the basis. You shake directly the foundation upon which rests 92 per cent. of all the business exchanges of the country,—confidence, credit, —and indirectly the trifling 8 per cent. as well which is transacted by the exchange of the metal itself or by government notes; for the standard article is the foundation for every exchange, both the ninety-two thousand and the eight thousand dollars. So, you see, if that be undermined, the vast structure, comprising all business, built upon it, must totter.

I have finished telling you about "money." We come now to apply the facts to the present situation, and here we enter at once upon the silver question; and I am sure you are all attention, for it is the most pressing of all questions now before you. You see that the race, in its progress, has used various articles as "money," and discarded them when better articles were found, and that it has finally reached coined pieces of valuable metal as the most perfect article. Only two metals are used among civilized nations as the standard metal—gold in some countries, silver in others. No country can have two standards. Centuries ago silver was adopted as the standard in China, India, and Japan, and more recently in the South American republics; and it still is the standard in these countries. When adopted it was a wise choice; silver had nearly double its present value, and was then steady, and it answered all the needs of a rural people.

The principal nations of Europe and our own country, being further advanced and having much greater business transactions, found the necessity for using as a standard a more valuable metal than silver, and gold was adopted; but as silver was used as money in many parts of the world as the standard, and used in these gold-basis countries for "small change," it was advisable for these nations to agree upon the value in gold which would be accorded to silver, and this was fixed at fifteen and one-half ounces of silver to one of gold. Please note that this was then as nearly as possible the market value of silver as a metal compared with gold as a metal. The nations did not attempt to give to silver any fictitious value, but only its own inherent value. And, more than this, each of these nations agreed, when the agreement came to an end, to redeem all the silver coin it had issued in gold at the value fixed. Everything went well under this arrangement for a long time. The more advanced nations were upon a gold basis, the less advanced nations upon a silver basis, and both were equally well served.

What, then, has raised this *silver question* which everybody is discussing? Just this fact: that while the supply, and therefore the value, of gold remained about the same, great deposits of silver were discovered, wonderful improvements made in mining machinery, and still more wonderful in the machinery for refining silver ore; and as more and more silver was produced at less cost, its value naturally fell more and more; one ounce of it, worth $1.33 in 1872, being worth to-day only $1.04. It has fallen as low as 93 cents. It has danced up and down; it has lost fixity of value. To all countries upon a silver basis there have come confusion and disaster in consequence. The question in India, with its two hundred and eighty-five millions of people, is most serious; and you see how our South American republics are troubled from this fall in the value of their basis-article, by which all other articles are measured. Even the European nations which are upon a gold basis are troubled by this "silver question," for under the agreement to rate fifteen and a half ounces of silver as worth an ounce of gold some of these nations have had enormous amounts of silver thrust upon them. Most of them saw what was coming many years ago, and ceased to increase their silver: some disposed of a great deal of what they had, and placed themselves strictly upon the gold basis; but there are still in European countries eleven hundred millions of dollars of silver legal-tender coins, not counting the amount of "token" silver money used for small change. It is not safe to say that less than twenty-five ounces of it would be found equal to one ounce of gold if put in the market, instead of the fifteen-and-a-half-ounce basis upon which these countries have obtained it.

All European countries have been, and are still, trying hard to escape from silver. In 1878 those comprising the Latin Union, which fixed the price of silver,—France, Belgium, Italy, Switzerland, and Greece,—finally closed their mints to legal-tender silver. Norway, Sweden, and Denmark in 1873 and 1875 ran out from under the silver avalanche, and now stand firmly upon a gold basis. Holland also, in 1875, took its stand practically upon gold. Austria-Hungary has not coined silver since 1879, except a small amount of "Levant silver thalers" for a special trade purpose. Even half-civilized Russia took the alarm, and ran as fast as she could out of the silver danger, for in 1876 she shut her mints to the further coinage of the dangerous metal, except such small amount as China wished to take promptly from her. So you see that all those countries that have tried silver and found out the evils which it produces, and its dangers, have been, and are now, using every means to rid themselves of it. For thirteen years it has been cast out of their mints, for during this long period no full legal-tender silver coins have been issued in Europe. Only our republic, among nations, is boldly plunging deeper and deeper into the dangers of silver coinage. When we have had the experience of older nations as to its operations, we may and, I think, surely will wish, like them, to retrace our steps when it is too late. So, you see, there is trouble wherever there is silver. What to do with their silver, which has fallen so low in value, is a serious problem in all these countries. It hangs like a dark cloud over their future.

So much has silver fallen in all parts of the world and disturbed everything that several conferences have been called by the nations in recent years, to which the United States has sent delegates. The object of these was to see whether the chief commercial nations could not agree again upon a new gold value for silver. But the conclusion has always been that it was too dangerous to attempt to fix a new value for silver until it could be more clearly seen what the future was to show about its supply and value, for perhaps it might fall so low that twenty-five or thirty ounces of it would not be worth more than an ounce of gold; no one can tell. As our country has already gone so far into the danger as to have four hundred and eighty-two millions of dollars in depreciated silver, we had to confer with our neighbours in misfortune, and appear as creditors have to appear at meetings held to try to support the bad business of a failing debtor.

Perhaps you are asking yourselves why, when I spoke of all the European countries in relation to silver, I did not state the amount of silver held in reserve by our principal rival, Great Britain. Listen one moment, and then ponder over the reply. *Not one dollar*. France has no less than six hundred and fifty millions of dollars in silver in her bank; but every dollar of Britain's reserves is in the one steady, unchangeable basis-article—gold. Wise old bird, the dear mother-land sits upon her perch, whistling away out of all danger from this silver trouble. She has made London the financial centre of the world. If anything be bought or sold in foreign lands, a draft upon London is demanded; because everyone knows that, come what may, it will be paid in the best article, which cannot fall in value—gold. No draft upon Paris or Vienna or New York for wise men. Why? Because the nations represented by these cities have become involved in great possible losses by their huge piles of silver, and may attempt by legislation to make drafts payable in that metal, which fluctuates so in value.

I wish the people of the United States would watch Britain carefully. She is keeping her own counsel; she is treating the silver-loaded nations with cool politeness in the conferences, which she graciously condescends to attend only because India, over which she rules, is unfortunately upon a silver basis; if it were not for that, she would probably politely decline. When they talk about fixing a gold value upon silver, she says that she really does not know what she will decide upon in the matter. What she is praying for is that the United States will continue to go deeper and deeper into silver until retreat is impossible, and she will keep her old policy, which has made her supreme in finance. Her only possible rival is not to be found in Europe, but here in the United States. What a grand thing for Britain if our country could be brought down to a silver basis—forced to relinquish the one standard which can alone give a nation front rank in the financial world! Silver for the republic, Gold for the monarchy: this is what Great Britain is hoping may come to pass, and what every American should resolve never shall. Governments may pass what laws they please about silver: the world heeds them not. Every business transaction between nations continues to be based on gold exclusively—nothing but gold—and will so continue. Britain knows this and acts accordingly.

I think I hear you ask indignantly: "How came our country to have three hundred and twelve millions of silver dollars in its vaults, like France, instead of having its reserves in the sure gold, like our rival, Britain, when, like Britain, we have gold as our basis?" That is a question every farmer and every toiler should ask, and demand an answer to, from his representative in Congress. The reason is easily given. Here is the history. Silver, as we have seen, had fallen in value, and was likely to fall still more. Europeon nations were loaded down with many hundreds of millions of dollars, and all anxious to get rid of it; owners of silver and of silver mines were alarmed; what was to be done to prop the falling metal? Evidently the government was the only power which could undertake the task; and towards that end all the influence and resources of the silver power were bent—alas! with eminent success; for the masses of the people were represented as in favour of silver. If true, they were going with the speculators against their own interests, in the most direct way possible.

The first act which aimed to give by legislation a value to silver was passed in 1878. It required our government to buy at least two million ounces of silver every month, while all other governments had stopped coining it, because it had become dangerously erratic in value. The silver men insisted that these purchases would raise its value; but were they right? No. It did not advance in price. What was to be done then? "Ah!" said these silver-tongued speculators, "the trouble is, the government has not gone far enough; only increase the amount; let the government buy four and a half million ounces per month of our silver instead of two million per month, and this will take all that the country's mines yield, and more too, and so silver must advance in value." They were right in stating that four and a half millions per month are more than the total yield of the United States silver mines; and then eight to ten millions of silver are taken and used every year for other purposes than coining into "money," leaving not more than, say, four millions per month for coinage. Many people were persuaded that if the government bought so much silver per month the value of silver must advance. The price did advance, because many of these mistaken people bought it upon speculation before the bill passed. Silver rose from 96 to 121—almost to its old rate in gold.

But what has been the result since the passage of the new bill? The answer is found in the quotation for silver to-day. It is back from 121 to 97, and here we are again. So, instead of being free from the silver trouble, as Britain is and we should have been, these men have succeeded in unloading upon the government already three hundred and ninety millions of dollars of their silver, and we are getting almost as badly off as France; but with this difference: France and other nations prudently stopped adding to their burdens of silver thirteen years ago, while our government is adding to its store four and one-half millions of ounces every month, costing a little more than that amount of dollars. The United States is trying to ignore the changed position of silver, and to make it equal to gold, against the judgment of all other first-class nations. To succeed, we shall have to buy not only what our own mines produce, but a great deal of what all other mines produce throughout the world, the total yield of silver being enough to make one hundred and sixty-eight millions of our silver dollars every year; and then we must, in addition, be prepared to buy the eleven hundred millions of dollars' worth with which European governments are now loaded down, and which they are anxious to sell.

So far from the government purchases of silver having raised its value, the government could not to-day sell the three hundred and thirteen millions of dollars' worth in its vaults without losing some millions upon the price it has paid the silver-owners for it. You will scarcely believe that the accounts of the treasury state that the government has made, so far, sixty-seven millions of profit upon its silver purchases. This is claimed because for the amount of silver put in a dollar it has paid only about eighty cents. All this "profit" is fictitious. You see, the nation has been led into very foolish purchases of silver. Four and a half millions of your earnings are taken through taxes every month, not for the constitutional purposes of government, but in an effort to bolster a metal by paying prices for it far higher than it otherwise would command. Your government is being used as a tool to enrich the owners of silver and silver mines. This is bad indeed, but hardly worth mentioning compared with the danger of panic and disaster it brings with it through the probable banishment of the steady gold basis and the introduction of the unsteady basis of silver.

The republic had the disgrace of slavery, and abolished it. Until this year it was disgraced in the eyes of the world because it had no law which secured to others than its own citizens the right to their literary productions. That disgrace has passed away also; but there has come upon it the disgrace of "debased coinage." The great republic issues dishonest coin, and it is the only nation in the world which does so, except Mexico, which still coins a little silver. But while the disgrace is upon us, the financial evils of "debased" coinage are yet to come; for, although the government issues debased coin, it agrees to receive it as worth a dollar in payment of duties and taxes, and makes it legal tender, and so it passes from hand to hand for the present as worth dollars. In this way the government has been able so far to prevent its depreciation. How long it can continue issuing four and a half millions more of these notes or coins every month and keep them equal to gold nobody can tell. But one thing is clear: ultimately the load must become too heavy, and, unless silver rises in value, or enough is put into the dollars to represent their value in gold, or the purchase of silver by the government is stopped, we must sooner or later fall from the gold basis to the condition of the Argentine and other South American republics.

This is how these silver dollars will act which have not metal enough to sell for dollars when the world begins to lose confidence in the ability of the government issuing them to pay gold for them when asked. Suppose a number of you had decided to carry a huge log from the woods, and you all got under, and, bending your necks, took its weight upon your shoulders, and then some doubted whether you really could stagger on under the load; and suppose two or three of you, after casting timid glances at each other, concluded you had better get from under: what would be the result? The lack of confidence would probably result in killing those who were foolish enough to remain. It is just so with this delicate question of the measure of values. A few speculators or "gold-bugs" will resolve that, come what may, they will make themselves safe and get from under.

Even in the mind of the most reckless there will be some doubt whether the United States alone can take the load of the world upon its shoulders and carry it, when all the other nations together are afraid to try it, and when no nation in the history of the world has ever succeeded in giving permanent value, as a standard for money, to a metal that did not in itself possess that value. Mark this: that our government has only succeeded so far in doing this with its silver dollars because it has issued only a limited quantity, and has been able to *redeem them in gold*—just as you could take a piece of paper and write on it, "This is good for one dollar, and I promise to pay it." That would be your "fiat" money. The question is, How long could you get people to take these slips for dollars? How soon would some suspicious man suggest that you were issuing too many? And then these slips would lose reputation; people would begin to doubt whether you could really pay all the dollars promised if called upon; and from that moment you could issue no more. Just so with governments: all can keep their small change afloat, although it may not contain metal equal to its face value; and it is a poor government which cannot go a little further and get the world to take something from it in the shape of "money" which is only partially so. But then, remember, any government will soon exhaust its credit if it continues to issue as "money" anything but what has intrinsic value as metal all the world over. Every nation has had eventually to recoin its "debased" coin or repudiate its obligations, and go through the perils and disgrace of loss of credit and position. In many instances the "debased" coin never was redeemed, the poor people who held it being compelled to stand the loss.

There is, however, one valuable feature of the present silver law which, if not changed, may stop the issue of many more "debased silver dollars." It requires that two millions of the four and a half millions of ounces of silver purchased each month shall be coined into money for one year. After that, only such amounts are to be coined as are found necessary to redeem the silver notes issued. As people prefer the notes to the silver, little or no coinage of silver dollars will be necessary, and only silver notes will be issued. When the government ceases to coin silver dollars, it will stand forth in its true character before the people—that of a huge speculator in silver, or, rather, as the tool of silver speculators, piling up in its vaults every month four and a half millions of ounces, not in the form of "money," but in bars. Surely this cannot fail to awaken the people to the true state of affairs, and cause them to demand that the reckless speculation shall cease.

It is in every respect much less dangerous, however, to keep the silver purchased in bullion than to coin it in "debased dollars," because it renders it easier at some future day to begin the coinage of honest silver dollars— that is, coins containing the amount of silver metal that commands a dollar as metal; instead of 371 grains of silver, 450, or 460, or more or less, should be used. This is just about the amount the government gets for each dollar. No possible act of legislation that I know of would produce such lasting benefit to the masses of the people of this country. But beyond material benefit something much higher is involved—the honour of the republic. The

stamp of its government should certify only that which
is true.

I do not suppose that there are many men in the
United States, except owners of silver, who would vote
that silver take the place of gold as the standard of value.
If the people understood that the question was whether
the one metal or the other—silver or gold—should be
elected as the standard, the vote would be almost unani-
mous for gold, its superiority is so manifest. Yet such
is surely the issue, although the advocates of silver dis-
claim any intention to disturb the gold standard, saying
they only desire to elevate silver and give it the position
which gold has as money. But you might as well try to
have two horses come in "first" in a race or to have two
"best" of anything. You might as well argue for two
national flags in one country. Just as surely as the citizen
has to elect the banner under which he stands or falls, so
surely must he elect gold or silver for his financial
standard. The standard article cannot be made to share
its throne with anything else, any more than the stars-
and-stripes can be made to share its sovereignty with
any other flag in its own country; for there is this law
about "money": the worst drives the best from the field.
The reason for this is very clear.

Suppose you get in change a five-dollar gold piece and
five dollars in silver, and there is some doubt whether
an act of Congress will really prove effective in keeping
silver equal to gold in value forever: ninety-nine people
out of a hundred may think that the law will give this
permanent value to silver, which the article itself does
not possess; but one man in a hundred may have doubts
upon the subject. I think the more a man knows about
"money," the more doubts he will have; and, although

you may have no doubts, still the fact that I have doubts, for instance, will lead you to say: "Well, he may be right; it is possible I may be wrong. I guess I will give Smith this silver for my groceries to-morrow, and give the old lady this beautiful bright golden piece to put by; it needs no acts of Congress—all the acts of Congress in the world cannot lessen its value; the metal in it is worth five dollars anywhere in the world, independent of the government stamp; these five pieces of silver are worth only three dollars and seventy-five cents as metal. Yes, I shall let Smith have the silver—*gold is good enough for me.*"

And you may be sure Smith unloads the silver as soon as he can upon Jones. And many people will believe and act so, and the gold in the country will disappear from business, and silver alone will be seen and circulate; every man that gets it giving it to another as soon as he can, and so keeping it in active circulation; and every man that gets a bit of gold holding it, and thus keeping it out of circulation. So instead of having more money, if we go in for trying by law to force an artificial value upon silver in order to use it as money, we shall really soon have less money in circulation. The seven hundred millions of gold which is now in circulation, and which is the basis of everything, will speedily vanish, the vast structure of credit built upon it be shaken, and the masses of the people compelled to receive silver dollars worth only seventy-eight cents, instead of being, as now, redeemable in gold and always worth one hundred cents. For, re-member, as I have told you, 92 per cent. of all operations conducted by "money" depends upon people having absolute confidence in the "money" being of unchange-able value.

Issue one hundred dollars of "debased" coin more than all men are sure can be kept of unchangeable value with gold—panic and financial revolution are upon you. More "money," you see, which could only be used in 8 per cent. of our smallest financial transactions, can easily be so issued as to overwhelm all the important business of the country by shaking "confidence," upon which 92 per cent. rests. To be always free from danger is to issue only such "money" as in itself has all the value certified by the stamp upon it. So jealously does Britain, our only rival, adhere to this that she is spending two millions of dollars just now to recoin gold coins which have lost a few cents of their value by wear. Her government stamp must always tell the truth. The republic should not be less jealous of its honor.

As you have seen, the silver-men were disappointed at the failure of acts of Congress to advance the value of their silver. Twice the government has been induced to do as they asked, under assurances that compliance would surely get the country out of its dangerous position as the owner of silver; twice it has been deceived. You would think the silver-owners would now admit their error and help the government to get back to safe ground with as little loss as possible. Far from it; instead of this they have taken the boldest step of all, and urged upon Congress what you have heard a great deal about—the "free coinage of silver." Now, what does that mean? It means that our government is to be compelled by law to open its mints and take all the silver with which European governments are loaded down, and part of all the silver mined in the world, and give for every seventy-eight cents' worth of it one of these coins, which you are compelled to take as a full dollar for your labour or

products. It means that the European merchant will send
silver over here, get it coined at our mints or get a silver-
dollar note for it, and then buy a full dollar's worth of
your wheat or corn, or anything he wants, for the silver
he could get only seventy-eight cents for in Europe or
anywhere else in the world. Europe is doing this every
day just now with India, the Argentine Republic, and
other countries upon a silver basis. The British merchant
buys wheat in India upon the depreciated silver basis,
takes it to Europe, and sells it upon the gold basis. He
has thus to pay so little for Indian wheat that it has
become a dangerous competitor to our own in Europe,
which it could not be except that by the fall in silver the
Indian farmer gets so little value for his products.

It is only a few months since the new Silver Bill was
passed requiring the government to more than double its
purchases, and already eight millions of dollars of silver
more than we have exported has been sent into this
country from abroad—something unknown for fifteen
years, for we have always exported more silver than we
have imported. Now we are buying all our own mines
furnish, and being burdened with some from Europe, for
which we should have received gold. In eighteen days of
the month of April we have sent abroad nine millions of
dollars in gold; so that under our present Silver Law you
see Europe has already begun to send us her depreciated
silver and rob us of our pure gold—a perilous exchange
for our country and one which should fill our legislators
with shame. Understand, please, that hitherto, under both
bills compelling the government to buy silver, bad as
these were, yet the government has got the metal at the
market price, now about seventy-eight cents for 371 1-4
grains; and only this amount the government has put

into the so-called dollar. Under "free coinage" all this
will change. The owner of the silver will then get the
dollar for seventy-eight cents' worth of silver. For pure,
cool audacity I submit that this proposition beats the
record; and yet when the Farmers' Alliance shouts for
free coinage, this is exactly what it supports—a scheme
to take from the people twenty-two cents upon each dollar
and put it into the pockets of the owners of silver. Surely
you will all agree that if seventy-eight cents' worth of
silver is to be made a dollar by the government, then the
government, and not the silver-owner, should get the
extra twenty-two cents' profit on each coin, if it succeeds.
The government needs it all; for, as I told you before,
the silver bought by the government only at market value
could not be sold to-day without a loss of millions.

If the free coinage of silver becomes law, our farmers
will find themselves just in the position of the Indian
farmer; and yet we are told that they are in favour of
silver. If this be true, there can be only one reason for
it—they do not understand their own interests. No class
of our people is so deeply interested in the maintenance
of the gold standard and the total sweeping-away of silver
purchases and debased coinage as the farmer, for many
of his products are sold in countries that are upon the
gold basis. If the American farmer agrees to take silver
in lieu of gold, he will enable the Liverpool merchant to
buy upon the lower silver basis, at present seventy-eight
cents for the dollar; while for all the articles coming
from abroad that the farmer buys he will have to pay
upon the gold basis. He will thus have to sell cheap and
buy dear. This is just what is troubling India and the
South American republics. Prices for this season's crops

promise to be higher than for years. *See that you get these upon the gold basis.*

Open our mints to the free coinage of silver, and thus offer every man in the world who has silver to sell a one-dollar coin stamped by the government, and taken by it for all dues, for which he gives only 371 1-2 grains of silver, worth seventy-eight cents, and every silver mine in the world will be worked day and night and every pound of silver obtained hurried to our shores. The nations of Europe, with eleven hundred millions of depreciated silver already on hand, will promptly unload it upon us; they will demand gold from us for all that we buy from them, and thus rob us of our gold while we take their silver. With "free coinage" in sight, we shall fall from the gold to the silver basis before the bill is passed. The last words of the late lamented Secretary Windom will prove true:—

"Probably before the swiftest ocean greyhound could land its silver cargo in New York, the last gold dollar within reach would be safely hidden in private boxes and in the vaults of safe-deposit companies, to be brought out only by a high premium for exportation."

It is a dangerous sea upon which we have embarked. You should ask yourselves why you should endanger the gold basis for silver. Does any one assert that the silver basis would be better for you or for the country? Impossible. No one dares go so far as this. All that the wildest advocate of the change ventures to say is that he believes that silver could be made as good as gold. Everybody knows that nothing could be made better. Let us ask why any one but an owner of silver should wish silver to be made artificially anything else than it is intrinsically.

What benefit to any one, except the owner of silver, that
the metal silver should not remain where natural causes
place it, like the metals copper and nickel? Why should
it be credited with anything but its own merits? There
was no prejudice in the mind of any one against it. It has
had a fair race with gold; the field is always open for it,
or for any metal, to prove itself better suited for the basis
of value. If silver became more valuable in the market
and steadier in value than gold, it would supplant gold.
Why not give the position to the metal that wins in fair
competition? Gold needs no bolstering by legislation; it
speaks for itself. Every gold coin is worth just what it
professes to be worth in any part of the world; no doubt
about it; no possible loss; and what is equally important,
no possible speculation; its value cannot be raised and
cannot be depressed. The speculator, having no chance to
gamble upon its ups and downs, does not favour it; but
this is the very reason you should favour that which gives
you absolute security of value all the time. Your interests
and the interests of the speculator are not the same.
Upon your losses he makes his gains.

One reason urged why silver should be purchased and
coined is that the country has not enough "money," and
that free coinage of silver will give it more. But if we
need more "money," the only metal which it is wise to
buy is gold. Why issue your notes for silver, which is
falling in value and involves unknown dangers, when for
these same notes you can get the solid, pure article itself,
real money, *gold,* which cannot possibly entail a loss upon
the country? But is it true that the country has not enough
"money"?—that is, you remember, the coined article used
for exchanging other articles. If so, it is a new discovery.
We have not suffered for want of coined money in times

past, and yet there is for each man, woman, and child five dollars more "money" in circulation than there ever was. We have more circulating medium—that is, "money"— per head than any country in Europe, with one exception, France, where the people do not use cheques and drafts as much as other similar countries—a fact which makes necessary many times more coined money than we require. Still there is little objection to having just as much coined money as is desired, provided it is not debased, but honest money; and the only way to be sure of that is to buy gold and coin it into "money"—not silver, the future value of which is so doubtful, and the purchases of which have so far been a losing speculation. Ask the advocate of more money why gold is not the best metal for the government to buy and coin into money for the people, and see what he has to say. Gold is as much an American product as silver; our mines furnish more than two millions of dollars of it every month. He could have no objection except that this would not tend to keep up the price of his own product, silver. He could not deny that it would give safer money for the people.

There is another plea urged on behalf of silver. Many public men tell us that silver coinage "is in the air," that people want it because they think that it will make money "cheap," and that, silver being less valuable than gold, the debts of people could be more easily paid. But let me call your attention to one point just here. The savings and the property of the people could only be thus reduced in value if the gold standard fell. As long as all government notes were kept equal to gold, as at present, no matter what amount of silver the government bought or coined, not the slightest change is possible. Only after the financial crisis had come, and the gold standard had gone down in the wreck, and every dollar of gold was withdrawn and held for high premiums, could any change occur to favour one class or another. If any man is vaguely imagining that he is to save or make in some way by the government becoming involved in trouble with its debased silver coin and silver purchases, let him remember that, in order that this vain expectation can be realized, there must first come to his government a loss of ability to make good its determination to keep its silver dollar equal to gold, when gold would at once vanish and command a premium. A wise Secretary of the Treasury has truly foretold the result:—

"This sudden retirement of $600,000,000 of gold, with the accompanying panic, would cause contraction and commercial disaster unparalleled in human experience, and our country would at once step down to the silver basis, when there would no longer be any inducement for coinage, and silver dollars would sink to their bullion value."

The man who tries to bring about this disaster in the hope to profit by it is twin brother to him who would wreck the express train for the chance of sharing its contents, or would drive the ship of state on the rocks for the chance of securing a part of the wrecked cargo. He is a wrecker and a speculator. His interests are opposed to the interests of the toiling masses.

Again, we are constantly told that the masses of the people favour "free silver coinage," or at least uphold the present silver laws, because they have received the impression, somehow or other, that the more silver there is coined the more money will come to them. Let us look into that. When the government buys silver bullion, it gives its own notes or silver dollars for it. Who gets

these? The owners of the silver bullion. How can these
be taken from their pockets and put into the pockets of
the people? From what we know of the silver men, we
cannot expect them to present many of their dollars to
anybody; it will only be when they buy the labour or the
products of the people that they will give these dollars
at the value of a hundred cents which have cost them
only seventy-eight. Will they give more of these seventy-
eight-cent dollars than they would have to give of one-
hundred-cent dollars for the same labour or products?
No, not until or unless the effort of the government to
give an artificial value to silver broke down, and our
money lost value, when a dollar might not be worth half
a dollar in purchasing power; calculated upon gold value,
they would always give less value than before. How,
then, can the working people or the farmers be benefited?
It is the owners of the silver, who will give the government seventy-eight cents' worth of bullion and get for it
a dollar, who will make the profit. Surely this is clear.
Up to this time the dollar which the farmer or workingman receives is still worth a dollar because the government has been able, by trying hard, to keep it worth this;
but when "free coinage of silver" comes, the silver dollar
must fall to its real value—seventy-eight cents—and the
farmer and workingman will be defrauded; so that the
interests of the farmer, mechanic, labourer, and all who
receive wages are that the "money" they get should be of
the highest value, and not cheap—gold, and not silver.

Up to this time we have held fast to gold as the
standard. Everything in the United States is based upon
gold to-day, all silver notes or coins being kept equal
to gold. Has that been a wise or an unwise policy? Would
it now be best to let the gold standard go, to which the

advanced nations cling, and especially Britain, and adopt
the silver standard of our South American neighbours?
Upon the solid rock of gold as our basis-article we have
built up the wealthiest country in the world, and the
greatest agricultural, manufacturing, and mining and
commercial country ever known. We have prospered beyond any nation the sun ever shone upon. In no country
are wages of labour so high or the masses of the people
so well off. Shall we discard the gold basis, or even endanger it? This is the question before the people of the
United States to-day.

The New York *Evening Post* is a free-trade organ, but
it has recently said that it would rather be the party to
pass ten McKinley Bills than one Silver Bill such as was
urged; and I, a Republican and a believer in the wisdom
of protection, tell you that I would rather give up the
McKinley Bill and pass the Mills Bill, if for the exchange
I could have the present Silver Bill repealed and silver
treated like other metals. In the next presidential campaign, if I have to vote for a man in favour of silver and
protection, or for a man in favour of the gold standard
and free trade, I shall vote and work for the latter, because my judgment tells me that even the tariff is not
half so important for the good of the country as the
maintenance of the highest standard for the money of the
people.

Would it not be well for you to listen to men who
have your confidence, and who have been compelled by
their official positions to investigate and study this silver
question well? President Harrison is well known as a
most conscientious man. He is not rich; he is poor. If he
has anything at heart, it is the good of the plain working
people of his country. He has had to study this subject,

and he tells you that he finds that the first thing a debased silver dollar will do is to go forth and cheat some poor man who has to take it for his products or labour. Ex-President Cleveland, like President Harrison, is a poor man; his sympathies are with the plain working people—the masses. He had to study the question that he might act upon it; and although many of his party have been led away into the crusade for silver,—temporarily, it is to be hoped (for to its credit, let me say, the Democratic party has hitherto been the staunch friend of the best money for the people),—Mr. Cleveland felt that he must tell the truth and denounce the free-silver-coinage idea, because he found that it must injure the workers of the nation. His recent letter gives another proof that he is a natural leader of men—a brave man and not a coward. His personal prospects he weighs not against the true welfare of the toilers who once made him President. In addition to these, no abler, purer, or grander Democrat ever managed the finances of this nation than Mr. Manning; no abler, purer, or grander Republican ever did so than Mr. Windom. These men were friends of the masses, if ever the masses had friends. Both had to investigate the silver question that they might learn what was best and act so as to promote the permanent welfare of the people. Both became deeply concerned about the impending danger of "debased money," and used all their powers to stop representatives in Congress from forcing the government to imperil the interests of the workingman, who must have the best money for his labour or products, or be the prey of speculators. These great men, two of them exalted to the highest political office upon the earth by your suffrages, had and have at heart only the good of the many as against the possible

enrichment of the few. Political opponents as they were
or are, that they should agree upon this question must
surely give every farmer, mechanic, and workingman in
the United States grave reason for believing that they,
and not the advocates of silver, are his wisest counsellors.

I close with one word of advice to the people. Unless
the government ceases to burden itself month by month
with more silver, or if the free coinage of silver be seriously entertained, *avoid silver;* when you lay by anything,
let it be in gold; when you deposit in the savings bank let
it be a gold deposit—ask the bank to give you a gold
receipt therefor. There is no use in the poor taking any
risk. If you do not thus act promptly, you will find no
gold left for you. The speculators and those closely
identified with business will have it all. It is a fact full
of warning that no bonds could be sold to advantage to-
day which were not made specially payable in *gold.* There
is danger ahead. Whatever happens, you can sleep
soundly upon gold. Silver will bring bad dreams to wise
men. Our government can do much; it is very strong; but
there are two things which it cannot do: it cannot—by
itself, against the world—permanently give to silver a
higher value than it possesses throughout the world as
metal, though this is what it is trying to do; and it cannot lessen the value of gold. Some day, perhaps, you may
have reason to thank me for the advice I have given you,
although I hope not.

Do not think, however, that I despair of the republic
—never; even if dragged into the difficulties inseparable
from silver, and matters become as bad with us as they
are to-day in the Argentine Republic, where one gold
dollar is worth two and a half currency dollars, there
is no occasion to fear the final result. The good sense

of the people will restore the gold basis after a time, and the republic will march on to the front rank among nations; but the silver experiment will cost much; and it is better that the direct loss should fall as much as possible upon the few of the moneyed class than upon the masses of the people. At best the latter must suffer most, for moneyed men know better than others can how to protect themselves. All this loss, I am sure, the people would prevent if they could only be made to understand the question; for their interests, far more than those of the rich, lie with honest money, and their wishes have only to be expressed to their representatives to prevent the threatened crisis.

Silver, owing to changes of value, has become the tool of the speculator. Steady, pure, unchangeable gold has ever been, and never was so much as now, the best instrument for the protection of the masses of the people.

I have written in vain if this paper does not do something to explain why this is so, and to impel the people to let their representatives in Congress clearly understand that, come what may, the stamp of the republic must be made true, the money of the American people kept the highest and surest in value of all money in the world, above all doubt or suspicion, its standard in the future, as in the past, not fluctuating Silver, but unchanging Gold.

THE COMMON INTEREST OF LABOUR AND CAPITAL

Employer and employe interdependent. The advantages of mutual trust. The employer who helps his workmen through education, recreation and social uplift, helps himself.

THE COMMON INTEREST OF LABOUR AND CAPITAL

ADDRESS TO WORKINGMEN

A GREAT philosopher has pointed out to us that in this life the chief, the highest reward that we can obtain, is the purchase of *satisfactions*. I have purchased a great satisfaction, one of the greatest I have ever acquired. I have been privileged to help some of my fellow-workmen help themselves. This Library [Braddock, Pa.] will give them an opportunity to make themselves more valuable to their employers, and so lay up intellectual capital that cannot be impaired or depreciated.

It is very unfortunate that the irresistible tendency of our age, which draws manufacturing into immense establishments, requiring the work of thousands of men, renders it impossible for employers who reside near to obtain that intimate acquaintance with employes which, under the old system of manufacturing in very small establishments, made the relation of master and man more pleasing to both.

When articles were manufactured in small shops by employers who required only the assistance of a few men and apprentices, the employer had opportunities to know every one, to become well acquainted with each, and to

From an Address to Workmen at Dedication of Carnegie Library, Braddock, Pa., January, 1889.

know his merits both as a man and as a workman; and on the other hand the workman being brought into closer contact with his employer, inevitably knew more of his business, of his cares and troubles, of his efforts to succeed, and, more important than all, they came to know something of the characteristics of the man himself. All this is changed.

Thus the employes become more like human machines, as it were, to the employer, and the employer becomes almost a myth to his men. From every point of view this is a most regrettable result, yet it is one for which I see no remedy. The free play of economic laws is forcing the manufacture of all articles of general consumption more and more into the hands of a few enormous concerns, that their cost to the consumer may be less.

There is no longer any room for conducting the manufacture of such articles upon a small scale; expensive works and machinery costing millions are required, as the amount per ton or per yard of what we call "fixed charges" is so great a factor in the total cost that whether a concern can run successfully or not in many cases depends upon whether it divides these fixed charges —which may be said to be practically the same in a large establishment as in a smaller—by a thousand tons per day or by five hundred tons per day of product. Hence the reason for the continual increase year by year in the product of your mills, not that the manufacturer wishes primarily to increase his product, but that the strain of competition forces him into extensions that he may thereby reduce more and more per ton or per yard these fixed charges, upon which the safety of his capital depends.

It being therefore impossible for the employers of

thousands to become acquainted with their men, if we are not to lose all feeling of mutuality between us, the employer must seek their acquaintance through other forms, to express his care for the well-being of those upon whose labour he depends for success, by devoting part of his earnings for institutions like this library, and for the accommodation of organizations such as the co-operative stores which occupy the lower floor of this building, and I hope in return that the employes are to show by the use which they make of such benefactions that they in turn respond to this sentiment upon the part of employers wherever it may be found. By such means as these we may hope to maintain to some extent the old feeling of kindliness, mutual confidence, respect and esteem which formerly distinguished the relations between the employer and his men. We are younger than Europe, and have still something to see from the older land in this respect; but I rejoice to see that many manufacturers in this country are awaking to the sense of duty to their employes; and what is even still more important are the evidences which we find among our workmen of a desire to establish societies which cannot but be beneficial to themselves. It is all well enough for people to help others, but the grandest result is achieved when people prove able to help themselves.

Another important feature, which may be referred to, is, that in Pittsburg labour, generally, is paid so well that the workman can save something every month, if he only will make the effort. Nothing can exceed the importance of saving part of his earnings. The workman who owns his own home, has already a sure foundation upon which to build the competence which is to give him comfort and independence in old age.

I have said how desirable it was that we should endeavour, by every means in our power, to bring about a feeling of mutuality and partnership between the employer and the employed. Believe me, the interests of Capital and Labour are one. He is an enemy of Labour who seeks to array Labour against Capital. He is an enemy of Capital who seeks to array Capital against Labour.

I have given the subject of Labour and Capital careful study for years, and I wish to quote a few paragraphs from an article I published years ago:

"The greatest cause of the friction which prevails between capital and labour, the real essence of the trouble, and the remedy I have to propose for this unfortunate friction:

"The trouble is that men are not paid at any time the compensation proper to that time. All large concerns necessarily keep filled with orders, say for six months in advance, and these orders are taken, of course, at prices prevailing when they are booked. This year's operations furnish perhaps the best illustration of the difficulty. Steel rails at the end of last year for delivery this year were $29 per ton at the works. Of course the mills entered orders freely at this price, and kept on entering them until the demand growing unexpectedly great carried prices up to $35 per ton. Now the various mills in America are compelled for the next six months or more to run upon orders which do not average $31 per ton, at the seaboard and Pittsburg, and say $34 at Chicago. Transportation, iron-stone, and prices of all kinds have advanced upon them in the meantime, and they must therefore run for the bulk of the year upon very small margins of profit. But the men noticing in the papers the 'great boom in steel rails,' very naturally demand their share of the advance, and under our existing faulty arrangements between capital and labour they have secured it. The employers, therefore, have grudgingly given what they know under proper arrangements they should not have been required to give; and there has been friction and still is dissatisfaction upon the part of the employers. Reverse this picture. The steel-rail market falls again. The mills have still six months' work at prices above the prevailing market, and can afford to pay men higher wages than the then existing state of the market would apparently justify. But having just been amerced in extra payments for labour which they should not have paid, they naturally attempt to reduce wages as the market price of rails goes down, and there arises discontent among the men, and we have a repetition of the negotiations and strikes which have characterized the beginning of this year. In other words, when the employer is going down the employe insists on going up, and *vice versa*. What we must seek is a plan by which men will receive high wages when their employers are receiving high prices for the product, and hence are making large profits; and *per contra*, when the employers are receiving low prices for product, and therefore small if any profits, the men will receive low wages. If this plan can be found, employers and employed will be 'in the same boat,' rejoicing together in their prosperity and calling into play their fortitude together in adversity. There will be no room for quarrels and instead of a feeling of antagonism there will be a feeling of partnership between employers and employed. There is a simple means of producing this result, and to its general introduction both employers and employed should steadily bend their energies. Wages should be based upon a sliding scale, in proportion to the net prices received for product month by month. It is impossible for Capital to defraud Labour under a sliding scale."

One advantage of this Library [Carnegie Library at Braddock, Pa.] will be that it will bring before you every local newspaper and every Trade Journal, and I beg you all to read these carefully. You will find many misstatements, many blunders. These are inseparable from the newspaper press, which must work hastily and report even rumours. But by studying the principal journals the tendency of affairs can be correctly seen. Newspapers will not give you a correct statement of the prices of material. Manufacturers are disposed to give the brightest colouring to the situation,—to report the highest sales made with a view to maintain prices and induce customers to purchase. They will probably not report how low they have been compelled to sell in order to meet competition and keep works running. Nevertheless, a careful perusal of the newspapers and Trade Journals, as I have said, will enable you to form a general opinion of the trend of events in the commercial world. If you read the papers to-day, you will know that out of thirteen mills engaged in the manufacture of steel rails in this country, not more than three are running to their capacity. Only one mill in all the West is making rails (North Chicago), and I am sorry to say that it seems probable that even that one will not be able to run continuously.

The most melancholy feature in all the disputes between labour and capital is that it is scarcely ever capital that succeeds in breaking down the price of labour, but, alas, it is labour which stabs labour. Look around you and see labour working for 10, 20 and even 30 per cent.

less in some mills, and at Johnstown and Harrisburg for less than one-half what we pay for skilled labour in this district; and then in your hearts blame not capital, but consider employers who regret those reductions in wages, who stand out against them and run for years at higher prices, as the best friends of labour, even although at last they must frankly confess that if they are to give their men steady employment and save their capital and works, they are forced to ask them to work at the rates obtained by their competitors. The first employer who reduces labour is labour's enemy; but the last employer to reduce labour may be labour's staunchest friend. The fatal enemy of labour is labour, not capital.

The greatest character in the public life of Britain, and the staunchest friend of the Republic in its hour of need, the Radical, John Bright, being once asked what was his most valuable acquisition, replied, "A taste for reading." I can truthfully say from my own experience that I agree with that great man. Most anxious to give you the best advice in my power, I advise you to cultivate the taste for reading. When I was a boy in my teens in Allegheny City, Col. Anderson, whose memory I must ever revere, who had a few hundred books, gave notice that he would lend these books every Saturday afternoon to boys and young men. You cannot imagine with what anxiety some of us who embraced this opportunity to obtain knowledge looked forward to every Saturday afternoon, when we could get one book exchanged for another. The principal partner with me in all our business, Mr. Phipps, equally with myself, had obtained access to the stores of knowledge by means of this benefactor. It is from personal experience that I feel that there is no human arrangement so powerful for good, there is no benefit that can be bestowed upon a community so great, as that which places within the reach of all the treasures of the world which are stored up in books.

We occasionally find traces even at this day of the old prejudice which existed against educating the masses of the people. I do not wonder that this should exist when I reflect upon what has hitherto passed for education. Men have wasted their precious years trying to extract education from an ignorant past whose chief province is to teach us, not what to adopt, but what to avoid. Men have sent their sons to colleges to waste their energies upon obtaining a knowledge of such languages as Greek and Latin, which are of no more practical use to them than Choctaw. I have known few college graduates that knew Shakespeare or Milton. They might be able to tell you all about Ulysses or Agamemnon or Hector, but what are these compared to the characters that we find in our own classics? One service Russell Lowell has done, for which he should be thanked—he has boldly said that in Shakespeare alone we have a greater treasure than in all the classics of ancient time. They have been crammed with the details of petty and insignificant skirmishes between savages, and taught to exalt a band of ruffians into heroes; and we have called them "educated." They have been "educated" as if they were destined for life upon some other planet than this. They have in no sense received instruction. On the contrary, what they have obtained has served to imbue them with false ideas and to give them a distaste for practical life. I do not wonder that a prejudice has arisen and still exists against such education. In my own experience I can say that I have known few young men intended for business who were not injured by a collegiate education. Had they gone into active work during the years spent at college they would have been better educated men in every true sense of that term. The fire and energy have been stamped out of them, and how to so manage as to live a life of idleness and not a life of usefulness has become the chief question with them. But a new idea of education is now upon us.

We have begun to realize that a knowledge of chemistry, for instance, is worth a knowledge of all the dead languages that ever were spoken upon the earth; a knowledge of mechanics more useful than all the classical learning that can be crammed into young men at college. What is the young man to do who knows Greek with the young man that knows stenography or telegraphy, for instance, or bookkeeping, or chemistry, or the law of mechanics, in these days? Not that any kind of knowledge is to be underrated. All knowledge is, in a sense, useful. The point I wish to make is this, that, except for the few, who have the taste of the antiquarian, and who find that their work in life is to delve among the dusty records of the past, and for the few that lead professional lives, the education given to-day in our colleges is a positive disadvantage.

The lack of education in its true sense has done more than all the other causes combined to prevent the universal recognition of labour. I remember that the great president, the greatest of all railway managers, Edgar Thomson, after whom the works here are called, once asked me to remove from Pittsburg to be master of machinery of the Pennsylvania Railroad. Well, you may smile. And I said to Mr. Thomson, "Why, Mr. Thomson, you amaze me. I know nothing whatever about machinery." "That is the reason I want you to take charge of it," he replied. "I have never known a mechanic with judgment and good sense except one." This was before the time of Captain Jones, so he could not have referred to the Captain. This lack of judgment in mechanics was because at that day in this country they had failed to receive an all-round education. I mean the true education and knowledge of matters and things in general, by which we are surrounded and with which we have to deal. The unprecedented success which has attended the development of the Bessemer works in this country has arisen from this cause, above all others, that, unlike the manufacture of iron, it has fallen into the hands of men of great scientific knowledge. The services of these men are recognized throughout the world and receive compensation which a few years ago would have been considered enormous, and in consequence they have lifted mechanical labour with them and served to dignify it in the eyes of the world. "The mechanic," "the mechanical engineer," the "manager of steel mills," are now titles of honour. If you want to make labour what it should be, educate yourself in useful knowledge. That is the moral I would emphasize. Get knowledge. Cultivate a taste for reading, that you may know what the world has done and is doing and the drift of affairs.

The value of the education which young men can now receive cannot be overestimated, and it is to this education, as given in technical schools, to which I wish to call your attention. Time was when men had so little knowledge that it was easy for one man to embrace it all, and the course in colleges bear painful evidence of this fact to-day. Knowledge is now so various, so extensive, so minute, that it is impossible for any man to know thoroughly more than one small branch. This is the age of the specialist; therefore you who have to make your living in this world should resolve to know the art which gives you support; to know that thoroughly and well, to be an expert in your specialty. If you are a mechanic, then from this library study every work bearing upon the subject of mechanics. If you are a chemist, then every work bearing upon chemistry. If you are at the blast furnaces, then every work upon the blast furnace. If in the mines, then every work upon mining. Let no man know more of your specialty than you do yourself. That should be your ideal. Then, far less important, but still important, to bring sweetness and light into your life, be sure to read promiscuously, and know a little about as many things as you have time to read about. Just as on his farm the farmer must first attend well to his potatoes and his corn and his wheat, from which he derives his revenue, and he may spend his spare hours as a labour of love in cultivating the flowers that surround his home. One domain your work, and the other your recreation.

In these days of transition and of struggles between labour and capital, to no better purpose can you devote a few of your spare hours than to the study of economic questions. There are certain great laws which will be obeyed: the law of supply and demand; the law of competition; the law of wages and of profits. All these you will find laid down in the text-books, and remember that there is no more possibility of defeating the operation of these laws than there is of thwarting the laws of nature which determine the humidity of the atmosphere or the revolution of the earth upon its axis.

The severe study of scientific books must not be permitted to exclude the equally important duty of reading the masters in literature; and by all means of fiction. The feeling which prevails in some quarters against fiction is, in my opinion, only a prejudice. I know that some, indeed most, of the most eminent men find in a good work of fiction one of the best means of enjoyment and of rest. When exhausted in mind and body, and especially in mind, nothing is so beneficial to them as to read a good novel. It is no disparagement of free libraries that most of the works read are works of fiction. On the contrary, it is doubtful if any other form of literature would so well serve the important end of lifting hard-working men out of the prosaic and routine duties of life. The works of Scott, Thackeray, Eliot, Dickens, Hawthorne, and others of the same class, are not to be rated below any other form of literature for workingmen.

You know how much manufacturing science is indebted to the improvements and inventions which owe their first suggestion to the workman himself. Now mark this important fact. These improvements and inventions come from the educated—educated in the true sense—and never from the ignorant workman. They must come, and they do come, from men who are in their special department men of more knowledge than their fellows. If they have not read, then they have *observed,* which is the best form of education. The important fact is that they must *know;* how the knowledge was acquired, it matters not. The fact that they know more about a problem than their fellows and are able to suggest the remedy or improvement, is what is of value to them and their employer. There is no means so sure for enabling the workman to rise to the foremanship, managership and finally partnership as knowledge of all

that has been done and is being done in the world to-day
in the special department in which he labours. From the
highest down to the lowest a better grade of service is
rendered by the intelligent man than it is possible for
the ignorant man to render. His knowledge always
comes in, and whether you have knowledge, on the part
of the manager who directs, or of the man who only
handles a shovel, you have in him a valuable employe in
proportion to his knowledge, other things being equal.
In the course of my experience as a manufacturer I
know our firm has made many mistakes by neglecting one
simple rule, "never to undertake anything new until your
managers have had an opportunity to examine everything that has been done throughout this world in that
department." Neglect of this has cost us many hundreds
of thousands of dollars, and we have become wise. Now
I say here to the man who is ambitious to learn, who,
perhaps, thinks that he has some improvement in his
mind, here in the rooms of this library, there is, or I
hope soon will be, the whole world's experience upon
that subject brought right before you down to a recent
date. In any question of mechanics or any question of
chemistry, any question of furnace practice, you will find
the records of the world at your disposal here. If you
are on the wrong track, these books will tell you; if you
are on the right track, they will tell you; if you
are on the right track, they will afford you encouragement. You can go through hall after hall in the patent
office in Washington, and see thousands of models of
inventions bearing upon all branches of human industry,
and ninety-nine out of every hundred would never have
been placed there had the ignorant inventor had at command such facilities as will be yours in this library.

I have heard employers say that there was great danger that the masses of the people might become too well educated to be content in their useful and necessary occupations. It has required an effort upon my part to listen to this doctrine with patience. It is all wrong; I give it an unqualified contradiction. The trouble between capital and labour is just in proportion to the ignorance of the employer and the ignorance of the employed. The more intelligent the employer the better, and the more intelligent the employed the better. It is never education, it is never knowledge, that produces collision. It is always ignorance on the part of one or the other of the two forces. Speaking from an experience not inconsiderable, I make this statement. Capital is ignorant of the necessities and the just dues of labour, and labour is ignorant of the necessities and dangers of capital. That is the true origin of friction between them. More knowledge on the part of capital of the good qualities of those that serve it, and some knowledge upon the part of the men of the economic laws which hold the capitalists in their relentless grasp, would obviate most of the difficulties which arise between these two forces, which are indispensably necessary to each other. I hope that those of our men who possess that inestimable prize, the taste for reading, will make it a point to study carefully a few of the fundamental laws from which there is no escape, either on the part of capital or labour. If this library be instrumental in the slightest degree in spreading knowledge in this department, it will have justified its existence.

I trust that you will not forget the importance of amusements. Life must not be taken too seriously. It is a great mistake to think that the man who works all the time wins in the race. Have your amusements. Learn to play a good game of whist or a good game of drafts, or a good game of billiards. Become interested in base-ball or cricket, or horses, anything that will give you innocent enjoyment and relieve you from the usual strain. There is not anything better than a good laugh. I attribute most of my success in life to the fact that, as my partners often say, trouble runs off my back like water from a duck. There is a poetical quotation from Shakespeare that is applicable. It is to "wear your troubles as your outsides—like your garments, care-lessly."

Many men are to be met with in this life who would have been great and successful had the world rated them at the value which they placed upon themselves. This class are the victims of an hallucination. Nobody in the world desires to keep down ability. Everybody in the world has an outstretched hand for it. Every employer of labour is studying the young men around him, most anxious to find one of exceptional ability. Nothing in the world so desirable for him and so profitable for him as such a man. Every manager in the works stands ready to grasp, to utilize the man that can do something that is valuable. Every foreman wants to have under him in his department able men upon whom he can rely and whose merits he obtains credit for, because the greatest test of ability in a manager is not the man himself, but the men with whom he is able to surround himself. These books on the shelves will tell you the story of the rise of many men from our own ranks. It is not the educated, or so-called classically educated man, it is not the aristocracy, it is not the monarchs, that have ruled the destinies of the world, either in camp, council, laboratory or workshop. The great inventions, the improvements, the discoveries in science, the great works in literature have sprung from the ranks of the poor. You can scarcely name a great invention, or a great discovery, you can scarcely name a great picture, or a great statue, a great song or a great story, nor anything great that has not been the product of men who started like yourselves to earn an honest living by honest work.

And, believe me, the man whom the foreman does not appreciate, and the foreman whom the manager does not appreciate, and the manager whom the firm does not appreciate, has to find the fault not in the firm, or the manager, or the foreman, but in himself. He cannot give the service that which is so invaluable and so anxiously looked for. There is no man who may not rise to the highest position, nor is there any man who, from lack of the right qualities or failure to exercise them, may not sink to the lowest. Employes have chances to rise to higher work, to rise to foremen, to be superintendents, and even to rise to be partners, and even to be chairmen in our service, if they prove themselves possessed of the qualities required. They need never fear being dispensed with. It is we who fear that the abilities of such men may be lost to us.

It is highly gratifying to know that the hours of labour are being gradually reduced throughout the country—eight hours to work, eight hours to play, eight hours to sleep, seems the ideal division. If we could only establish by law that all manufacturing concerns which run day and night should use three turns, it would be most desirable. You know we tried to do so for several years at a cost of some hundreds of thousands of dollars, but were finally compelled by our competitors to give up the struggle; the best plan, perhaps, is to reach it by slow degrees through State laws. No one firm can do much. All its competitors in the various states must be compelled to do likewise, for in our days profits are upon so narrow a margin that no firm can run its works except under similar conditions with its competitors. It is necessary, therefore, that laws should be secured binding upon all. We should be glad to support such a law; but, even as at present, if workmen use well the time they have at their disposal they will soon rise to higher positions. You need not work twelve hours very long; most of us have worked more hours than twelve in our youth.

The workman has many advantages to-day over his predecessors. A sliding scale for his labour ranks him higher than before as a man and a citizen. The proportion of the joint earnings of capital and labour given to labour never was so great and is constantly rising, the earnings of capital never were so low. The cost of living never was so low in recent times.

I hope the future is to add many more advantages and that the toilsome march which labour has had to make on its way from serfdom, when our fore-fathers were bought and sold with the mines and factories they worked, up to its present condition, is not yet ended, but that it is destined to continue and lead to other important results for the benefit and dignity of labour.

[The sliding scale proposed was afterwards introduced by Mr. Carnegie ten years ago and has been in operation ever since. Mr. Carnegie considers it the best plan of all.]

THRIFT AS A DUTY

THE DUTIES OF RICH MEN

Thrift an evidence of civilization. Saving one of the highest duties of citizenship. The accumulation of a competence a duty; the acquirement of vast wealth not a virtue but a great responsibility.

THRIFT AS A DUTY

THE DUTIES OF RICH MEN

THE importance of the subject is suggested by the fact that the habit of thrift constitutes one of the greatest differences between the savage and the civilized man. One of the fundamental differences between savage and civilized life is the absence of thrift in the one and the presence of it in the other. When millions of men each save a little of their daily earnings, these petty sums combined make an enormous amount, which is called capital, about which so much is written. If men consumed each day of each week all they earned, as does the savage, of course there would be no capital—that is, no savings laid up for future use.

Now, let us see what capital does in the world. We will consider what the shipbuilders do when they have to build great ships. These enterprising companies offer to build an ocean greyhound for, let us say, £500,000, to be paid only when the ship is delivered after satisfactory trial trips. Where or how do the shipbuilders get this sum of money to pay the workmen, the wood merchant, the steel manufacturer, and all the people who furnish material for the building of the ship? They get it from the savings of civilized men. It is part of the money saved for investment by the millions of industrious people. Each man, by thrift, saves a little, puts

From *The Youth's Companion,* September, 1900.

the money in a bank, and the bank lends it to the ship-builders, who pay interest for the use of it. It is the same with the building of a manufactory, a railroad, a canal, or anything costly. We could not have had anything more than the savage had, except for thrift.

THRIFT THE FIRST DUTY

Hence, thrift is mainly at the bottom of all improvement. Without it no railroads, no canals, no ships, no telegraphs, no churches, no universities, no schools, no newspapers, nothing great or costly could we have. Man must exercise thrift and save before he can produce anything material of great value. There was nothing built, no great progress made, as long as man remained a thriftless savage. The civilized man has no clearer duty than from early life to keep steadily in view the necessity of providing for the future of himself and those dependent upon him. There are few rules more salutary than that which has been followed by most wise and good men, namely, "that expenses should always be less than income." In other words, one should be a civilized man, saving something, and not a savage, consuming every day all that which he has earned.

The great poet, Burns, in his advice to a young man, says:

To catch Dame Fortune's golden smile,
    Assiduous wait upon her:
And gather gear by every wile
    That's justified by honour.

Not for to hide it in a hedge,
    Not for a train attendant;
But for the glorious privilege
    Of being independent.

That is sound advice, so far as it goes, and I hope the reader will take it to heart and adopt it. No proud, self-respecting person can ever be happy, or even satisfied, who has to be dependent upon others for his necessary wants. He who is dependent has not reached the full measure of manhood and can hardly be counted among the worthy citizens of the republic. The safety and progress of our country depend not upon the highly educated men, nor the few millionnaires, nor upon the greater number of the extreme poor; but upon the mass of sober, intelligent, industrious and saving workers, who are neither very rich nor very poor.

THRIFT DUTY HAS ITS LIMIT

As a rule, you will find that the saving man is a temperate man, a good husband and father, a peaceful, law-abiding citizen. Nor need the saving be great. It is surprising how little it takes to provide for the real necessities of life. A little home paid for and a few hundred pounds—a very few—make all the difference. These are more easily acquired by frugal people than you might suppose. Great wealth is quite another and a far less desirable matter. It is not the aim of thrift nor the duty of men to acquire millions. It is in no respect a virtue to set this before us as an end. Duty to save ends when just money enough has been put aside to provide comfortably for those dependent upon us. Hoarding millions is avarice, not thrift.

Of course, under our industrial conditions, it is inevitable that a few, a very few men, will find money coming to them far beyond their wants. The accumulation of millions is usually the result of enterprise and judgment, and some exceptional ability for organization. It does not come from savings in the ordinary sense of that word. Men who in old age strive only to increase their already great hoards, are usually slaves of the habit of hoarding formed in their youth. At first they own the money they have made and saved. Later in life the money owns them, and they cannot help themselves, so overpowering is the force of habit, either for good or evil. It is the abuse of the civilized saving instinct and not its use that produces this class of men.

No one need be afraid of falling a victim to this abuse of the habit if he always bears in mind that whatever surplus wealth may come to him is to be regarded as a sacred trust, which he is bound to administer for the good of his fellows. The man should always be master. He should keep money in the position of a useful servant. He must never let it master and make a miser of him.

A man's first duty is to make a competence and be independent. But his whole duty does not end here. It is his duty to do something for his needy neighbours who are less favoured than himself. It is his duty to contribute to the general good of the community in which he lives. He has been protected by its laws. Because he has been protected in his various enterprises he has been able to make money sufficient for his needs and those of his family. All beyond this belongs in justice to the protecting power that has fostered him and enabled him to win pecuniary success. To try to make the world in some way better than you found it, is to have a noble motive in life. Your surplus wealth should contribute to the development of your own character and place you in the ranks of nature's noblemen.

It is no less than a duty for you to understand how important it is, and how clear your duty is, to form the habit of thrift. When you begin to earn, always have some part of your earnings, like a civilized man, instead of spending all, like the poor savage.

The advantages of an early start. College education not necessary to business success. Poor boys the successful men of to-day. Men of business ability sure of recognition.

HOW TO WIN FORTUNE

LABOUR is divided into two great armies—the agricultural and the industrial. In these diverse forces are in operation. In the former everything tends to a further distribution of land among the many; in the latter everything tends to a concentration of business in the hands of the few. One of the two great fallacies upon which "Progress and Poverty"—Mr. George's book—is founded, is that the land is getting more and more into the hands of the few. Now the only source from which Mr. George could obtain correct information upon this point is the census; and this tells us that in 1850 the average extent of farms in the United States was 203 acres; in 1860, 199 acres; in 1870, 153 acres, and that in 1880 it was still further reduced to 134 acres. The reason is obvious for this rapid distribution of the land. The farmer who cultivates a small farm by his own labour is able to drive out of the field the ambitious capitalist who attempts to farm upon a large scale with the labour of others. In Great Britain nothing has been more significant than that the tillers of small farms have passed through the agricultural depression there far better than those who cultivated large farms. So in both countries we have proof that under the free play of equal laws land is becoming more and more divided among the masses of the people. In the whole range of social

From *The New York Tribune,* April 13, 1890.

questions no fact is more important than this, and nothing gives the thoughtful student greater satisfaction. The triumph of the small proprietor over the large proprietor insures the growth and maintenance of that element in society upon which civilization can most securely depend, for there is no force in a nation so conservative of what is good, so fair, so virtuous, as a race of men who till the soil they own. Happily for mankind experience proves that man cannot work more soil profitably than he can till himself with the aid of his own family.

When we turn to the other army of labour—the industrial—we are obliged to confess that it is swayed by the opposite law, which tends to concentrate manufacturing and business affairs generally in a few vast establishments. The fall in prices of manufactured articles has been startling. Never were the principal articles of consumption so low as they are to-day. This cheapening process is made possible only by concentration. We find 1,700 watches per day turned out by one company, and watches are sold for a few dollars apiece. We have mills making many thousand yards of calico per day, and this necessary article is to be had for a few cents per yard. Manufacturers of steel make 2,500 tons per day, and four pounds of finished steel are sold for 5 cents. And so on through the entire range of industries. Divide the huge factories into smaller establishments, and it will be found impossible to manufacture some of the articles at all, the success of the process being often dependent on its being operated upon a large scale, while the cost of such articles as could be produced in small establishments would be two or three times their present prices. There does not appear to be any counteracting force to this law of concentration in the industrial world. On the contrary, the active forces at work seem to demand greater and greater output or turn-over from each establishment in order that the minimum of cost should be reached. Hence comes the rapid and continuous increase of the capital of manufacturing and commercial concerns, five, ten, fifteen, and even twenty millions being sometimes massed in one corporation.

Has the Young Man Now a Chance?

This has given rise to a complaint which is often heard, but which I hope to show has no foundation. The young practical man points to these, and says to himself: "It is no longer possible for our class without capital to rise beyond the position of employes upon salaries. There is a lion in the path which leads to independent commands or to partnership, and this lion is the huge establishments already existing, which are an impassable barrier to our advancement." The man engaged in the agricultural army, as we have seen, has nothing to fear from capital. With a small sum, which is not very difficult for him to save or borrow, he can begin farming, the only competition with which he has to contend being that of others of his own class situated like himself. It is certainly more difficult for a mechanic or practical man to establish a new business, or to win partnership in one that exists, than it is for the young farmer to begin his business; yet the difficulties are not insuperable, nor greater than have hitherto existed. They are not such as to stimulate the ambitious; and this is always to be taken into account, that if the race in the industrial and business world be harder to win, the prize is infinitely greater.

Before considering the prospects of the mechanic in the industrial, of the clerk in the mercantile, commercial and financial worlds, let me show that no classes other than these two have had much to do with establishing the factories, business houses and financial institutions which are best known in the United States to-day. And first, as to the part of trained mechanics. I select the best-known industrial establishments in each department, many of them the most extensive works of their kind and of world-wide reputation: Baldwin Works, for locomotives; Sellers & Co., Bement & Dougherty, for mechanical tools; Disston's Works, for saws; works of the Messrs. Dobson, and of Thomas Dolan, Philadelphia, and Gary, of Baltimore, textile fabrics; Fairbanks, for scales; Studebakers, for waggons, who count their waggons by the acre; Pullman, of Chicago; Allison, of Philadelphia, for cars; Washburn & Moen, and Cleveland Rolling Mills, steel wire, etc.; Bartlett, iron founder, Baltimore; Sloanes, also Higgins, carpets; Westinghouse, electrical apparatus; Peter Henderson & Co., and Landreth & Co., seeds; Harper Brothers, publishers; Babbitt, for Babbitt's metal; Otis Works, Cleveland, boiler steel; the Remington Works, and Colt's Works, Hartford, firearms; Singer Company, Howe, Grover, sewing machines; McCormick Works, of Chicago; Balls, of Canton, and Walter A. Woods, for agricultural implements; steamship building, Roach, Cramp, Neafie, on the Atlantic; Scott upon the Pacific; Parkhurst, Wheeler, Kirby, McDugall, Craig, Coffinberry, Wallace, the leading officials of shipbuilding companies on our great lakes; horseshoes, Burdens; Atterbury Works, for glass; Groetzingers, tanning; Ames Works, for shovels; Steinway, Chickering and Knabe, pianos.

Every one of these great works was founded and managed by mechanics, men who served their apprenticeship. The list could be greatly extended, and if we were to include those which were created by men who entered life as office-boys or clerks, we should embrace almost every famous manufacturing concern in the country. Edison, for instance, was a telegraph operator. Corliss, of Corliss engine; Cheney, of Cheney silk; Roebling, of wire fame; Spreckels, in sugar refining—all and many more captains of industry—were poor boys with natural aptitude, to whom a regular apprenticeship was scarcely necessary.

In the mercantile, commercial and financial branches of business, which are all under the law which drives business affairs into large concerns, the poor clerk takes the place of the trained mechanic in the industrial world. Claflin's, Jaffray's, Sloan's, the Lords, the Taylors, the Phelpses, the Dodges, the gigantic houses of Jordan & Marsh in Boston, of Field in Chicago, Barr in St. Louis, Wanamaker in Philadelphia, Meldrum & Anderson, Buffalo; Newcomb, Endicott & Co., Detroit; Taylor, Cleveland; Daniels & Fisher, Denver; Horne, and Campbell & Dick, Pittsburg, all these and the corresponding houses throughout the country, as far as I am able to trace their history, have the same story to tell. Wanamaker, Claflin, Jordan, Lord, Field, Barr and the others all poor boys in the store, and Phelps and Dodge both poor clerks.

In banking and finance, it is an oft repeated story that our Stanfords, Rockefellers, Goulds, Sages, Fields, Dillons, Seligmans, Wilsons, and Huntingtons came from the ranks. The millionnaires who are in active control started as poor boys, and were trained in that sternest but most efficient of all schools—poverty.

Where Is the College-Made Man?

I asked a city banker to give me a few names of presidents and vice-presidents and cashiers of our great New York city banks who had begun as boys or clerks. He sent me thirty-six names, and wrote he would send me more next day. I cannot take the reader's time with a complete list, but here are a few of the best known: Williams, president Chemical Bank; Watson & Lang, Bank of Montreal; Tappen, president Gallatin National; Brinkerhoff, president Butchers' and Drovers' Bank; Clark, vice-president American Exchange; Jewitt, president Irving National; Harris, president Nassau Bank; Crane, president Shoe and Leather Bank; Nash, president Corn Exchange Bank; Cannon, president Chase National; Cannon, vice-president Fourth National; Montague, president Second National; Baker, president First National; Hamilton, vice-president Bowery Bank, and so on.

The absence of the college graduate in this list should be deeply weighed. I have inquired and searched everywhere in all quarters, but find small trace of him as the leader in affairs, although not seldom occupying positions of trust in financial institutions. Nor is this surprising. The prize-takers have too many years the start of the graduate; they have entered for the race invariably in their teens—in the most valuable of all the years for learning—from fourteen to twenty; while the college student has been learning a little about the barbarous and petty squabbles of a far-distant past, or trying to master languages which are dead, such knowledge as seems adapted for life upon another planet than this, as far as business affairs are concerned—the future captain of industry is hotly engaged in the school of experience, obtaining the very knowledge required for his future triumphs.

I do not speak of the effect of college education upon young men training for the learned professions, for which it is, up to a certain point, almost indispensable in our day for the average youth, but the almost total absence of the graduate from high position in the business world seems to justify the conclusion that college education as it exists seems almost fatal to success in that domain. It is to be noted that salaried officials are not in a strict sense in business—a captain of industry is one who makes his all in his business and depends upon success for compensation. It is in this field that the graduate has little chance, entering at twenty, against the boy who swept the office, or who begins as shipping clerk at fourteen. The facts prove this. There are some instances of the sons of business men, graduates of colleges, who address themselves to a business life and succeed in managing a business already created, but even these are few compared with those who fail in keeping the fortune received.

There has come, however, in recent years, the polytechnic and scientific school, or course of study, for boys, which is beginning to show most valuable fruits in the manufacturing branch. The trained mechanic of the past, who has, as we have seen, hitherto carried off most of the honours in our industrial works, is now to meet a rival in the scientifically educated youth, who will push him hard—very hard indeed. Three of the largest steel manufacturing concerns in the world are already under the management of three young educated men—students of these schools who left theory at school for practice in the works while yet in their teens. Walker, Illinois Steel Company, Chicago; Schwab, Edgar Thomson Works; Potter, Homestead Steel Works, Pittsburg, are types of the new product—not one of them yet thirty. Most of the chiefs of departments under them are of the same class. Such young educated men have one important advantage over the apprenticed mechanic—they are open-minded and without prejudice. The scientific attitude of mind, that of the searcher after truth, renders them receptive of new ideas. Great and invaluable as the working mechanic has been, and is, and will always be, yet he is disposed to adopt narrow views of affairs, for he is generally well up in years before he comes into power. It is different with the scientifically trained boy; he has no prejudices, and goes in for the latest invention or newest method, no matter if another has discovered it. He adopts the plan that will beat the record and discards his own devices or ideas, which the working mechanic superintendent can rarely be induced to do. Let no one, therefore, underrate the advantage of education; only it must be education adapted to the end in view, and must give instruction bearing upon a man's career if he is to make his way to fortune.

Thus in the financial, commercial and mercantile branches of business, as in manufacturing, we have to ask, not what place the educated mechanic and practical men occupy, but what these two types have left for others throughout the entire business world. Very little, indeed, have they left.

In the industrial department the trained mechanic is the founder and manager of famous concerns. In the mercantile, commercial and financial it is the poor office-boy who has proved to be the merchant prince in disguise, who surely comes into his heritage. They are the winning classes. It is the poor clerk and the working mechanic who finally rule in every branch of affairs, without capital, without family influence, and without college education. It is they who have risen to the top and taken command, who have abandoned salaried positions and boldly risked all in the founding of a business. College graduates will usually be found under salaries, trusted subordinates. Neither capital, nor influence, nor college learning, nor all combined have proved able to contend in business successfully against the energy and indomitable will which spring from all-conquering poverty. Lest anything here said may be construed as tending to decry or disparage university education let me clearly state that those addressed are the fortunate poor young men who have to earn a living; for such as can afford to obtain a university degree and have means sufficient to insure a livelihood the writer is the last man to advise its rejection—compared with which all the pecuniary gains of the multi-millionnaire are dross —but for poor youth the earning of a competence is a duty and duty done is worth even more than university education, precious as that is. Liberal education gives a man who really absorbs it higher tastes and aims than the acquisition of wealth, and a world to enjoy, into

which the mere millionnaire cannot enter; to find therefore that it is not the best training for business is to
prove its claim to a higher domain. True education can
be obtained outside of the schools; genius is not an in-
digenous plant in the groves academic—a wild flower
found in the woods all by itself, needing no care from
society—but average man needs universities.

Are Corporations to Disappear?

The young practical man of to-day working at the
bench or counter, to whom the fair goddess, Fortune,
has not yet beckoned, may be disposed to conclude that
it is impossible to start business in this age. There is
something in that. It is, no doubt, infinitely more difficult
to start a new business of any kind to-day than it was.
But it is only a difference in form, not in substance. It is
infinitely easier for a young practical man of ability to
obtain an interest in existing firms than it has ever been.
The doors have not closed upon ability; on the contrary,
they swing easier upon their hinges. Capital is not
requisite. Family influence, as before, passes for nothing.
Real ability, the capacity for doing things, never was
so eagerly searched for as now, and never commanded
such rewards.

The law which concentrates the leading industries and
commercial, mercantile and financial affairs in a few
great factories or firms contains within itself another
law not less imperious. These vast concerns cannot be
successfully conducted by salaried employes. No great
business of any kind can score an unusually brilliant
and permanent success which is not in the hands of
practical men pecuniarily interested in its results. In the

industrial world the days of corporations seem likely to
come to an end. It has been necessary for me to watch
closely most of my life the operations of great establishments owned by hundreds of absent capitalists, and
conducted by salaried officers. Contrasted with these I
believe that the partnership conducted by men vitally
interested and owning the works will make satisfactory
dividends when the corporation is embarrassed and
scarcely knows upon which side the balance is to be at
the end of a year's operations. The great dry-goods
houses that interest their most capable men in the profits
of each department succeed, when those fail that endeavour to work with salaried men only. Even in the
management of our great hotels, it is found wise to take
into partnership the principal men. In every branch of
business this law is at work, and concerns are prosperous,
generally speaking, just in proportion as they succeed in
interesting in the profits a larger and larger proportion
of their ablest workers. Co-operation in this form is fast
coming in all great establishments. The manufacturing
business that does not have practical manufacturing
partners had better supply the omission without delay,
and probably the very men required are the bright young
mechanics who have distinguished themselves while
working for a few dollars per day or the youths from
the polytechnic school. Instances constantly occur where
the corporation unwilling to interest a promising practical man loses his services, and sees an interest given
him by some able individual manufacturer or commercial
firm who are constantly on the lookout for that indispensable article—ability. It has not hitherto been the
practice for corporations properly to reward these
embryo managers, but this they must come to, if they

are to stand the competition of works operated by those interested in the profits.

Corporations, on the other hand, as I desire to point out to practical young men, have one advantage. Their shares are sold freely. If a worker wishes to become interested in any branch of manufacturing in America to-day, the path is easy. For $50 or $100 he can become a stockholder. It is becoming more and more common for workers so to invest their savings. There are many well-managed corporations whose assets and prestige enable them to earn satisfactory returns, and no better evidence of capacity and of good judgment can a workman give to his employers than that furnished by the presence of his name upon the books as a shareholder in the concern.

Workingmen have a prejudice against showing their employers that the wages they earn suffice to enable them to save; but this is a mistake. The saving workman is the valuable workman, and the wise employer regards the fact that he does save as prima facie evidence that there is something exceptionally valuable in him. It should be the effort of every corporation to induce its principal workers to invest their savings in its shares. Only in this way can corporations hope to cope successfully with individual manufacturers who have already discovered one of the valuable secrets of unusual success, viz.: to share their profits with those who are most instrumental in producing them. The day of the absent capitalist stockholder, who takes no interest in the operation of the works beyond the receipt of his dividend, is certainly passing away. The day of the valuable active worker in the industrial world is coming. Let, therefore, no young, practical workman be dis-

couraged. On the contrary, let him be cheered. More and
more it is becoming easier for the mechanic or practical
man of real ability to dictate terms to his employers.
Where there was one avenue of promotion, there are
now a dozen. The enormous concern of the future is to
divide its profits, not among hundreds of idle capitalists
who contribute nothing to its success, but among hundreds of its ablest employes, upon whose abilities and
exertions success greatly depends. The capitalist absent
stockholder is to be replaced by the able and present
worker.

As to the qualifications necessary for the promotion
of young practical men, one cannot do better than quote
George Eliot, who put the matter very pithily: "I'll tell
you how I got on. I kept my ears and my eyes open, and
I made my master's interest my own."

The condition precedent for promotion is, that the
man must first attract notice. He must do something
unusual, and especially must this be beyond the strict
boundary of his duties. He must suggest, or save, or
perform some service for his employer which he could
not be censured for not having done. When he has thus
attracted the notice of his immediate superior, whether
that be only the foreman of a gang, it matters not; the
first great step has been taken, for upon his immediate
superior promotion depends. How high he climbs is his
own affair.

We often hear men complaining that they get no
chance to show their ability, and when they do show
ability that it is not recognized. There is very little in
this. Self-interest compels the immediate superior to give
the highest place under him to the man who can best
fill it, for the officer is credited with the work of his

department as a whole. No man can keep another down. It will be noticed that many of the practical men who have earned fame and fortune have done so through holding on to improvements which they have made. Improvements are easily made by practical men in the branch in which they are engaged, for they have the most intimate knowledge of the problems to be solved there. It is in this way that many of our valuable improvements have come. The man who has made an improvement should always have an eye upon obtaining an interest in the business rather than an increase of salary. Even if the business up to this time has not become very prosperous, if he has the proper stuff in him, he believes that he could make it so, and so he could. All forms of business have their ups and downs. Seasons of depression and buoyancy succeed each other, one year of great profits, several years with little or none. This is a law of the business world, into the reasons of which I need not enter. Therefore the able young practical man should not have much regard as to a choice of the branch of business. Any business properly conducted will yield during a period of years a handsome return.

Dangers to Young Men

There are three great rocks ahead of the practical young man who has his foot upon the ladder and is beginning to rise. First, drunkenness, which, of course, is fatal. There is no use in wasting time upon any young man who drinks liquor, no matter how exceptional his talents. Indeed, the greater his talents are the greater the disappointment must be. The second rock ahead is speculation. The business of a speculator and that of a

manufacturer or man of affairs, are not only distinct
but incompatible. To be successful in the business world,
the manufacturer's and the merchant's profits only
should be sought. The manufacturer should go forward
steadily, meeting the market price. When there are
goods to sell, sell them; when supplies are needed, purchase them, without regard to the market price in either
case. I have never known a speculative manufacturer
or business man who scored a permanent success. He
is rich one day, bankrupt the next. Besides this, the
manufacturer aims to produce articles, and in so doing
to employ labour. This furnishes a laudable career. A
man in this avocation is useful to his kind. The merchant is usefully occupied distributing commodities; the
banker in providing capital. The third rock is akin to
speculation—indorsing. Business men require irregular
supplies of money, at some periods little, at others
enormous sums. Others being in the same condition,
there is strong temptation to indorse mutually. This
rock should be avoided. There are emergencies, no
doubt, in which men should help their friends, but there
is a rule that will keep one safe. No man should place
his name upon the obligation of another if he has not
sufficient to pay it without detriment to his own business. It is dishonest to do so. Men are trustees for those
who have trusted them, and the creditor is entitled to
all his capital and credit. For one's own firm, "your
name, your fortune, and your sacred honour"; but for
others, no matter under what circumstances, only such
aid as you can render without danger to your trust. It
is a safe rule, therefore, to give the cash direct that you
have to spare for others and never your indorsement
or guarantee.

One great cause of failure of young men in business is lack of concentration. They are prone to seek outside investments. The cause of many a surprising failure lies in so doing. Every dollar of capital and credit, every business thought, should be concentrated upon the one business upon which a man has embarked. He should never scatter his shot. It is a poor business which will not yield better returns for increased capital than any outside investment. No man or set of men or corporation can manage a business man's capital as well as he can manage it himself. The rule, "Do not put all your eggs in one basket," does not apply to a man's life work. Put all your eggs in one basket, and then watch that basket, is the true doctrine—the most valuable rule of all. While business of all kinds has gone and is still going rapidly. into a few vast concerns, it is nevertheless demonstrated every day that genuine ability, interested in the profits, is not only valuable but indispensable to their successful operation. Through corporations whose shares are sold daily upon the market; through partnerships that find it necessary to interest their ablest workers; through merchants who can manage their vast enterprises successfully only by interesting exceptional ability; in every quarter of the business world, avenues greater in number, wider in extent, easier of access than ever before existed, stand open to the sober, frugal, energetic and able mechanic, to the scientifically educated youth, to the office boy and to the clerk—avenues through which they can reap greater successes than were ever before within the reach of these classes in the history of the world.

When, therefore, the young man, in any position or

in any business, explains and complains that he has not
opportunity to prove his ability and to rise to partnership, the old answer suffices:

"The fault, dear Brutus, is not in our stars,
But in ourselves, that we are underlings."

WEALTH AND ITS USES

*Poverty an incentive to great achieve-
ment. Surplus wealth allows merely an
elaboration of the simple needs of life.
Wealth helps consolidation and cheapens
production.*

WEALTH AND ITS USES

Wealth," as Mr. Gladstone has recently said, "is the business of the world." That the acquisition of money is the business of the world arises from the fact that, with few unfortunate exceptions, young men are born to poverty, and therefore under the salutary operation of that remarkably wise law which makes for their good: "Thou shalt earn thy bread by the sweat of thy brow."

It is the fashion nowadays to bewail poverty as an evil, to pity the young man who is not born with a silver spoon in his mouth; but I heartily subscribe to President Garfield's doctrine, that "The richest heritage a young man can be born to is poverty." I make no idle prediction when I say that it is from that class from whom the good and the great will spring. It is not from the sons of the millionnaire or the noble that the world receives its teachers, its martyrs, its inventors, its statesmen, its poets, or even its men of affairs. It is from the cottage of the poor that all these spring. We can scarcely read one among the few "immortal names that were not born to die," or who has rendered exceptional service to our race, who had not the advantage of being cradled, nursed, and reared in the stimulating school of poverty. There is nothing so enervating, nothing so deadly in its

From a Lecture at Union College, Schenectady, N. Y., Jan'y, 1895.

effects upon the qualities which lead to the highest achievement, moral or intellectual, as hereditary wealth. And if there be among you a young man who feels that he is not compelled to exert himself in order to earn and live from his own efforts, I tender him my profound sympathy. Should such an one prove an exception to his fellows, and become a citizen living a life creditable to himself and useful to the State, instead of my profound sympathy I bow before him with profound reverence; for one who overcomes the seductive temptations which surround hereditary wealth is of the "salt of the earth," and entitled to double honour.

One gets a great many good things from the New York *Sun,* the distinguished proprietor and editor of which you had recently the pleasure, benefit, and honour of hearing. I beg to read this to you as one of its numerous rays of light:

"Our Boys

"Every moralist hard up for a theme asks at intervals: What is the matter with the sons of our rich and great men? The question is followed by statistics on the wickedness and bad endings of such sons.

"The trouble with the moralists is that they put the question wrong end first. There is nothing wrong with those foolish sons, except that they are unlucky; but there is something wrong with their fathers.

"Suppose that a fine specimen of an old deerhound, very successful in his business, should collect untold deer in the park, fatten them up, and then say to his puppies: 'Here, boys, I've had a hard life catching these deer, and I mean to see you enjoy yourselves. I'm so used to racing through the woods and hunting that I can't get out of the habit, but you boys just pile into that park and help yourselves.' Such a deerhound as that would be scorned by every human father. The human father would say to such a dog: 'Mr. Hound, you're simply ruining those puppies. Too much meat and no exercise will give them the mange and seventeen other troubles; and if distemper doesn't kill them, they will be a knock-kneed, watery-eyed lot of disgraces to you. For heaven's sake keep them down to dog-biscuit and work them hard.'

"That same human father does with great pride the very thing that he would condemn in a dog or a cat. He ruins his children, and then, when he gets old, profusely and sadly observes that he has done everything for them, and yet they have disappointed him. He who gives to his son an office which he has not deserved and enables him to disgrace his father and friends, deserves no more sympathy than any Mr. Fagin deliberately educating a boy to be dishonest.

"The fat, useless pug-dogs which young women drag wheezing about at the end of strings are not to blame for their condition, and the same thing is true of rich men's sons. The young women who overfeed the dogs and the fathers who ruin their sons have themselves to thank.

"No man would advocate the thing, perhaps; but who can doubt that if there could be a law making it impossible for a man to inherit anything but a good education and a good constitution, it would supply us in short order with a better lot of men?"

This is sound. "If you see it in *The Sun* it is so." At least it is in this case.

It is not the poor young man who goes forth to his

work in the morning and labours until evening that we should pity. It is the son of the rich man to whom Providence has not been so kind as to trust with this honourable task. It is not the busy man, but the man of idleness, who should arouse our sympathy and cause us sorrow. "Happy is the man who has found his work," says Carlyle. I say, "Happy is the man who has to work and to work hard, and work long." A great poet has said: "He prayeth best who loveth best." Some day this may be parodied into: "He prayeth best who worketh best." An honest day's work well performed is not a bad sort of prayer. The cry goes forth often nowadays, "Abolish poverty!" but fortunately this cannot be done; and the poor we are always to have with us. Abolish poverty, and what would become of the race? Progress, development, would cease. Consider its future if dependent upon the rich. The supply of the good and the great would cease, and human society retrograde into barbarism. Abolish luxury, if you please, but leave us the soil, upon which alone the virtues and all that is precious in human character grow; poverty—honest poverty.

I will assume for the moment, gentlemen, that you were all fortunate enough to be born poor. Then the first question that presses upon you is this: What shall I learn to do for the community which will bring me in exchange enough wealth to feed, clothe, lodge, and keep me independent of charitable aid from others? What shall I do for a living? And the young man may like, or think that he would like, to do one thing rather than another; to pursue one branch or another; to be a business man or craftsman of some kind, or minister, physician, electrician, architect, editor, or lawyer. I have no doubt some of you in your wildest flights aspire to be journal-

ists. But it does not matter what the young man likes or
dislikes, he always has to keep in view the main point:
Can I attain such a measure of proficiency in the branch
preferred as will certainly enable me to earn a livelihood
by its practice?

The young man, therefore, who resolves to make
himself useful to his kind, and therefore entitled to receive in return from a grateful community which he
benefits the sum necessary for his support, sees clearly
one of the highest duties of a young man. He meets the
vital question immediately pressing upon him for decision, and decides it rightly.

So far, then, there is no difference about the acquisition of wealth. Every one is agreed that it is the first
duty of a young man to so train himself as to be self-
supporting. Nor is there difficulty about the next step,
for the young man cannot be said to have performed the
whole of his duty if he leaves out of account the con-
tingencies of life, liability to accident, illness, and trade
depressions like the present. Wisdom calls upon him to
have regard for these things; and it is a part of his duty
that he begin to save a portion of his earnings and
invest them, not in speculation, but in securities or in
property, or in a legitimate business in such form as will,
perhaps, slowly but yet surely grow into the reserve upon
which he can fall back in emergencies or in old age, and
live upon his own savings. I think we are all agreed as
to the advisability—nay, the duty—of laying up a competence, and hence to retain our self-respect.

Besides this, I take it that some of you have already
decided just as soon as possible to ask "a certain young
lady" to share his lot, or perhaps his lots, and, of course,
he should have a lot or two to share. Marriage is a

very serious business indeed, and gives rise to many weighty considerations. "Be sure to marry a woman with good common-sense," was the advice given me by my mentor, and I just hand it down to you. Common sense is the most uncommon and most valuable quality in man or woman. But before you have occasion to provide yourself with a helpmate, there comes the subject upon which I am to address you—"Wealth"—not wealth in millions, but simply revenue sufficient for modest, independent living. This opens up the entire subject of wealth in a greater or less degree.

Now, what is wealth? How is it created and distributed? There are not far from us immense beds of coal which have lain for millions of years useless, and therefore valueless. Through some experiment, or perhaps accident, it was discovered that black stone would burn and give forth heat. Men sank shafts, erected machinery, mined and brought forth coal, and sold it to the community. It displaced the use of wood as fuel, say at one-half the cost. Immediately every bed of coal became valuable because useful, or capable of being made so; and here a new article worth hundreds, yes, thousands of millions was added to the wealth of the community. A Scotch mechanic one day, as the story goes, gazing into the fire upon which water was boiling in a kettle, saw the steam raise the lid, as hundreds of thousands had seen before him; but none saw in that sight what he did—the steam engine, which does the work of the world at a cost so infinitely trifling compared with what the plans known before involved, that the wealth of the world has been increased one dare not estimate how much. The saving that the community makes is the root of wealth in any branch of material development. Now, a young man's labour or service to the community creates wealth just in proportion as his service is useful to the community, as it either saves or improves upon existing methods. Commodore Vanderbilt saw, I think, thirteen different short railway lines between New York and Buffalo, involving thirteen different managements, and a disjointed and tedious service. Albany, Schenectady, Utica, Syracuse, Auburn, Rochester, etc., were heads of some of these companies. He consolidated them all, making one direct line, over which your Empire State Express flies fifty-one miles an hour, the fastest time in the world; and a hundred passengers patronize the lines where one did in olden days. He rendered the community a special service, which, being followed by others, reduces the cost of bringing food from the prairies of the West to your doors to a trifling sum per ton. He produced, and is every day producing, untold wealth to the community by so doing, and the profit he reaped for himself was but a drop in the bucket compared with that which he showered upon the State and the nation.

Now, in the olden days, before steam, electricity, or any other of the modern inventions which unitedly have changed the whole aspect of the world, everything was done upon a small scale. There was no room for great ideas to operate upon a large scale, and thus to produce great wealth to the inventor, discoverer, originator, or executive. New inventions gave this opportunity, and many large fortunes were made by individuals. But in our day we are rapidly passing, if we have not already passed, this stage of development, and few large fortunes can now be made in any part of the world, except from one cause, the rise in the value of real estate.

Manufacturing, transportation both upon the land and upon the sea, banking, insurance, have all passed into the hands of corporations composed of hundreds and in many cases thousands of shareholders. The New York Central Railroad is owned by more than ten thousand shareholders, the Pennsylvania Railroad is owned by more people than the vast army which it employs, and nearly one-fourth of the number are the estates of women and children. It is so with the great manufacturing companies; so with the great steamship lines; it is so, as you know, with banks, insurance companies, and indeed with all branches of business. It is a great mistake for young men to say to themselves, "Oh! we cannot enter into business." If any of you have saved as much as $50 or $100, I do not know any branch of business into which you cannot plunge at once. You can get your certificate of stock and attend the meeting of stockholders, make your speeches and suggestions, quarrel with the president, and instruct the management of the affairs of the company, and have all the rights and influence of an owner. You can buy shares in anything, from newspapers to tenement-houses; but capital is so poorly paid in these days that I advise you to exercise much circumspection before you invest. As I have said to workingmen and to ministers, college professors, artists, musicians, and physicians, and all the professional classes: Do not invest in any business concerns whatever; the risks of business are not for such as you. Buy a home for yourself first; and if you have any surplus, buy another lot or another house, or take a mortgage upon one, or upon a railway, and let it be a first mortgage, and be satisfied with moderate interest. Do you know that out of every hundred that attempt

business upon their own account statistics are said to
show that ninety-five sooner or later fail? I know that
from my own experience. I can quote the lines of
Hudibras and tell you, as far as one manufacturing
branch is concerned, that what he found to be true is
still true to an eminent degree to-day:

> "Ay me! What perils do environ
> The man that meddles with cold iron."

The shareholders of iron and steel concerns to-day
can certify that this is so, whether the iron or steel be
hot or cold; and such is also the case in other branches
of business.

The principal complaint against our industrial conditions of to-day is that they cause great wealth to flow
into the hands of the few. Well, of the very few, indeed,
is this true. It was formerly so, as I have explained,
immediately after the new inventions had changed the
conditions of the world. To-day it is not true. Wealth
is being more and more distributed among the many.
The amount of the combined profits of labour and
capital which goes to labour was never so great as to-
day, the amount going to capital never so small. While
the earnings of capital have fallen more than one-half,
in many cases have been entirely obliterated, statistics
prove that the earnings of labour were never so high as
they were previous to the recent unprecedented depression in business, while the cost of living,—the necessaries of life,—have fallen in some cases nearly one-half.
Great Britain has an income tax, and our country is to
be subject to this imposition for a time. The British returns show that during the eleven years from 1876 to
1887 the number of men receiving from $750 to $2,500

per year, increased more than 21 per cent., while the number receiving from $5,000 to $25,000 actually decreased 2 1-2 per cent.

You may be sure, gentlemen, that the question of the distribution of wealth is settling itself rapidly under present conditions, and settling itself in the right direction. The few rich are getting poorer, and the toiling masses are getting richer. Nevertheless, a few exceptional men may yet make fortunes, but these will be more moderate than in the past. This may not be quite as fortunate for the masses of the people as is now believed, because great accumulations of wealth in the hands of one enterprising man who still toils on are sometimes most productive of all the forms of wealth. Take the richest man the world ever saw, who died in New York some years ago. What was found in his case? That, with the exception of a small percentage used for daily expenses, his entire fortune and all its surplus earnings were invested in enterprises which developed the railway system of our country, which gives to the people the cheapest transportation known. Whether the millionnaire wishes it or not, he cannot evade the law which under present conditions compels him to use his millions for the good of the people. All that he gets during the few years of his life is that he may live in a finer house, surround himself with finer furniture, and works of art which may be added: he could even have a grander library, more of the gods around him; but, as far as I have known millionnaires, the library is the least used part of what he would probably consider "furniture" in all his mansion. He can eat richer food and drink richer wines, which only hurt him. But truly the modern millionnaire is generally a man of very simple tastes and even miserly habits. He spends little upon himself, and is the toiling bee laying up the honey in the industrial hive, which all the inmates of that hive, the community in general, will certainly enjoy. Here is the true description of the millionnaire, as given by Mr. Carter in his remarkable speech before the Behring Sea tribunal at Paris:

"Those who are most successful in the acquisition of property and who acquire it to such an enormous extent are the very men who are able to control it, to invest it, and to handle it in the way most useful to society. It is because they have those qualities that they are able to engross it to so large an extent. They really own, in any just sense of the word, only what they consume. The rest is all held for the benefit of the public. They are the custodians of it. They invest it; they see that it is put into this employment, that employment, another employment. All labour is employed by it and employed in the best manner, and it is thus made the most productive. These men who acquire these hundreds of millions are really groaning under a servitude to the rest of society, for that is practically their condition; and society really endures it because it is best for them that it should be so."

Here is another estimate by a no less remarkable man. Your friend, Mr. Dana, justly said at Cornell:

"That is one class of men that I refer to, the thinkers, the men of science, the inventors; and the other class is that of those whom God has endowed with a genius for saving, for getting rich, for bringing wealth together, for accumulating and concentrating money, men against whom it is now fashionable to declaim, and against whom legislation is sometimes directed. And yet is there any benefactor of humanity who is to be envied in his achievements, and in the memory and the monuments he has left behind him, more than Ezra Cornell? Or, to take another example that is here before our eyes, more than Henry W. Sage? These are men who knew how to get rich, because they had been endowed with that faculty; and when they got rich, they knew how to give it for great public enterprises, for uses that will remain living, immortal as long as man remains upon earth. The men of genius and the men of money, those who prepare new agencies of life, and those who accumulate and save the money for great enterprises and great public works, these are the peculiar and the inestimable leaders of the world, as the twentieth century is opening upon us."

The bees of a hive do not destroy the honey-making bees, but the drones. It will be a great mistake for the community to shoot the millionnaires, for they are the bees that make the most honey, and contribute most to the hive even after they have gorged themselves full. Here is a remarkable fact, that the masses of the people in any country are prosperous and comfortable just in proportion as there are millionnaires. Take Russia, with its population little better than serfs, and living at the point of starvation upon the meanest possible fare, such fare as none of our people could or would eat, and you do not find one millionnaire in Russia, always excepting the Emperor and a few nobles who own the land, owing to their political system. It is the same, to a great extent, in Germany. There are only two millionnaires known to me in the whole German Empire. In France, where the people are better off than in Germany, you cannot count one half-dozen millionnaires in the whole country. In the old home of our race, in Britain, which is the richest country in all Europe—the richest country in the world save one, our own—there are more millionnaires than in the whole of the rest of Europe, and its people are better off than in any other. You come to our own land: we have more millionnaires than in all the rest of the world put together, although we have not one to every ten that is reputed so. I have seen a list of supposed millionnaires prepared by a well-known lawyer of Brooklyn, which made me laugh, as it has made many others. I saw men rated there as millionnaires who could not pay their debts. Many should have had a cipher cut from their $1,000,000. Some time ago I sat next Mr. Evarts at dinner, and the conversation touched upon the idea that men should distribute their wealth during their lives for the public good. One gentleman said that was correct, giving many reasons, one of which was that, of course, they could not take it with them at death.

"Well," said Mr. Evarts, "I do not know about that. My experience as a New York lawyer is that, somehow or other, they do succeed in taking at least four-fifths of it." Their reputed wealth was never found at death.

Whatever the ideal conditions may develop, it seems to me Mr. Carter and Mr. Dana are right. Under our present conditions the millionnaire who toils on is the cheapest article which the community secures at the price it pays for him, namely, his shelter, clothing, and food.

The inventions of to-day lead to concentrating industrial and commercial affairs into huge concerns. You cannot work the Bessemer process successfully without employing thousands of men upon one spot. You could not make the armour for ships without first expending seven millions of dollars, as the Bethlehem Company has spent. You cannot make a yard of cotton goods in competition with the world without having an immense factory and thousands of men and women aiding in the process. The great electric establishment here in your town succeeds because it has spent millions, and is prepared to do its work upon a great scale. Under such conditions it is impossible but that wealth will flow into the hands of a few men in prosperous times beyond their needs. But out of fifty great fortunes which Mr. Blaine had a list made of he found only one man who was reputed to have made a large fortune in manufacturing. These are made from real estate more than from all other causes combined; next follows transportation, banking. The whole manufacturing world furnished but one millionnaire.

But assuming that surplus wealth flows into the hands of a few men, what is their duty? How is the struggle for dollars to be lifted from the sordid atmosphere surrounding business and made a noble career? Now, wealth has hitherto been distributed in three ways: The first and chief one is by willing it at death to the family. Now, beyond bequeathing to those dependent upon one the revenue needful for modest and independent living, is such a use of wealth either right or wise? I ask you to think over the result, as a rule, of millions given over to young men and women, the sons and daughters of the millionnaire. You will find that, as a rule, it is not good for the daughters; and this is seen in the character and conduct of the men who marry them. As for the sons, you have their condition as described in the extract

which I read you from *The Sun*. Nothing is truer than
this, that as a rule the "almighty dollar" bequeathed to
sons or daughters by millions proves an almighty curse.
It is not the good of the child which the millionnaire
parent considers when he makes these bequests, it is his
own vanity; it is not affection for the child, it is self-
glorification for the parent which is at the root of this
injurious disposition of wealth. There is only one thing
to be said for this mode, it furnishes one of the most
efficacious means of rapid distribution of wealth ever
known.

There is a second use of wealth, less common than the
first, which is not so injurious to the community, but
which should bring no credit to the testator. Money is
left by millionnaires to public institutions when they
must relax their grasp upon it. There is no grace, and
can be no blessing, in giving what cannot be withheld.
It is no gift, because it is not cheerfully given, but only
granted at the stern summons of death. The miscarriage
of these bequests, the litigation connected with them,
and the manner in which they are frittered away seem
to prove that the Fates do not regard them with a kindly
eye. We are never without a lesson that the only mode
of producing lasting good by giving large sums of
money is for the millionnaire to give as close attention
to its distribution during his life as he did to its acquisition. We have to-day the noted case of five or six millions of dollars left by a great lawyer to found a public
library in New York, an institution needed so greatly
that the failure of this bequest is a misfortune. It is
years since he died; the will is pronounced invalid
through a flaw, although there is no doubt of the intention of the donor. It is sad commentary upon the

folly of men holding the millions which they cannot use until they are unable to put them to the end they desire. Peter Cooper, Pratt of Baltimore, and Pratt of Brooklyn, and others are the type of men who should be taken by you as your model; they distributed their surplus during life.

The third use, and the only noble use of surplus wealth, is this: That it be regarded as a sacred trust, to be administered by its possessor, into whose hands it flows, for the highest good of the people. Man does not live by bread alone, and five or ten cents a day more revenue scattered over thousands would produce little or no good. Accumulated into a great fund and expended as Mr. Cooper expended it for the Cooper Institute, it establishes something that will last for generations. It will educate the brain, the spiritual part of man. It furnishes a ladder upon which the aspiring poor may climb; and there is no use whatever, gentlemen, trying to help people who do not help themselves. You cannot push any one up a ladder unless he be willing to climb a little himself. When you stop boosting, he falls, to his injury. Therefore, I have often said, and I now repeat, that the day is coming, and already we see its dawn, in which the man who dies possessed of millions of available wealth which was free and in his hands ready to be distributed will die disgraced. Of course I do not mean that the man in business may not be stricken down with his capital in the business, which cannot be withdrawn, for capital is the tool with which he works his wonders and produces more wealth. I refer to the man who dies possessed of millions of securities which are held simply for the interest they produce, that he may add to his hoard of miserable dollars. By administering surplus wealth during life great wealth may become a blessing to the community, and the occupation of the business man accumulating wealth may be elevated so as to rank with any profession. In this way he may take rank even with the physician, one of the highest of our professions, because he too, in a sense, will be a physician, looking after and trying not to cure, but to prevent, the ills of humanity. To those of you who are compelled or who desire to follow a business life and to accumulate wealth, I commend this idea. The epitaph which every rich man should wish himself justly entitled to is that seen upon the monument to Pitt:

> He lived without ostentation,
> And he died poor.

Such is the man whom the future is to honour, while he who dies in old age retired from business, possessed of millions of available wealth, is to die unwept, unhonoured, and unsung.

I may justly divide young men into four classes:

First, those who must work for a living, and set before them as their aim the acquisition of a modest competence—of course, with a modest but picturesque cottage in the country and one as a companion "who maketh sunshine in a shady place" and is the good angel of his life. The motto of this class, No. 1, might be given as "Give me neither poverty nor riches." "From the anxieties of poverty as from the responsibilities of wealth, good Lord, deliver us."

Class No. 2, comprising those among you who are determined to acquire wealth, whose aim in life is to belong to that much-talked-of and grandly abused class, the millionaires, those who start to labour for the greatest good of the greatest number, but the greatest number always number one, the motto of this class being short and to the point: "Put money in thy purse."

Now, the third class comes along. The god they worship is neither wealth nor happiness. They are inflamed with "noble ambition;" the desire of fame is the controlling element of their lives. Now, while this is not so ignoble as the desire for material wealth, it must be said that it betrays more vanity. The shrine of fame has many worshippers. The element of vanity is seen in its fiercest phase among those who come before the public. It is well known, for instance, that musicians, actors, and even painters—all the artistic class—are peculiarly prone to excessive personal vanity. This has often been wondered at; but the reason probably is that the musician and the actor, and even the painter, may be transcendent in his special line without being even highly educated, without having an all-around brain. Some peculiarities, some one element in his character, may give him prominence or fame, so that his love of art, or of use through art, is entirely drowned by a narrow, selfish, personal vanity. But we find this liability in a lesser degree all through the professions, the politician, the lawyer, and, with reverence be it spoken, sometimes the minister; less, I think, in the physician than in any of the professions, probably because he, more than in any other profession, is called to deal with the sad realities of life face to face. He of all men sees the vanity of vanities. An illustration of this class is well drawn in Hotspur's address:

By heavens, methinks it were an easy leap,
To pluck bright honour from the pale-faced moon;
Or dive into the bottom of the deep,
Where fathom-line could never touch the ground,
And pluck up drowned honour by the locks;
So he that doth redeem her thence might wear
Without corrival all her dignities.

Mark, young gentlemen, he cares not for use; he cares not for state; he cares only for himself, and, as a vain peacock, struts across the stage.

Now, gentlemen, it does not seem to me that the love of wealth is the controlling desire of so many as the love of fame; and this is matter for sincere congratulation, and proves that under the irresistible laws of evolution the race is slowly moving onward and upward. Take the whole range of the artistic world, which gives sweetness and light to life, which refines and adorns, and surely the great composer, painter, pianist, lawyer, judge, statesman, all those in public life, care less for millions than for professional reputation in their respective fields of labour. What cared Washington, Franklin, Lincoln, or Grant and Sherman for wealth? Nothing! What cared Harrison or Cleveland, two poor men, not unworthy successors? What care the Judges of our Supreme Court, or even the leading counsel that plead before them? The great preachers, physicians, great teachers, are not concerned about the acquisition of wealth. The treasure they seek is in the reputation acquired through their service to others, and this is certainly a great step from the millionnaire class, who struggle to old age, and through old age to the verge of the grave, with no ambition, apparently, except to add to their pile of miserable dollars. But there is a fourth class, higher than all the preceding, who worship neither at the shrine of wealth nor fame, but at the noblest of all shrines, the shrine of service—service to the race. Self-abnegation is its watchword. Members of this inner and higher circle seek not popular applause, are concerned not with being popular, but with being right. They say with Confucius: "It concerneth me not that I have not high office; what concerns me is to make myself worthy of office." It is not cast down by poverty, neither unduly elated by prosperity. The man belonging to this class simply seeks to do his duty day by day in such manner as may enable him to honour himself, fearing nothing but his own self-reproach. I have known men and women not prominently before the public, for this class courts not prominence, but who in their lives proved themselves to have reached this ideal stage. Now, I will give you for this class the fitting illustration from the words of a Scotch poet who died altogether too young:

> I will go forth 'mong men, not mailed in scorn,
> But in the armour of a pure intent.
> Great duties are before me, and great songs;
> And whether crowned or crownless when I fall,
> It matters not, so as God's work is done.
> I've learned to prize the quiet lightning deed,
> Not the applauding thunder at its heels
> Which men call fame.

Then, gentlemen, standing upon the threshold of life, you have the good, better, best presented to you—the three stages of development, the natural, spiritual, and celestial, they may fitly be called. One has success in material things for its aim—not without benefit this for the race as a whole, because it lifts the individual from the animal and demands the exercise of many valuable qualities: sobriety, industry, and self-discipline. The second rises still higher: the reward sought for being things more of the spirit—not gross and material, but invisible; and not of the flesh, but of the brain, the spiritual part of man; and this brings into play innumerable virtues which make good and useful men.

The third or celestial class stands upon an entirely different footing from the others in this, that selfish considerations are subordinated in the select brotherhood of the best, the service to be done for others being the first consideration. The reward of either wealth or fame is unsought, for these have learned and know full well that virtue is its own and the only exceeding great reward; and this once enjoyed, all other rewards are not worth seeking. And so wealth and even fame are dethroned; and there stands enthroned the highest standard of all—your own approval flowing from a faithful discharge of duty as you see it, fearing no consequences, seeking no reward.

It does not matter much what branch of effort your tastes or judgment draw you to, the one great point is that you should be drawn to some one branch. Then perform your whole duty in it and a little more—the "little more" being vastly important. We have the words of a great poet for it, that the man who does the best he can, can whiles do more. Maintain your self-respect as the most precious jewel of all and the only true way to win the respect of others, and then remember what Emerson says, for what he says here is true: "No young man can be cheated out of an honourable career in life unless he cheat himself."

THE BUGABOO OF TRUSTS

What is a Trust? Combinations the order of the day. Trusts that increase production and reduce prices.

THE BUGABOO OF TRUSTS

We must all have our toys; the child his rattle, the adult his hobby, the man of pleasure the fashion, the man of art his Master; and mankind in its various divisions requires a change of toys at short intervals. The same rule holds good in the business world. We have had our age of "consolidations" and "watered stocks." Not long ago everything was a "syndicate;" the word is already becoming obsolete and the fashion is for "Trusts," which will in turn no doubt give place to some new panacea, that is in turn to be displaced by another, and so on without end. The great laws of the economic world, like all laws affecting society, being the genuine outgrowth of human nature, alone remain unchanged through all these changes. Whenever consolidations or watered stocks, or syndicates, or Trusts endeavour to circumvent these, it always has been found that after the collision there is nothing left of the panaceas, while the great laws continue to grind out their irresistible consequences as before.

It is worth while to inquire into the appearance and growth of Trusts and learn what environments produce them. Their genesis is as follows: a demand exists for a certain article, beyond the capacity of existing works to supply it. Prices are high, and profits tempting. Every manufacturer of that article immediately proceeds to enlarge his works and increase their producing power. In

addition to this the unusual profits attract the attention
of his principal managers or those who are interested to
a greater or less degree in the factory. These communi-
cate the knowledge of the prosperity of the works to
others. New partnerships are formed, and new works
are erected, and before long the demand for the article
is fully satisfied, and prices do not advance. In a short
time the supply becomes greater than the demand, there
are a few tons or yards more in the market for sale than
required, and prices begin to fall. They continue falling
until the article is sold at cost to the less favourably situated or less ably managed factory; and even until the
best managed and best equipped factory is not able to
produce the article at the prices at which it can be sold.
Political economy says that here the trouble will end.
Goods will not be produced at less than cost. This was
true when Adam Smith wrote, but it is not quite true
to-day. When an article was produced by a small manufacturer, employing, probably at his own home, two or
three journeymen and an apprentice or two, it was an
easy matter for him to limit or even to stop production.
As manufacturing is carried on to-day, in enormous establishments with five or ten millions of dollars of capital
invested, and with thousands of workers, it costs the
manufacturer much less to run at a loss per ton or per
yard than to check his production. Stoppage would be
serious indeed. The condition of cheap manufacture is
running full. Twenty sources of expense are *fixed
charges,* many of which stoppage would only increase.
Therefore the article is produced for months, and in
some cases that I have known for years, not only without profit or without interest upon capital, but to the
impairment of the capital invested. Manufacturers have

balanced their books year after year only to find their capital reduced at each successive balance. While continuing to produce may be costly, the manufacturer knows too well that stoppage would be ruin. His brother manufacturers are of course in the same situation. They see the savings of many years, as well perhaps as the capital they have succeeded in borrowing, becoming less and less, with no hope of a change in the situation. It is in soil thus prepared that anything promising relief is gladly welcomed. The manufacturers are in the position of patients that have tried in vain every doctor of the regular school for years, and are now liable to become the victims of any quack that appears. Combinations—syndicates—Trusts—they are willing to try anything. A meeting is called, and in the presence of immediate danger they decide to take united action and form a Trust. Each factory is rated as worth a certain amount. Officers are chosen, and through these the entire product of the article in question is to be distributed to the public, at remunerative prices.

Such is the genesis of "Trusts" in manufactured articles. In transportation the situation, while practically the same, differs in some particulars. Many small railway lines are built under separate charters. A genius in affairs sees that the eight or ten separate organizations, with as many different ideas of management, equipment, etc., are as useless as were the two hundred and fifty petty kings in Germany, and, Bismarck-like, he sweeps them out of existence, creates a great through line, doubles the securities or stock, the interest upon which is paid out of the saving effected by consolidation, and all is highly satisfactory, as in the case of the New York Central. Or a line is built and managed with such sagacity as distinguishes the Pennsylvania Railroad, and it succeeds in developing the resources of the States so extensively that upon a line of three hundred and fifty miles between Pittsburg and Philadelphia it nets about thirteen millions of dollars per annum. Twelve millions of dollars of this it shows upon its books. From one to two millions extra are expended in making one of the best lines in the world out of a road which was originally designed as a horse-railroad. We do not call our railroad combinations Trusts, but they are substantially such, since they aim at raising and maintaining transportation rates in certain districts. They are "combinations" or "systems" which aim at monopolies within these districts.

During the recent Presidential campaign it suited the purpose of one of the parties to connect Trusts with the doctrine of protection. But Trusts are confined to no country, and are not in any way dependent upon fiscal regulations. The greatest Trust of all just now is the Copper Trust, which is French, and has its headquarters in Paris. The Salt Trust is English, with its headquarters in London. The Wire-rod Trust is German. The Steel-rail Trust that ever existed was an international one which embraced all the works in Europe. Trusts, either in transportation or manufactures, are the products of human weakness, and this weakness is co-extensive with the race.

There is one huge combination classed with Trusts which is so exceptional in its origin and history that it deserves a separate paragraph. I refer to the Standard Oil Company. So favourable an opportunity to control a product perhaps never arose as in the case of petroleum. At an early stage a few of the ablest business men that the world has ever seen realized the importance of the discovery, and invested largely in the purchase of property connected with it. The success of the petroleum business was phenomenal, and so was the success of these people. The profits they made, and, no doubt, as much capital as they could borrow, were fearlessly reinvested, and they soon became the principal owners, and finally, substantially the only owners of the territory which contained this great source of wealth. The Standard Oil Company would long ago have gone to pieces had it not been managed, upon the whole, in harmony with the laws which control business. It is generally admitted that the prices of oil to the consumer are as low to-day, and many think that they are even lower, than could have been attained had the business not been grouped and managed as one vast concern in the broad spirit for which the Standard Oil managers are famous. They are in the position somewhat of the Colemans, of Pennsylvania, who possess the chief source of the ore supply in the East. They own the Cornwall deposit of ore as the Standard Oil Company owns the source of the oil deposit. But as the company has continually to deal with the finding of oil in other localities, the price of its existence and success is the continuance of that exceptional ability in its councils and management displayed by its founders. Threatened opposition arises every now and then, and the chances are greatly in favour of the Standard Oil Company losing its practical monopoly, and going the way of all huge combinations. It is a hundred to one whether it will survive when the present men at the head retire; or perhaps I should say when the present man retires, for wonderful organizations imply a genius at the head, a commander-in-chief, with exceptionally able corps commanders no doubt, but still a Grant at the head. To those who quote the Standard Oil Company as an evidence that Trusts or combinations can be permanently successful, I say, wait and see. I have spoken thus freely of that company, because I am ignorant of its management, profits, and modes of action. I view it from the outside, as a student of political economy only, and as such have endeavoured to apply to it the principles which I know *will* have their way, no matter how formidable the attempt made to defeat their operations.

We have given the genesis of Trusts and combinations in their several forms. The question is, Do they menace the permanent interest of the nation? Are they a source of serious danger? Or are they to prove, as many other similar forms have proved, mere passing phases of unrest and transition? To answer this question let us follow the operation of the manufacturing Trust which we have in imagination created, salt or sugar, nails, beans, or lead or copper; it is all the same. The sugar refiners, let us say, have formed a Trust after competing one with another through years of disastrous business, and all the sugar manufactured in the country in existing factories is sold through one channel at advanced prices. Profits begin to grow. Dividends are paid, and those who before saw their property vanishing before their eyes are now made happy. The dividends from that part of a man's capital invested in the sugar business yield him profit far above the capital he has invested in various other affairs. The prices of sugar are such that the capital invested in a new factory would yield enormously. He is perhaps bound not to enlarge his factory or to enter into a new factory, but his relatives and acquaintances soon discover the fresh opportunity for gain. He can advise them to push the completion of a small factory, which, of course, must be taken into the Trust. Or, even if he does not give his friends this intimation, capital is always upon the alert, especially when it is bruited about that a Trust has been formed, as in the case of sugar, and immediately new sugar manufactories spring up, as if by magic. The more successful the Trust, the surer these off-shoots are to sprout. Every victory is a defeat. Every factory that the Trust buys is the sure creator of another, and so on *ad infinitum,* until the bubble bursts. The sugar refiners have tried to get more from capital in a special case than capital yields in general. They have endeavoured to raise a part of the ocean of capital above the level of the surrounding waters, and over their bulwarks the floods have burst, and capital, like water, has again found its level. It is true that to regain this level a longer or a shorter period may be required, during which the article affected may be sold to the consumer in limited quantities at a higher rate than before existed. But for this the consumer is amply recompensed in the years that follow, during which the struggle between the discordant and competitive factories becomes severer than it ever was before, and lasts till the great law of the survival of the fittest vindicates itself. Those factories and managers that can produce to the best advantage eventually close the less competent. Capital wisely managed yields its legitimate profit. After a time the growth of demand enables capital to receive an unusual profit. This in turn attracts fresh capital to the manufacture, and we have a renewal of the old struggle, the consumer reaping the benefit.

Such is the law, such has been the law, and such promises to be the law for the future; for, so far, no device has yet been devised that has permanently thwarted its operation. Given freedom of competition, and all combinations or trusts that attempt to exact from the consumer more than a legitimate return upon capital and services, write the charter of their own defeat. We have many proofs that this great law does not sleep, and that it will not be suppressed. Some time ago, as I have stated, the steel rail manufacturers of Europe formed a trust and advanced the price of rails to such an extent that American manufacturers were able for the first, and perhaps for the last time, to export steel rails to Canada in competition with the European. But the misunderstandings and quarrels, inseparable from these attempted unions of competitors, soon broke the Trust. With vindictive feelings, added to what was before business rivalry, the struggle was renewed, and the steel rail industry of Europe has never recovered. It was found that the advance in prices had only galvanized into life concerns which never should have attempted to manufacture rails; and so that Trust died a natural death.

During the great depression which existed for several years in this country in the steel rail trade many anxious meetings were held under circumstances described in the genesis of Trusts, and it was resolved that the plan of restricting production should be tried. Fortunately reaction soon came. A demand for rails set in before the plan went into operation, and, as a matter of fact, no restriction of product was ever attempted, and the steel rail industry was thus saved from a great error.

We have recently seen the lead industry of this country shattered and its chief owners bankrupted. The newspapers a few weeks ago were filled with accounts of the convention of the growers of cattle in St. Louis, resolved to break down the combination of slaughterers and shippers in Chicago and Kansas City. No business

was poorer in this country for many years than the manufacture of nails. It was overdone. To remedy this the
manufacturers did not form a Trust so far as the sale of
product was concerned, but they restricted production. A
certain percentage of their machines was kept idle. This
percentage was increased from time to time, and only
the quantity made that the market would take at a certain
price. But the result was that there were soon more
machines in America for the manufacture of iron nails
added to the works than the demand for nails will require
for many years to come, and this combination of nail
manufacturers went the way of all Trusts, and left the
business in a worse plight than it was before.

The Sugar Trust has already a noted competitor at its
heels. The Copper Trust is in danger. All stand prepared
to attack a "Trust" or "combine" if it proves itself worth
attacking; in other words, if it succeeds in raising its
profits above the natural level of profits throughout the
country it is subject to competition from every quarter,
and must finally break down. It is unnecessary to devote
much attention to the numerous Trusts in minor articles
which one reads of, a new one appearing every few days
and others passing out of existence, because they are all
subject to the great law. The newspapers charge that
Trusts exist or have existed in wall paper, shoe laces,
lumber, coal, coke, brick, screws, rope, glass, school-
books, insurance and hardware, and twenty more articles;
but the fitting epitaph for these ephemeral creations is

> "If I was so soon to be done for,
> I wonder what I was begun for!"

We may exclaim with Macbeth, as he watched the
shadowy descendants of Banquo filing past, "What, will

the line stretch out to the crack of doom?" But as with Banquo's procession, so with Trusts, it is comforting to remember that as one approaches another disappears. They come like shadows, and so depart.

So much for Trusts in the manufacturing department. Let us now examine the railways, whose "pools" and "combinations" and "differentials" alarm some people. In all their various forms, these are the efforts of capital to protect itself from the play of economic forces, centred in free competition. In most cases the stocks of railways have been watered. Calculated upon the real capital invested the dividends of railway lines have been unusual, and much above the return which capital generally has yielded in other forms of investment. The entire capital stock of railways in the West as a rule has cost little or nothing, the proceeds of the bonds issued having been sufficient to build them. The efforts of railway managers to-day are therefore directed to obtain a return upon more capital than would be required to duplicate their respective properties. Their combinations and agreements of various kinds, which come to naught a few months after they are solemnly entered into, are evidences of this attempt. But, just as enormous profits on capital, received from the manufacture of any article, are sure to attract additional capital into the production of the article, so, in like manner, the unusual success of these railroads attracts new capital into their territory. New York Central paying dividends upon its eighty per cent. stock dividend culminates in the West Shore. The Pennsylvania Railroad, earning, as I have said, something like thirteen millions per annum upon its line in Pennsylvania, has its South Pennsylvania. One line between Chicago and Milwaukee being greatly profitable, fortunately

brought into existence a parallel road. The two being
unusually profitable, fortunately resulted in a third.
There was one line between these points, and now there
are six; and should the six combine to-morrow and exact
from the public one per cent. more return upon capital
than the average return, there would soon be seven, and
very properly so.

This proves once more that there is no possibility of
evading the great law, provided capital is free to embark
in competing lines. In Great Britain and throughout
Europe generally a different policy has been pursued in
regard to railways from that of the free-to-all policy
which we have followed. The railways and other transportation routes of Great Britain, in order to get permission to build, have cost nearly as much per mile as our
cheapest Western lines have cost to build. Manchester,
for instance, has recently decided to construct a canal,
thirty miles long, to Liverpool, and the expense incurred
in obtaining permission from Parliament to embark
capital in this enterprise has cost nearly half a million of
dollars up to this date. The Government, through a committee of Parliament, determines whether a proposed
line is actually needed, and to settle this point everybody
connected with existing transportation facilities in the
neighbourhood appears before the committee to prove
that it is not needed, while the promoters of the scheme
are at enormous expense to prove by hundreds of experts
that it is. The empirical decision of the committee of the
House of Commons on this question is not to be compared with the unerring decision of the capitalists interested. They know much better than any committee of the
Legislature are likely to know whether the work in
question will pay a fair dividend, and this is the best

proof that it is required. The result of the American policy is seen in the fact that notwithstanding all the attempts upon the part of our railways to thwart the economic laws, nevertheless, the American people enjoy the cheapest transportation in the world. The railway rates upon freight in Europe, compared with those in America, show startling contrasts. The cost of freightage on English lines is upon the average more than double the American charge, and in many cases which I have examined it is three times as great. In not a few cases the British charge is far beyond three times the American.

A friend bought a cargo of grain at Leith, which had paid one dollar per ton freight from New York; it cost him ninety-six cents per ton to transport it thirty-five miles inland. Another purchased six hundred tons charcoal pig-iron upon Lake Superior, which cost four dollars per ton freight to Liverpool; he paid $2.87 per ton to carry it eighty miles inland by rail to his mills. For this amount our trunk lines carry rails five hundred and sixty miles, as against eighty miles in Britain. If Europe enjoyed our advantages of free competition in its transportation system, the development of its resources would be surprising, even at this late day in its history. There is, in my opinion, only cause for hearty congratulation as regards our railway policy. Its evils are trifling; its advantages over all other systems in the world enormous.

The people of America can smile at the efforts of all her railway magnates and of all her manufacturers to defeat the economic laws by Trusts or combinations, or pools, or "differentials," or anything of like character. Only let them hold firmly to the doctrine of free competition. Keep the field open. Freedom for all to engage in railroad building when and where capital desires, subject to conditions open to all. Freedom for all to engage in any branch of manufacturing under like conditions.

There can be no permanent extortion of profit beyond the average return from capital, nor any monopoly, either in transportation or manufacturing. Any attempt to maintain either must end in failure, and failure ultimately disastrous just in proportion to the temporary success of the foolish effort. It is simply ridiculous for a party of men to meet in a room and attempt by passing resolutions to change the great laws which govern human affairs in the business world, and this, whether they be railway presidents, bankers or manufacturers.

The fashion of Trusts has but a short season longer to run, and then some other equally vain device may be expected to appear when the next period of depression arrives; but there is not the slightest danger that serious injury can result to the sound principles of business from any or all of these movements. The only people who have reason to fear Trusts are those foolish enough to enter into them. The Consumer and the Transporter, not the Manufacturer and the Railway owner, are to reap the harvest.

Even since the foregoing was written, a new form has appeared on the stage in the shape of "The Presidents' Agreement—an agreement among gentlemen," in which the parties engage to control, strangle and restrict the future development of our magnificent railway system under the laws of natural growth, at a time when the country requires this development as much as it ever did. These gentlemen are not going to engage in building lines which will give the public the benefit of healthy competition, or permit such to be built hereafter. It is safe to say that very soon this toy will be discarded, like its predecessors, for another, and that the very men apparently most pleased with this new rattle will then regard it with the greatest contempt, and go foward in the good work, as hitherto, developing the railway system wherever and whenever they think they see a fair chance for profit. Whenever existing railways exact from the public more than a fair return upon the actual capital invested, or upon the capital which would be required to duplicate existing lines, competing lines will be built—fortunately for the interests of the country—which is much more concerned in getting cheap transportation than it is in insuring dividends for capitalists; and whenever a percentage is to be obtained by the negotiation of railway securities, bankers will be found—also, fortunately for the best interests of the country—who will gladly find a market for them without stopping to inquire whether monopolies are to be overthrown by the new lines.

It is not in the power of man to exact for more than a brief season, and a very brief season indeed, unusual profit upon actual capital invested either in Transportation or Manufacture, so long as all are free to compete, and this freedom, it may safely be asserted, the American people are not likely to restrict.

ANGLO-AMERICAN TRADE RELATIONS

Contrasting the commercial methods of the two countries. The part the tariff plays in trade. Protective tariff in the United States; free trade in Britain, a comparison of results.

ANGLO-AMERICAN TRADE RELATIONS

Upon the threshold of this great question we encounter that evergreen subject of discussion, Free Trade versus Protection. There is only one kind of Free Trade, but there are two kinds of Protection. First: the British kind, and then the American variety, very different indeed in theory and in practice. Protection in Britain simply means that the food of the people should be permanently made dearer to the consumer, and consequently that the value of land should be permanently and artificially enhanced. Now the American idea of Protection is that foreshadowed by Mill. It adheres to Adam Smith's great doctrine that the end to be aimed at is the best supply of an article at the lowest price under the free exchange of commodities. Thus he keeps ever in view the consumer. If we have reason to believe that the resources of a country are such as only need development to furnish a better and cheaper supply of an article than has ever been or could ever be obtained from other lands, we believe with Adam Smith that it is sometimes advisable to pay dearer for that article for a time, if the end be the conquest of a greater market. Adam Smith was not a wild dogmatist upon the subject of Free Trade: indeed, he has recorded his opinion that he might as well expect Utopia upon earth as the establishment of complete Free Trade, even in Britain; and where changes were to be

From a Speech before the Chamber of Commerce, Halifax, Sept., 1900.

made in fiscal laws, he is clear always upon this point: that these must be slowly made and without serious injury to trade as it exists. Here are two examples to illustrate the difference between Protection in England and America. During the war for the Union the American people were hurt and incensed by hostility shown, not by the British people, but by the British Government. They determined to limit the use of British products as much as possible and especially to be independent in the supply of iron and steel, the sinews of war, since, by England's warlike attitude and the building of the *Alabama,* it was not as certain as, thank the Fates! it is now that war between the two countries could not come—thus does wrong done nations or people bring retribution and every foe created is a danger ready to explode. The *Alabama* gave us thirty years' continuous protection, and enables us to invade Britain successfully with our steel. The Government asked manufacturers how much duty would be required to induce them to enter the new business of making steel. Up to that time we had made none successfully. Thirty per cent. duty was asked and obtained. All know the result; not only is the American supplied with cheaper steel than any nation in the world, Britain not excepted, but it is certain that a large part of the wants of the world is to be supplied by this country. It is beyond all question the country which can best produce steel to-day. Now we think that temporary Protection given and which has been reduced to one-fourth its first extent is here fully vindicated. Take the other case: the best men of every nation must ever labour to advance the material progress of that nation by introducing new manufactures, and it was thought that with proper Protection for a time the Union would grow a full supply of sugar cheaper than it could be brought from abroad. This experiment, however, resulted in failure. We were mistaken, therefore Protection was abandoned and sugar made free. In the one case Protection was a success, in the other a failure. I think that what has taken place in the United States may be expected to take place in other nations one after the other as they develop. Every nation will try to produce within its own borders an article when there is a probability of its being able to make it cheaper and better than it could be had from abroad, and we must wait patiently the result of these trials. Just as the United States abandoned the protection of sugar, so I believe other nations will come to the American idea of Protection, that it is folly to protect forever, that the attempt of a nation to benefit itself by a permanent tax upon any article as a matter of protection is akin to the attempt of a man to raise himself by pulling up his suspenders. Thorough believer as I am in the theory that sometimes it is wise for a young nation to induce capital and brains to engage in the experiment of manufacturing something new, which is always attended with special risks, I am none the less a believer in Adam Smith's great doctrine that the end must be the free exchange of commodities by all the nations of the world, subject only to the necessity of revenue, but this matter of revenue is important.

You remember Mr. Chamberlain was at one time carried away with the idea of a Zollverein of the Empire; you were to have free trade within its bounds as we have within the forty-five States embraced in the Union, a brilliant idea at first sight; but after conferring with the Colonials at the Jubilee, Mr. Chamberlain announced that he could not be induced to touch the subject with tongs. It is well for a statesman to change his opinions when he finds them wrong. The British colonies to-day feel that they have to raise most of their revenue from taxing imports, and therefore a Zollverein did not seem practicable—and there are other objections. For instance, the United States adds to its duties upon sugar an amount equal to the bounty paid by any nation upon its growth,—this is considered only fair to our own producers of sugar.

It is probable, therefore, that for the present, probably for our own day, the needs of revenue and the impracticability of collecting it from internal taxes will cause the British Colonies to continue high duties upon imports, especially such as may be classed as luxuries, which mean the finest things of all grades; in other words, things used not by the masses of the poor, but by the rich few. Such is certainly a popular policy, and it is well known how potent votes are to the politician. The same influences will, I believe, prevail in the United States. I know of no mode of raising revenue so easy, or one so satisfactory to the voters. It may be a surprise, but I believe it is true, that under our present tariff policy the masses of the American people practically escape taxation. They use almost—indeed, I might say wholly—home-made articles: home tobacco, wine, spirits and beer, home-made cotton and woollen cloths and silks, serviceable, but not so fine as the foreign, and all these are to-day surprisingly cheap. I had a proof of that recently. A family in comfortable circumstances, not rich, went to England each year with their five children to visit parents. Formerly, the cost of their passage was saved by the purchase of clothing and other articles. The lady told us she bought nothing on the other side now, she could

clothe her children cheaper in New York. There is much
testimony tending to bear this out. We find our servants
who pass with us to and fro buying many articles in New
York, but pray remember, not fine luxurious articles, in
which people with ample means indulge. Upon these,
about which there need be no fear our rich class will
ever forego, we can by high duties raise a large amount
of needed revenue, without greatly restricting the demand. The rich classes of the Republic hesitate little
about cost in their luxuries, and fine silks, fine linen, fine
lace, finest woollen fabrics, fine wines or Scotch whiskey
and British beer are among our luxuries.

Pray note this policy will no longer be pursued
primarily for protection, but for revenue only. Even if
Protection as a policy were discarded, it is probable such
articles would be taxed—the masses would demand this.
It is a great mistake to think that it is the few and not
the many who favour taxing the imported articles used
by the few rich. It is my opinion that there can be no
abolition of such duties in our day. This is the most
popular of all means of raising revenue.

There is a new revelation in trade between nations
which cannot be overlooked. It may now be taken as
established that raw materials in favoured parts of the
world have now attained the power to attract to them
capital and ability, so that they will as a rule be manufactured close at hand. The various peoples display un-
suspected capacity for manufacturing; the poor men and
women of India, the Peons of Mexico, the Negroes of
America, make satisfactory mill operatives. The Chinese
and Japanese are becoming so, also. Britain and the
United States furnish a few heads of departments, automatic machines need little skill in the mere workers. We

must expect great changes to flow from this fact. It behooves Britain, long the chief, and at one time, indeed, almost the sole manufacturing nation of importance, and the United States, also, to keep our standard of efficiency at the very highest in every department. There may come changes amounting to revolution from this cause. Sir Sutherland, of the P. & O., recently spoke to his shareholders of the probability of ordering steamships in the Far East. I think, however, he will first obtain these from Britain and America—it is a far cry to the Far East.

While we may not look for any great increase in the foreign trade of nations, nothing comparable, for instance, to the growth of their domestic trade, since the tendency is for nations to supply their chief wants, still, I believe that the increase of the population and of wealth, creating new wants and extending the field of present wants, must be such as to keep the exchange of articles not only at its present volume, but with a small ratio of increase. How small foreign trade is at best, as compared to internal trade! In the case of the United States, notwithstanding it exported manufactures last year (1899) to the extent of 80 millions sterling ($400,-000,000), this was not quite a paltry five per cent. of the total value of its manufactures, above 1,800 millions. There is little to fear as to the wants of the world; Britain's only concern is to remain and become the country which can best supply them.

So much for Anglo-American trade relations. In these days of bitter partisanship and sectarianism, it seems almost essential that there should arise a body of intelligent men in each centre who know neither rank, wealth, party nor creed in their deliberations as members of such body, who subordinate all other issues to those which concern the peace and prosperity of their country; which extends its view to all peoples of all lands, rightly regarding men everywhere as a brotherhood, bound together and therefore dependent in greater or less degree in a common prosperity; and which sees in the peace and prosperity of other nations results not antagonistic but tributary to their own, discarding these narrow conceptions of the ordinary politician who sees in war against other lands benefit to his own, and, I fear, sees even more clearly popularity for himself. It is essentially true concerning commercial nations especially, such as Great Britain long has been and must remain, and such as our newer republic is becoming, which is fast sharing with the mother country the business of the world—that there is no measure of prosperity in any part of the world in which we do not share. The whole world pays tribute to the nations which supply in any considerable degree its wants. Hence the greatest interest of Britain and of America is peace. Hence, also, a wise policy to sustain peace, a grave error of policy to disturb it, since we cannot destroy the prosperity of any nation without impairing our own. Any seeming temporary gain from the injury of others is really loss in the end. This is perhaps what may be called a view for the future, but steps toward its acceptance are being taken even in our own day. The first step lies in exploding the idea that trade follows the flag; the fact is that trade scents the best bargain. Trade is no respecter of flags; loyal Canada buys her Union Jacks in New York. She trades with the Republic to three times the extent she trades with England and to a greater extent than with all other nations combined. In vain does any nation seek political or nominal control over foreign territory with a view to permanent commercial advantage under free trade or equal laws for all. She secures or holds only the market which she can best supply. To spend millions of money and thousands of lives for the political control of new territory may be considered necessary sometimes for political reasons, but never for the requirements of trade. We shall have gained one step forward then when it is freely recognized that political acquisition is not essential for acquiring the trade of new territory. This truth even America just now needs to relearn, since she is trying to acquire political control of the Philippines. British and American interests are safeguarded when equal laws for all nations are secured. Thus the interests of both countries in foreign trade have become the same and should lead to a common policy— the Open Door and Peace, allowing all nations, all peoples to follow their own laws of development in perfect freedom. We have had many proofs recently of the familiar adage that blood is thicker than water, very much thicker as I believe, between the members of our own race. In the evident drawing together of the English-speaking race and all that this implies we see the dawn of a new sentiment rising—the Patriotism of Race, a sentiment of pride and devotion in the race now given by one half of the race to the Union Jack, and by the other half of the race to the Stars and Stripes—the other of the two flags which unitedly hold sway over all English-speaking men, for no community exists speaking our tongue which does not owe allegiance to one or the other of these symbols. The silver lining to the clouds of war in which, alas! the two branches of our race are at present engaged, is that it has so turned out that these now stand closer to each other than at any time since they separated.

We may safely, I believe quite safely, assume that no question can even arise between the two nations but one people, which will not be amicably settled, that no government can ever exist in either land strong or wicked enough to resist the demand of the best of the people of both that the settlement of differences shall not be by the brutal arbitrament of the sword. The day has passed when English-speaking men will ever be called upon to kill each other in battle. The sun is never again to shine upon such a spectacle. We have passed that stage and turned down the pages of that horrid story forever.

What then of the future charged with this potent new sentiment of race patriotism which seems dawning upon us? Our own race especially is prone to the disease known as land hunger. Great Britain has spread the red spots of sovereignty all over the world; we have stretched from the shores of the Atlantic three thousand miles to the Pacific, from the St. Lawrence to the Gulf of Mexico, and, not content, I fear following Britain's perilous example, we are trying to annex foreign territory. The truth is that we have taken the Scripture much to heart, which tells us that the meek shall inherit the earth, and which, our humorist Mark Twain said, explained it all —our race is so meek; at all events we seem to have lost no time in discovering that the true and only reliable proof of the true inheritors was whether they spoke English.

This expanding epoch must soon pass. It is the law of development that each country shall eventually rule itself. Canada does so, Australia is about to assume sovereign sway, both have their own fiscal tariffs, against even England's products. The seventeen Republics of South America only recently governed by Spain are now all independent and self-governing. It is only during the periods of development that distant Powers can govern and hold sway over a people, but during this stage such may be the benign effects of the government that even after practical control has been taken over by the new community, the ties between mother and child may not only remain unbroken, but stronger than ever before. Of this Canada and Australia give ample proof. By the wise, kind, peaceful, and conciliatory policy pursued a race patriotism has been created within the Empire which depends upon moral forces, the most enduring of all, not upon law but upon love. The success of Britain's colonial policy in recent times is one of the grandest triumphs ever achieved by a nation perhaps the grandest of all. It has been possible only by peaceful, not by warlike means, a victory much more renowned than any conquest by force and more enduring, as the future is to show.

The flag of great Britain floats over Canada and Australia; by the desire of their people they are part of the solid united whole, and the question now is whether this federation of the race is to stop within the Empire, or finally develop into a federal council for the entire race governing international relations which involve the peace of the world, and leaving home rule to each country in all other affairs, even as to the form of government itself, a crowned or uncrowned republic. I am on record as having predicted years ago that our English-speaking race would one day be again united, and it was not so very long since. Here is a fit field for our Chamber of Commerce to cultivate, for it lies in the direction of peace and goodwill. For the present at least they can exert their influence to strengthen the good feeling, the drawing together of the two branches. I failed to mention one of the best, perhaps the best, of all the results of our temporary policy of Protection. It has brought to us so many British manufacturers to establish industries and thus develop our resources—the Clarks and the Coats of Paisley, the Dolans of Yorkshire, the Sandersons of Sheffield, and last, but certainly not least, a great prize from Halifax. Who could expect us not to extol our idea of Protection if we capture the Firths? We must not line them up for a king's ransom, we need as many of the Halifax quality as can be had. Whenever our tariffs suit, all may take a sweeping revenge, come over, and enjoy perfect free trade in the forty-five nations of the Union and be happy. The Republic calls them to come one, come all. It taxes highest the gems and precious things imported, but these jewels beyond price are admitted duty free.

It is not only for their value industrially that they should be valued, but as links binding the old and the new lands, the mother and child together. Some of the younger members of the firm settle among us, their children marry Americans, or when they visit the old home, contract alliances there, and the true Anglo-American is the result, who is not unlikely to prove the coming man, possessed of the virtues and strength of both races and the vices or weaknesses of neither, and who, at all events, we may rest assured, will be the foremost disciple of race patriotism and labour for the coming of the day of common citizenship within the wide and ever expanding boundaries of our race.

"BUSINESS"

Business is a large word and in its primary meanings covers the whole range of man's efforts. The same principles of thrift, energy, concentration and brains win success in any branch of business from medicine to dry goods.

"BUSINESS"

Business is a large word, and in its primary meaning covers the whole range of man's efforts. It is the business of the preacher to preach, of the physician to practise, of the poet to write, the business of the university professor to teach, and the business of the college student, one might sometimes think, from the amount of attention bestowed upon it, to play football. I am not to speak of "business" in this wide sense, but specifically as defined in the Century Dictionary:

"Mercantile and manufacturing pursuits collectively; employment requiring knowledge of accounts and financial methods; the occupation of conducting trade; or monetary transactions of any kind."

The illustration which follows is significant, and clearly defines this view of business. It reads:

"It seldom happens that men of a *studious turn* acquire any degree of reputation for their knowledge of *business.*"

But we must go one step further, more strictly to define business, as I am to consider it. Is a railway president receiving a salary, or the president of a bank, or a salaried officer of any kind, in business? Strictly speak-

From a Lecture delivered at Cornell University, January 11, 1896.

ing, he is not; for a man, to be in business, must be at
least part owner of the enterprise which he manages and
to which he gives his attention, and chiefly dependent for
his revenues not upon salary but upon its profits. This
view rules out the entire salaried class. None of these
men are now men in business, but many of them have
been, and most successful therein. The business man pure
and simple plunges into and tosses upon the waves of
human affairs without a life-preserver in the shape of
salary; he risks all.

Choice of a Career

There is no great fortune to come from salary, however high, and the business man pursues fortune. If he
be wise he puts all his eggs in one basket, and then
watches that basket. If he is a merchant in coffee, he
attends to coffee; if a merchant in sugar, he attends to
sugar and lets coffee alone, and only mixes them when he
drinks his coffee with sugar in it. If he mine coal and
sell it, he attends to the black diamonds; if he own and
sail ships, he attends to shipping, and he ceases to insure
his own ships just as soon as he has surplus capital and
can stand the loss of one without imperilling solvency; if
he manufacture steel, he sticks to steel, and severely lets
copper alone; if he mine ironstone, he sticks to that, and
avoids every other kind of mining, silver- and gold-
mining especially. This is because a man can thoroughly
master only one business, and only an able man can do
this. I have never yet met the man who fully understood
two different kinds of business; you cannot find him any
sooner than you can find a man who thinks in two

languages equally and does not invariably think only in one.

Subdivision, specialization, is the order of the day.

Every Man to His Trade or His Specialty

I have before me many representatives of all classes of students. If I could look into your hearts, I should find many differing ambitions; some aiming at distinction in each of the professions; some would be lawyers, some ministers, some doctors, some architects, some electricians, some engineers, some teachers, and each sets before him, as models, honoured names that have reached the highest rank in these professions. The embryo lawyers before me would rival Marshall and Story of the past, or Carter and Choate of the present; the preacher would be a Brooks or a Van Dyke; the physician a Janeway or a Garmany; the editor would be a Dana; the architect a Richardson, and, having reached the top of his darling profession, his ambition then would be satisfied. At least, so he thinks at present. With these classes I have nothing whatever to do directly to-day, because all these are professional enthusiasts. Nevertheless, the qualities essential for success in the professions being in the main the same which insure success in business, much that I have to say applies equally to you all.

There remain among you those who would sail the uncertain sea of business, and devote themselves to making money, a great fortune, so that you shall be millionnaires. I am sure that while this may be chiefly in your thoughts, it is not all you seek in a business career; you feel that in it there is scope for exercise of great abilities, of enterprise, energy, judgment, and all the best traits of human nature, and also that men in business perform useful service to society.

I am to try to shed a little light upon the path to success, to point out some of the rocks and shoals in that treacherous sea, and give a few hints as to the mode of sailing your ship, or rowing your shell, whether, for instance, the quick or the slow stroke is surer to win in the long race.

The Start in Life

Let us begin, then, at the beginning. Is any would-be business man before me content in forecasting his future, to figure himself as labouring all his life for a fixed salary? Not one, I am sure. In this you have the dividing line between business and non-business; the one is a master, and depends upon profits, the other a servant, and depends upon salary. Of course, you have all to begin as servants with salary, but you have not all to end there.

You have some difficulty in obtaining a start, great difficulty as a rule, but here comes in the exceptional student. There is not much difficulty for him; he has attracted the attention of his teachers who know many men of affairs; has taken prizes; he is head of his class; has shown unusual ability, founded upon characteristics which are sure to tell in the race; he has proved himself self-respecting, has irreproachable habits, good sense, method, untiring industry, and his spare hours are spent in pursuing knowledge, that being the labour in which he most delights.

One vital point more: his finances are always sound, he rigorously lives within his means, and last, but not least, he has shown that his heart is in his work. Besides all this, he has usually one strong guarantee of future industry and ambitious usefulness, he is not burdened with wealth; it is necessary that he make his own way in the world. He is not yet a millionnaire, but is only going to be one. He has no rich father, or, still more dangerous, rich mother, who can, and will, support him in idleness should he prove a failure; he has no life-preserver, and therefore must sink or swim. Before that young man leaves college he is a marked man. More than one avenue is open for him. The door opens before he is ready to knock; he is waited for by the sagacious employer. Not the written certificate of his professor, for certificates have generally to be read, and are read within the lines; but a word or two spoken to the business man who is always on the lookout for the exceptional young graduate, has secured the young man all that a young man needs—a start. The most valuable acquisition to his business which an employer can obtain is an exceptional young man; there is no bargain so fruitful for him as this.

It is, of course, much more difficult for only the average student; he has generally to search for employment, but finally he also gets a start.

OPENINGS TO SUCCESS

It is the career of the exceptional student which illustrates the pathway to success. We need not render ourselves anxious about him; he is all right. He has been thrown into the sea, but he does not need any life-preserver; he does not need to be coddled, he will swim; he was not born to be drowned, and you see him breast the waves year after year until he is at the head of a great business. His start, of course, is not at the head, he is at the foot; fortunately so, for that is the reason his progress has always been upward. If he had started high he would not have had the chance to make a continual ascent. It does not matter much how he starts, for the qualities in him are such as to produce certain effects in any field he enters. He goes forward upon a very small salary, performing certain small uses, indeed, much smaller than he thinks himself capable of performing, but these he performs thoroughly.

Some day in some way something happens that brings him to the notice of his immediate superior. He objects to some plan proposed, and thinks it can be bettered in some way, or he volunteers to assist in a department other than his own; or, he stays, one day, later at his work than usual, or goes some morning sooner, because there was some part of the business that had not been entirely settled the night before, or there was something to start next morning that he was afraid might not be ready or just right, and he "just goes down early to be sure." His employer has been somewhat anxious upon the same point, and he, too, goes down early that morning and finds his salaried young man, showing that he does not work for salary alone; it is not solely an affair of "hire and salary" with him; he is not that kind of a young man; he is working for the success of the business. Or it may be that some day his employer proposes a certain mode of action in regard to a customer's account; perhaps the young man has started in the office, and has been asked to look after the credits, a most important part. His employers wish to close this credit, which, perhaps, would embarrass the customer. This young man, known to the customer, has had to visit his place occasionally in the course of business, collecting his accounts, or trying to collect them, and the young man modestly says he is a splendid fellow, bound to succeed, does his business upon fair and wise methods, and only needs a little temporary indulgence to come out all right.

The employer has faith in the young man's judgment and ability, thinks it a rather strong suggestion for a clerk to make, but says to him: "You look out for this matter, and see that we do not lose; but, of course, we do not wish to injure one of our customers; if we can help him without risk we wish to do it." The young man takes the matter in hand, and results prove he was quite right; the customer becomes one of the very best of all their customers, and one that it would require a great deal to take away from the firm.

Or, perhaps, the bright young man may have noted the insurance policies upon the works, and their dates of expiration; he finds the fact has been overlooked— that some of the insurances have lapsed and are invalid. It is none of his business; he is not paid to look after the insurance of the firm; in one sense—the narrow sense —that is the business of some other man, but he ventures to call attention to the fact, and suggests that the premiums should be paid. But now mark the advantage of general reading and education. This young man has read the newspapers and reviews, and learns of several "sharp business practices" by which the insurer is sometimes defrauded of his insurance, and especially has he read of new methods and cheap plans of insurance. He suggests that it would be well to change this and that policy to another and very solid old company. You see, gentlemen, the business man of this day has to read, yes, and study, and go to the roots of many things, that he may avoid the pitfalls that surround business upon every side. He would not be an employer worth having that did not note what kind of a young man that was, although now in the humble guise of a clerk.

The Second Step Upward

Suppose he is an electrician or engineer, and comes from Sibley, which is a good place to come from. In the great manufacturing concern so fortunate as to secure his services, he has to do with some humble branch of the work, but he discovers that there are a few boilers which are not quite safe, and that the engines or motors are built upon false mechanical principles, and are very wasteful of fuel, and that one of the engines will soon give trouble; there is a foundation under it upon which he finds that the contractor has not done honest work; or dropping into the works one night just to see that all is going well, perhaps he discovers that a man trusted by the firm has fallen into bad habits, and is not fit for duty, or perhaps is not on duty, and that an accident might thus happen. He feels it to be his duty to take action here and safeguard the business from the danger of an accident. He draws the plans which show some defects in the machinery, lays them before his employers with suggestions how to cure these, made upon the latest scientific principles that he had been taught in Sibley. The employer, of course, is very averse to spend money, and angry to learn that his machinery is not what it should be. But although his anger explodes and envelops the young man for a moment, he is not shooting at him; when the *debris* clears off he sits down and learns from the young man what a few thousand dollars now might save, and the result is that he tells the Sibley boy he wishes him to take up this subject and attend to it, and be sure to make all right.

Already that young man's fortune is almost as good as made. He could not hide his light under a bushel if he tried, and the coming business man is not excessively liable to that sin, and does not want to; he is business all over. There is no affectation or false modesty about him. He knows his business, and he feels fully conscious and proud of the fact that he knows it, and that is one of the many advantages Sibley gives him, and he is determined that his employer should not, at least upon that point, know less than he does. You must never fail to enlighten your employer. You cannot keep such a young man as that back; and this let me tell you, no employer wishes to keep him back. There is only one person as happy at finding this young man as the young man is in finding himself, and that is his employer. He is worth a million more or less, but of course, it would not be good for him to get it, while so young.

He has now made two steps upward. First, he has got a start, and, secondly, he has satisfied his employer that he renders exceptional service, a decisive step; as the French say, "he has arrived," and he is there to stay. His foot is upon the ladder; how high he climbs is his own affair. He is among the few within the very threshold of the whole business.

There is a good deal to be done after this, however. This young man has zeal and ability, and he has shown that he has also that indispensable quality—judgment; and he has shown another indispensable quality—that his heart is in the business; that no other cause takes him

from it; that he pushes aside the very seductive temptations which surround young men, and concentrates his
attention, his time, his efforts, upon the performance of
his duties to his employer. All other studies, occupations,
and all amusements are subordinate to the business, which
holds paramount sway. His salary, of course, increases. If
he has happened to engage with an employer who does
not fully appreciate such services as he has rendered, and
is ready to render, other employers have not failed to
note that here is that rare article, the exceptional young
man, in the service of their rival, and it is possible that
our young hero may have to change employers. It does
not often happen, but it does sometimes, that a young
man has to do so. As a rule, the employer is only too
thankful that such a young man has come to him, and he
makes it his interest to remain. Confidence is a matter of
slow growth, however, and it is a far cry from a high
salary as a hireling, into equality as a partner.

THE CRUCIAL QUESTION

Let us trace him a little further. This young man's
services to the firm have been such as to render it necessary some day that he should visit his employer at his
house. It is not long before many occasions arise which
call the young man to the house, where he is now favoured
upon his merits by the household, and to whom his nature
soon becomes known, and the master soon begins to ask
himself whether he might not some day make him a
partner, and then comes the question of questions: *Is he
honest and true?* Let me pause here one moment. Gentlemen, this is the crucial question, the keystone of the arch;
for no amount of ability is of the slightest avail without

honour. When Burns pictured the Genius of Scotland in "The Vision," these marvellous words came to him:

> Her eye, ev'n turn'd on empty space,
> Beam'd keen wi' honour.

No concealment, no prevarication, no speculation, trying to win something for which no service is given; nothing done which, if published, would involve your shame. The business man seeks first in his partner "the soul of honour," one who would swerve from the narrow path even to serve him would only forfeit his confidence. Is he intelligent? Is he capable of forming a correct judgment, based upon knowledge, upon distant and far-reaching issues? Young men, yes, and old men also, sometimes marry in haste, which is very foolish in both classes. But there is this to be said for the partnership—it is rarely entered upon in a hurry. It is not one or two qualities which insure it, but an all-round character, desirable in many respects, highly objectionable in none, and with special ability in one or two.

We often hear in our day that it is impossible for young men to become owners, because business is conducted upon so great a scale that the capital necessary reaches millions, and, therefore, the young man is doomed to a salaried life. Now there is something in that view only so far as the great corporations are concerned, because an interest in these is only attainable by capital; you can buy so many shares for so many dollars, and as the class of young men I address are not willing to remain forever salaried men, but are determined sooner or later to become business men upon their own account, as masters, I do not believe that employment in a great corporation is as favourable for them as with private owners, because, while a young man can look forward to a large salary in their service, that is all to which he can aspire. Even the presidents of these corporations, being only salaried men, are not to be classed as strictly business men at all. How, then, can a young man under them be anything but a salaried man his life long?

Where to Look for Opportunities

Many a business which has long been successful as a partnership is put into a joint stock concern, and the shares are offered in the market, and professional men, guilelessly innocent of business, and, sometimes, women of a speculative turn, and, I am sorry to say, many times clergymen, and artists, are deluded into purchasing. The public buys the business, but they should have bought the man or men who made the business.

You remember the Travers story? A friend called Travers in to see a dog that he wished to buy to clear his conservatory of rats, and when the dog-fancier undertook to show him how this dog demolished these pests, one great, big old rat chased the dog. Travers's friend said to him:

"What would you do?"

Travers replied: "B-b-b-buy the rat."

The public often buys the wrong thing.

It would be an excellent study for you to read frequently the stock-lists of miscellaneous companies. You will find some of the newspapers give the list, and then note the par value of the shares and the price at which you may purchase them. It may be said that this par value is upon fictitious capital. That is so only in some instances; in manufacturing companies especially I think the reverse is the rule. The capital does not fully represent the cost of the properties.

But there are many corporations which are not corporations, many instances of partnership in which the corporate form has been adopted, and yet the business continued substantially as a partnership, and comparing such institutions with the great corporations whose ownership is here, there, and everywhere, we find a most notable difference. Take, for instance, the great steamship lines of the world. Most of these, as those of you who read well know, fail to make returns to their shareholders. The shares of some of the greatest companies have been selling at one-half and sometimes one-third their cost. These are corporations, pure and simple, but if we look at other lines engaged upon the same oceans, which are managed by their owners and in which, generally, one great business man is deeply interested and at the head, we find large dividends each year and amounts placed to the reserve fund. It is the difference between individualism and communism applied to business, between the owners managing their own business as partners, and a joint stock concern of a thousand shifting owners ignorant of the business.

The same contrast can be drawn in every branch of business, in merchandising, in manufacturing, in finance, in transportation by land as well as by sea. It is so with banks. Many banks are really the property of a few business men. These soon become the leading banks, and their shares are invariably quoted at the highest premium, especially if the president of the bank be the largest owner, as he is in many of the most remarkable cases of success. In such partnership corporations there is every opportunity for the coming business man to obtain ownership which exists in pure partnerships, for the owners of both manage affairs and are on the constant watch for ability.

Do not be fastidious; take what the gods offer. Begin, if necessary, with a corporation, always keeping your eye open for a chance to become interested in a business of your own. Remember every business can be made successful, because it supplies some essential want of the community; it performs a needed office, whether it be in manufacturing which produces an article, or in gathering and distributing it by the merchant; or the banker, whose business is to take care of and invest capital.

There is no line of business in which success is not attainable.

A Secret of Success

It is a simple matter of honest work, ability, and concentration. There is no question about there being room at the top for exceptional men in any profession. These have not to seek patronage; the question is, rather, how can their services be secured, and, as with every profession, so in every line of business, there is plenty of room at the top. Your problem is how to get there. The answer is simple: conduct your business with just a little more ability than the average man in your line. If you are only above the average your success is secured, and the degree of success is in ratio to the greater degree of ability and attention which you give above the average. There are always a few in business who stand near the top, but there are always an infinitely greater number at and near the bottom. And should you fail to ascend, the fault is not in your stars, but in yourselves. Those who fail may say that this or that man had great advantages, the fates were propitious, the conditions favourable. Now, there is very little in this; one man lands in the middle of a stream which he tries to jump, and is swept away, and another tries the same feat, and lands upon the other side.

Examine these two men.

You will find that the one who failed, lacked judgment; he had not calculated the means to the end; was a foolish fellow; had not trained himself; could not jump; he took the chances. He was like the young lady who was asked if she could play the violin, she said she "did not know, she had never tried." Now, the other man who jumped the stream had carefully trained himself; he knew about how far he could jump, and there was one thing "dead sure" with him, he knew he could, at any rate, jump far enough to land at a point from which he could wade ashore, and try again. He had shown judgment.

Prestige is a great matter, my friends. A young man who has the record of doing what he sets out to do will find year after year his field of operations extended, and the tasks committed to him greater and greater. On the other hand, the man who has to admit failure and comes to friends trying to get assistance in order to make a second start is in a very bad position, indeed.

College Graduates in Business

The graduates of our colleges and universities in former years graduated while yet in their teens. We have changed this, and graduates are older, as a rule, when they enter upon life's struggle, but they are taught much more. Unless the young university man employs his time to the very best advantage in acquiring knowledge upon the pursuit which he is to make the chief business of his life, he will enter business at a disadvantage with younger men who enter in their teens, although lacking in university education. This goes without saying. Now, the question is: Will the graduate who has dwelt in the region of theory overtake the man who has been for a year or two in advance of him, engaged in the hard and stern educative field of practice?

That it is possible for the graduate to do so also goes without saying, and that he should in after life possess views broader than the ordinary business man, deprived of university education, is also certain, and, of course, the race in life is to those whose record is best at the end; the beginning is forgotten and is of no moment. But if the graduate is ever to overtake the first starter in the race, it must be by possessing stronger staying-powers; his superior knowledge leading to sounder judgment must be depended upon to win the race at the finish. A few disadvantages he must strenuously guard against, the lack of severe self-discipline, of strenuous concentration, and intense ambition, which usually characterizes the man who starts before the habits of manhood are formed. The habits of the young man at college, after he is a man, and the habits of the youngster in the business arena are likely to differ.

There is another great disadvantage which the older man has to overcome in most successful business establishments. There will be found in operation there a strict civil-service system and promotion without favour. It is, therefore, most difficult to find admission to the service in any but the lowest grades. One has to begin at the foot, and this is better for all parties concerned, especially the young graduate.

The exceptional graduate should excel the exceptional non-graduate. He has more education, and education will always tell, the other qualities being equal. Take two men of equal natural ability, energy, and the same ambition and characteristics, and the man who has received the best, widest, most suitable education has the advantage over the other, undoubtedly.

BUSINESS MEN AND SPECULATORS

All pure coins have their counterfeits; the counterfeit of business is speculation. A man in business always gives value in return for his revenue, and thus performs a useful function. His services are necessary and benefit the community; besides, he labours steadily in developing the resources of the country, and thus contributes to the advancements of the race. This is genuine coin. Speculation, on the contrary, is a parasite fastened upon the labour of business men. It creates nothing and supplies no want. When the speculator wins he takes money without rendering service, or giving value therefor, and when he loses, his fellow-speculator takes the money from him. It is a pure gambling operation between them, degrading to both. You can never be an honest man of business and a speculator. The modes and aims of the one career are fatal to the other. No business man can honestly speculate, for those who trust him have a right to expect strict adherence to business methods. The creditor takes the usual risks of business, but not those of speculation. The genuine and the counterfeit have nothing in common.

That 95 per cent. fail of those who start in business upon their own account seems incredible, and yet such are said to be the statistics upon the subject. Although it is said that figures will say anything, still it is a fact that the proportion is very great. Do not think that I wish to discourage you against attempting to be your own masters and having a business of your own; very far from it. Besides, the coming business man is not to be discouraged by anything that anybody can say. He is a true knight who says with Fitzjames:

> If the path be dangerous known,
> The danger self is lure alone.

The young man who is determined to be a business man will not be thwarted, neither will he be diverted into any other channel, and he is going to start and have a trial; he will "make a spoon or spoil a horn" trying to make it. He must go ahead and find it out. Time enough to confine yourself to a life-long bondage as mere receivers of a salary after you have tried business, and really discovered whether or no you are one of the gifted who possess all the necessary qualities.

I have tried to sketch the path of the exceptional graduate from salary to partnership. It is no fancy sketch; there is not a day passes without changes in many firms which raise young men to partnership, and in every single city no first of January passes without such promotions. Business requires fresh young blood for its existence. If any of you are discouraged upon this point, let me give you two stories within my own experience, which should certainly cheer you.

A Sketch from Life

There is a large manufacturer, the largest in the world in his line. I know him well, a splendid man, who illustrates the business career at its best. Now, like all sensible business men, as he grew in years he realized that fresh blood must be introduced into his business; that while it was comparatively easy for him to manage the extensive business at present, it was wise to provide for its continuance in able hands after he had retired. Rich men seldom have sons who inherit a taste for business. I am not concerned to say whether this is well or otherwise. Looking at the human race as a whole, I believe it is for good.

If rich men's sons had poor men's necessities, and, hence, their ambitious abilities, there would be less chance for the students of college than there is. It was not to any member of his family that this man looked for the new young blood. A young man in the service of a corporation had attracted his attention in the management of certain business matters connected with the firm. The young man had to call upon this gentleman frequently. The wise man did not move hastily in the matter. About his ability he was soon satisfied, but that covered only one point of many. What were the young man's surroundings, habits, tastes, acquirements? Beyond his immediate business, what was his nature? He found everything in these matters just as he would have it. The young man was supporting a widowed mother and a sister; he had as friends some excellent young men, and some older than himself; he was a student; he was a reader; had high tastes, of course; I need hardly say that he was a young gentleman, highly self-respecting, the soul of honour, incapable of anything low or vulgar; in short, a model young man, and of course poor—that goes without saying.

The young man was sent for, and the millionnaire told him that he should like very much to try him in his service, and asked the young man if he would make the trial. The millionnaire stated frankly what he was looking for—a young business man who might develop, and finally relieve him of much care. The arrangement was that he should come for two years as a clerk, subject to clerk's rules, which in this case was very hard, because he had to be at the factory a few minutes before seven in the morning. He was to have a salary somewhat larger than he had received, and if at the end of two years nothing had been said on either side, no obligations were weaved, each was free. He was simply on trial. The young man proudly said he would not have it otherwise.

The business went on. Before the two years expired the employer was satisfied that he had found that exceedingly rare thing, a young business man. What a number of qualities this embraces, including judgment, for without judgment a business man amounts to nothing. The employer stated to the young man that he was delighted with him, pleased with his services, and expressed his joy at having found him. He had now arranged to interest him in the firm. But to his amazement the young man replied:

"Thanks, thanks, but it is impossible for me to accept."

"What is the matter? You suit me; do I not suit you?"

"Excuse me, sir, but for reasons which I cannot explain,

I am to leave your service in six months, when my two years are up, and I intended to give you notice of this, that you might fill my place."

"Where are you going?"

"I am going abroad."

"Have you made any engagement?"

"No, sir."

"Do you not know where you are going?"

"No, sir."

"Nor what you are to do?"

"No, sir."

"Sir, I have treated you well, and I do think I am entitled to know the real reason. I think it is your duty to tell me."

The reason was dragged out of the young man: "You have been too good to me. I would give anything to be able to remain with you. You even invited me to your house; you have been absent travelling; you asked me to call often to take your wife and daughter to such entertainments as they wished to attend, and I cannot stand it any longer."

Well, the millionnaire, of course, discovered what all of you have suspected, just what you would have done under the circumstances; he had fallen in love with the daughter. Now in this country that would not have been considered much of an indiscretion, and I do not advise any of you to fight much against it. If you really love, you should overlook the objection that it is your employer's daughter who has conquered, and that you may have to bear the burden of riches; but in the land of which I speak it would have been considered dishonourable for a young clerk to make love to any young lady without the parents' permission.

"Have you spoken to my daughter?" was the question. The young man scarcely deigned to reply to that.

"Of course not."

"Never said a word, or led her to suspect in any way?"

"Of course not."

"Well," he said, "I do not see why you should not; you are the very kind of son-in-law I want if you can win my daughter."

Very strange, but somehow or other, the young lady did not differ from papa; he was the kind of husband she wanted. Now that young man is a happy business man to-day.

Romance in Business

I have another story which happened in another country. Both the fathers-in-law told me these stories themselves, and proud men they are, and proud am I of their friendship. You see business is not all this hard prosaic life that it is pictured. It bears romance and sentiment in it, and the greater the business, the more successful, the more useful, in my experience, there is found more romance and imagination. The highest triumphs even in business flow from romance, sentiment, imagination, particularly in the business of a world-wide firm.

The other story is so similar to the first that successful telling is impossible. You will all jump to the conclusion, and the details in these cases are nothing. It is as when I began to tell my young nephews about the battle of ᴦ innockburn; there were the English, and there stood the ᴐcotch.

"Which whipped, uncle?" cried the three at once—

details unnecessary. But there was no battle in this case. I infer it was all settled by amicable arbitration.

I shall not tell it at length, as I did the other, but it is precisely the same, except that the young man in this other case was not employed except in the ordinary manner. The young man's services were needed, and he was employed. He finally became private secretary to the millionnaire, and with equally fatal results. In this case, however, the father asked this exemplary and able young man to look after his sons during his absence. This necessitated visits to the residence at the country house, and sports and games with the sons. My friend forgot he had a daughter, and he should not have done this. When you become not only heads of business but heads of families, you should make a note of this, and not think your sons everything. The private secretary, who was requested to attend to the sons, somehow or other, getting his instructions verbally, seems to have understood them as having a slightly wider range. The daughter apparently needed most of his attention. But note this: These two young men won the confidence and captured the judgment and admiration of their employers—business men—first, and then fell in love with the daughters. You will be perfectly safe if you take matters in the same order of precedence.

Value of a Business Career

Perhaps I may be permitted, without going too far beyond the scope of my text, to make a few remarks upon the influence of a business career upon men, as compared with other pursuits.

First, then, I have learned that the artistic career is

most narrowing, and produces such petty jealousies, un-
bounded vanities, and spitefulness, as to furnish me with
a great contrast to that which I have found in men of
affairs. Music, painting, sculpture, one would think,
should prove most powerful in their beneficent effects
upon those who labour with them as their daily vocation.
Experience, however, is against this. Perhaps because
the work, or the performance, of artists is so highly personal, so clearly seen, being brought directly before the
public, that petty passions are stimulated; however that
may be, I believe it will not be controverted that the
artistic mind becomes prejudiced and narrow. But, understand, I speak only of classes and of the general
effect; everywhere we find exceptions which render the
average still more unsatisfactory. In regard to what are
called the learned professions, we notice the effect produced by specialization in a very marked degree.

In the ministerial class this is not so marked in our
day, because leaders in that great function permit themselves a wider range of subjects than ever before, and
are dealing less with creeds and formulas and more and
more with the practical evils and shortcomings of human
life in its various phases. This naturally broadens the
mind. It has been held that the legal profession must
tend to make clear, but narrow, intellects, and it is
pointed out that great lawyers have seldom arisen to
commanding position and power over their fellows. This
does not mean that men who study law become unsatisfactory legislators or statesmen and rulers. If it did, our
country, of all others, should be in a bad way, because
we are governed by lawyers. But the most famous Americans who have been great men, were not great lawyers;
that is, they have seldom attained the foremost rank in

the profession, but have availed themselves of the inestimable advantage which the study of law confers upon a statesman, and developed beyond the bounds of the profession. We are reminded that the great lawyer and the great judge must deal with rules and precedents already established; the lawyer follows precedents, but the ruler of men makes precedents.

Merchants and Professional Men

The tendency of all professions, it would seem, must be to make what is known as the professional mind clear, but narrow. Now what may be claimed for business as a career is that the man in business is called upon to deal with an ever-changing variety of questions. He must have an all-round judgment based upon knowledge of many subjects. It is not sufficient for the great merchant and business man of our day that he know his country well, its physical conditions, its resources, statistics, crops, waterways, its finances, in short, all conditions which affect not only the present, but which give him data upon which he can predict, with some degree of certainty, the future.

The merchant whose operations extend to various countries must also know these countries, and also the chief things pertaining to them. His view must be world-wide; nothing can happen of moment which had not its bearing upon his action—political complications at Constantinople; the appearance of the cholera in the East; monsoon in India; the supply of gold at Cripple Creek; the appearance of the Colorado beetles or the fall of a ministry; the danger of war; the likelihood of arbitration compelling settlement—nothing can happen in any part of the world which he has not to consider. He must possess one of the rarest qualities—be an excellent judge of men—he often employs thousands, and knows how to bring the best out of various characters; he must have the gift of organization—another rare gift—must have executive ability; must be able to decide promptly and wisely.

Now, none of these rare qualities are so absolutely essential to the specialist in any branch or profession. He follows a career, therefore, which tends not only to sharpen his wits, but to enlarge his powers; different, also, from any other careers, that it tends not to specialization and the working of the mind within narrow grooves, but tends to develop in a man capacity to judge upon wide data. No professional life embraces so many problems, none other requires so wide a view of affairs in general. I think, therefore, that it may justly be said, for the business career, that it must widen and develop the intellectual powers of its devotee.

On the other hand, the professional career is immeasurably nobler in this: that it has not for its chief end the ignoble aim of money-making and is free from the gravest danger which besets the career of business, which is in one sense the most sordid of all careers if entered upon in the wrong spirit. To make money is no doubt the primary consideration with most young men who enter it. I think if you will look into your hearts you will find this to be true. But while this may be the first, it should not be the last consideration.

There is the great use which a man can perform in developing the resources of his country; in furnishing employment to thousands; in developing inventions which prove of great benefit to the race, and help it forward. The successful man of affairs soon rises above the mere desire to make money as the chief end of his labours; that is superseded by thoughts of the uses he performs in the line which I have just mentioned. The merchant soon finds his strongest feeling to be that of pride in the extent of his international operations; in his ships sailing every sea. The manufacturer finds in his employes, and in his works, in machinery, in improvements, in the perfection of his factories and methods his chief interest and reward. The profitable return they make is chiefly acceptable not because this is mere money, but because it denotes success.

There is a romantic as well as prosaic side to business. The young man who begins in a financial firm and deals with capital invested in a hundred different ways—in bonds upon our railway systems, in money lent to the merchant and to the manufacturer to enable them to work their wonders—soon finds romance in business and unlimited room for the imagination. He can furnish credit world-wide in its range. His simple letter will carry the traveller to the farthest part of the earth. He may even be of service to his country in a crisis, as Richard Morris, the great merchant in Philadelphia, was to General Washington in the Revolutionary Cause, or as in our own day our great bankers have been in providing gold to our Government at several crises to avert calamity.

The Vanished Prejudice Against Trade

If the young man does not find romance in his business, it is not the fault of the business, but the fault of the young man. Consider the wonders, the mysteries

connected with the recent developments in that most spiritual of all agents—electricity—with its unknown, and,
perhaps, even unguessed of powers. He must be a dull and
prosaic young man who, being connected with electricity
in any of its forms, is not lifted from humdrum business
to the region of the mysterious. Business is not all
dollars; these are but the shell—the kernel lies within
and is to be enjoyed later, as the higher faculties of the
business man, so constantly called into play, develop and
mature. There was in the reign of militarism and barbarous force much contempt for the man engaged in
trade. How completely has all this changed! But, indeed,
the feeling was of recent origin, for if we look further
back we find the oldest families in the world proud of
nothing but the part they played in business. The woolsack and the galley still flourish in their coat-of-arms.
One of the most—perhaps the most—influential statesman in England to-day is the Duke of Devonshire, because he has the confidence of both parties. He is the
president of the Barrow Steel Company. The members
of the present Conservative cabinet were found to hold
sixty-four directorships in various trading, manufacturing, and mining companies. In Britain to-day not how
to keep out of trade, but how to get in it, is the question. The President of the French Republic, a man with
a marvellous career, has been a business man all his days.
The old feeling of aversion has entirely gone.

You remember that the late Emperor of Germany
wished to make his friend, the steel manufacturer,
Krupp, a Prince of the empire, but that business man
was too proud of his works, and the son of his father,
and begged the Emperor to excuse him from degrading
the rank he at present held as King of Steel. Herr

Krupp's son, who has now succeeded to his father's throne, I doubt not, would make the same reply to-day. At present he is a monarch equal to his Emperor, and from all I know of the young King Krupp, just as proud of his position.

The old prejudice against trade has gone even from the strongholds in Europe. This change has come because trade itself has changed. In old days every branch of business was conducted upon the smallest retail scale, and small dealings in small affairs breed small men; besides, every man had to be occupied with the details, and, indeed, each man manufactured or traded for himself. The higher qualities of organization and of enterprise, of broad views and of executive ability, were not brought into play. In our day, business in all branches is conducted upon so gigantic a scale that partners of a huge concern are rulers over a domain. The large employer of labour sometimes has more men in his industrial army than the petty German kings had under their banners.

It was said of old that two of a trade never agree; to-day the warmest friendships are formed in every department of human effort among those in the same business; each visits the other's counting-house, factory, warehouse; and are shown the different methods; all the improvements; new inventions, and freely adapt them to their own business.

Affairs are now too great to breed petty jealousies, and there is now allied with the desire for gain the desire for progress, invention, improved methods, scientific development, and pride of success in these important matters; so that the dividend which the business man seeks and receives to-day is not alone in dollars. He receives with the dollar something better, a dividend in the shape of satisfaction in being instrumental in carrying forward to higher stages of development the business which he makes his life-work.

Rewards of a Business Career

I can confidently recommend to you the business career as one in which there is abundant room for the exercise of man's highest power, and of every good quality in human nature. I believe the career of the great merchant, or banker, or captain of industry, to be favourable to the development of the powers of the mind, and to the ripening of the judgment upon a wide range of general subjects; to freedom from prejudice, and the keeping of an open mind. And I do know that permanent success is not obtainable except by fair and honourable dealing, by irreproachable habits and correct living, by the display of good sense and rare judgment in all the relations of human life, for credit and confidence fly from the business man, foolish in word and deed, or irregular in habits, or even suspected of sharp practice. There may be room for a foolish man in every profession—foolish as a child beyond the range of his specialty, and yet successful in that—but no man ever saw a foolish business man successful. If without sound, all-round judgment, he must fail.

The business career is thus a stern school of all the virtues, and there is one supreme reward which it often yields which no other career can promise; I point to noble benefactions which it renders possible. It is to business men following business careers that we chiefly owe our universities, colleges, libraries, and educational institutions, as witness Girard, Lehigh, Chicago, Harvard, Yale, Cornell, and many others.

What monument can a man leave behind him productive of so much good, and so certain to hand his name down to succeeding generations, hallowed with the blessings of thousands in each decade who have within its walls received that most precious possession, a sound and liberal education? These are the works of men who recognized that surplus wealth was a sacred trust, to be administered during the life of its possessor for the highest good of his fellows.

If, then, some business men may fall subject to the reproach of grasping, we can justly claim for them as a class what honest Thomas Cromwell claimed for the great cardinal, and say: "If they have a greed of getting yet in bestowing they are most princely, as witness these seats of learning."

STEEL MANUFACTURE IN THE UNITED STATES IN THE NINETEENTH CENTURY

Some reasons why the United States has become the greatest steel-producing country in the world. Comparative costs of raw material and manufacture of steel in this country and abroad.

STEEL MANUFACTURE IN THE UNITED STATES IN THE NINETEENTH CENTURY

To WRITE of the manufacture of steel in the United States during the last century is indeed to begin at the beginning. From Mr. Swank's standard work, "Iron in All Ages," we learn that the Legislature of Pennsylvania as late as 1786 lent Mr. Humphreys £300 for five years to enable him to try to make bar iron into steel "as good as in England." As late as 1810 there were produced in the whole country only 917 tons of steel, Pennsylvania's share being 531 tons, or more than half of the whole. It is remarkable that the good old Keystone State still makes about the same percentage. Even in 1831 the production of steel was only 1,600 tons, an amount which was said then to equal the whole amount imported, so that the market for steel was divided equally with the foreigner seventy years ago. But this steel was made chiefly by cementation; crucible steel was to come later. From 1831 until as late as 1860 little progress was made in developing the manufacture of steel, for the total product in Pennsylvania in 1850 was only 6,000 tons, still principally blister steel. In 1840 Isaac Jones and William Coleman began its manufacture

From the Review of the Century number of the New York *Evening Post,* January 12, 1901.

in Pittsburg and succeeded. In 1853 Singer, Nimick & Co. produced successfully the usual grades of cast steel for saws, machinery, etc., and for kindred purposes Hussey, Wells & Co. in 1860 made out of American iron crucible steel of first quality as a regular product, and in 1862 came Park Brother & Co., with the biggest crucible steel plant of all up to that time, and several hundred English workmen were imported to insure success. This firm also used American iron. All these concerns were in Pittsburg.

Henceforth the struggle with foreign steel became severe until the invader was finally driven from the field. At first European makers could "dump their surplus" upon the market and force American makers to accept for their entire output the extreme low rates which had only to be taken by the invader for a small part of his. The party in control of a profitable home market can most successfully invade the foreign markets. In recent years it is the American manufacturer who is "dumping his surplus" in foreign territory. First conquer your home market and the foreign market will probably be added to you is the rule with manufacturers in international trade.

As I write of Coleman, Jones, Nimick, Singer, Hussey, and Park I am carried back to boyhood, when as a messenger boy in the telegraph office in Pittsburg I delivered to them many a telegram and received coveted recognition from these great men of my youth. Every one passed before my eyes as I wrote his name as vividly as if I were still in daily intercourse with him. Were they in the next room and to speak I could tell each voice before the word was ended. All are gone except the younger brother Singer, still my partner and friend.

These are the fathers of steel in the United States. They "have done the State some service." Peace to their ashes!

It was not till 1864, when the last century was almost two-thirds gone, that the revolution in steel manufacture came to us, and the Iron Age began to give way to the new King Steel, for our first Bessemer steel was made in that notable year, and steel hitherto costing from six to seven cents per pound for ordinary grades has since sold at less than one cent per pound, while steel billets by the hundred thousand tons have sold at "three pounds of steel for two cents." Into this steel for each pound enter two pounds of iron ore mined and transported by rail and water 1,000 miles, one pound of coke, requiring one and one-third pounds of coal to be mined, coked, and transported 50 miles, and one-third of a pound of limestone quarried and transported 140 miles; so that three and a third pounds of raw material have been made into one pound of steel and given to the consumer for two-thirds of one cent, three pounds for two cents being $15 for 2,240 pounds—the gross ton.

Were the writer to be asked how this miracle is performed he could not tell, for never can he dispel the doubt, when he thinks of it, that there must be some mistake, and that the concern which bestows this precious metal upon an ungrateful people for such a trifle must soon go to the wall. So, indeed, it would if this extremely low price had to be taken for any length of time or for all forms of steel. There is not sufficient profit to cover the risks of business in three pounds of steel for two cents. Still, some of the largest concerns of the United States, which own all their raw materials and their own ships and railways and are properly equipped and managed, might reach this as their cost price, allowing nothing for dividends or for interest upon the capital invested. Interest approaches two dollars per ton and in most cases exceeds it. The risks of manufacturing, accidents and renewals, and of sales should be rated at two dollars per ton.

This low cost was made possible by the invention of Sir Henry Bessemer. Bessemer steel was enthroned as king, and no monarch seemed so sure of a long and undisputed reign, supplemented as the Bessemer process was by the invention of a young genius, my friend Sidney Gilchrist Thomas, who added the basic process, by which impure ores could be used in the manufacture of Bessemer steel.

Various contributory causes have made steel billets at $15 a ton possible, among which automatic machinery ranks first, and in this the American excels; continuous processes come second. Workshops 1,100 and 1,200 feet long are becoming common, in which the raw material enters at one end and emerges finished at the other without handling, and often without even stopping except for reheating. The writer hears of plans to-day for new works upon such a scale that a mile and a quarter of land is required, one shop alone being 3,000 feet in length. One essential for cheap production is magnitude. Concerns making one thousand tons of steel per day have little chance against one making ten. We see this law in all departments of industry. It evolves the twenty-thousand-ton steamship and the fifty-ton railroad car. Improved engines and the use of electricity as a motor, the new loading and unloading machinery, are all contributory causes to the cheapening of steel.

There is one element of cost, however, which every student of sociology will rejoice to know has not been cheapened, and that is human labour. It has risen and the tendency is to higher earnings per man. In one of the largest steel works last year the average wages per man, including all the paid-by-the-day labourers, boys, and mechanics, exceeded $4 per day for 311 days. Fewer men being required the labour cost per ton is less, and contrary to the opinion often expressed these men are of higher quality than ever as men. It is a mistake to suppose that men are becoming mere machines; the workman of former days would be unable to take charge of the complicated machinery of to-day or to meet the demands made by present methods upon his brain and alertness.

Five years ago, had one asked the steelmakers of the country whether there was any likelihood of the Bessemer process being rivalled, not one in a thousand would have hesitated to reply with an emphatic never! But the one in a thousand, conversant with recent experiments, would have been less emphatic and would have intimated that perhaps even the Bessemer process might not remain without a rival.

The merits of the Siemens-Martin open-hearth furnace had been noted by at least one firm whose representative had seen it at work abroad. To Cooper, Hewitt & Co. is due the credit of having been the first to experiment with it in the United States. This was in 1868. The cost of open-hearth steel was necessarily greater than that of Bessemer, and so was restricted to few uses, but a new plant was needed on a large scale to place the new process securely upon its feet as a rival to the Bessemer, ready to benefit by the numerous improvements which clever men would make in the course of development. The Thomas basic process was found to be remarkably well adapted to the open-hearth furnace. The first basic open-hearth steel in this country was made by the firm of Carnegie, Phipps & Co., Limited, at Homestead, in 1888. There are now two kinds of steel made in the open hearth, the acid and the basic, the latter much cheaper than the former, though even purer, since the basic process eliminates impurities thoroughly. Basic open-hearth steel is now used as a substitute for Swedish iron in many instances, even for horseshoes. Armour is made of it. The East River bridge is to be built of acid steel, for which a higher price is to be paid, but this is solely because its engineer is not open to demonstration. The great advantage to the United States of the basic open-hearth process is that our enormous deposits of iron ores high in phosphorus can be used for steel, while the Bessemer process in American practice requires ores comparatively free from phosphorus, the supply of which is limited. The production of open-hearth steel is rapidly increasing.

Thus the age of iron, which passed away during the last century, was succeeded by the age of Bessemer steel, which enjoyed a reign of only thirty-six years, beginning, as it did, in 1864, and is in turn now passing away to be succeeded by the age of Siemens open-hearth steel. Already the product of the open-hearth is far beyond that of Bessemer in Britain, and such the writer ventures to predict will soon be the case in the United States.

The passing away of the Bessemer age has brought the South into prominence as a possible manufacturer of steel, when otherwise it never would have been in the field, its ores being unsuitable for the Bessemer process, but probably soon to be proved to be adapted to the open-hearth process. Until the new steel works of the Tennessee Company have been fully started and run for some time it cannot be completely demonstrated whether steel can be made there cheap enough to make the South a great centre for its manufacture. The experimental stage has not yet been clearly passed, since only part of the plant has been operated, but there seems little reason to doubt that any difficulties which may be met will finally be overcome and that the South is soon to become an important factor in steel manufacture.

The present centre of steel is in the square made by a line drawn from Pittsburg to Wheeling, northward to Lorain, eastward to Cleveland, and south again to Pittsburg. In this territory most of the steel is made. Allegheny County alone, including Pittsburg, produced in 1899 nearly one-quarter of all the pig iron made in the United States, almost half of the open-hearth steel, and almost 39 per cent. of the total production of all kinds of steel. As far as the writer sees there is little chance of this region being soon displaced. Colorado will, no doubt, expand as the Western coast is developed. Chicago's position as a steel manufacturer is assured. There is no sign of the great Southwest making steel to any extent. As late as the middle of the last century the Eastern States upon the Atlantic constituted the home of steel manufacture. Even in Pennsylvania about one-half of all its steel was made east of the Alleghany Mountains. Since then the trend has been constant and rapid to the region known as the Central West, which has Pittsburg as its metropolis. The transfer of the great Lackawanna Iron and Steel Works of Scranton, Pa., to Buffalo, and the splendid triumphs of the Bethlehem Steel Company, in Pennsylvania, in armour, guns, and forgings as specialties, which gave it a unique and commanding position, are proofs that for the making of ordinary steel the

East is not a favourable location. The history of the steel works at Troy is another case in point. There is one exception to this march westward, at Harrisburg, in Eastern Pennsylvania, which remains a prosperous and important centre of manufacture. The Maryland Steel Company at tide-water has advantages for export, but probably more important for the future of that company is its development in shipbuilding, for which its plant is well located. So far as the writer sees there is nothing to change the centre of steel manufacture in this country in the new century; it is in the Central West already described, and there it is likely to remain.

In that centre itself there are causes at work which may lead to some important changes. The wonderful growth of the lake cities on the northern border of the Central West region is shown by the recent census. These possess the advantages of the extremely low cost of lake transportation and by the Welland Canal, by which vessels of considerable tonnage can load at Conneaut and other lake ports direct for Europe, and above all the low rates which the Erie Canal insures manufactures for more than half the year. These are attracting attention, especially since an effort is being made to weld the trunk railway lines into one directorate to enable them to exact higher rates of freight when lower prices for service or articles seem to be the prevailing law. The selection of Buffalo by the Lackawanna Iron and Steel Company for its new works is evidence of a movement to the lakes. The policy of the railroad combination will inevitably operate in favour of the southern ports and to the advantage of New York. The differential of 3c. per hundred in favour of Baltimore and 2c. in favour of

Philadelphia over New York certainly means that the traffic will continue to seek these ports, and that New York's percentage of the shipping trade will steadily fall, as it has been doing. It is not to be supposed, however, that the City and State of New York will fail to protect their position by improving the weapon which New York State alone of all the States has in her waterway from the lakes to the port of New York. The writer takes this for granted, and consequently predicts a great development in steel manufacture in that part of the Central West lying along the southern border of Lake Erie, which will inure to the benefit of New York as being the port which may be reached cheapest from the Central West by water.

One of the features of the new century is to be a return to water transport for heavy materials. Lake ships of 7,000 tons' burden already exist. Barges will ply upon the Ohio River, soon to be slackwatered, and upon the enlarged Erie Canal, and also upon the canal from Chicago to the Mississippi, and many other waterways will be opened upon which the raw materials for steel and the finished article itself are to be carried for manufactures at rates already reached upon the lakes, one-third and often one-fourth those charged by rail.

It is scarcely within the bounds of belief that any cheaper or better process of making steel remains to be discovered, or that improvements upon present methods can possibly be such as to greatly reduce the cost and enable steel to be made without loss at less than 3 pounds for 2 cents. The twentieth century, with all its wonders yet to be revealed, will probably end with the manufacture of steel substantially as it is now, by the open hearth. There does not seem room for much improvement.

The last few years have witnessed the export of steel from our country to other lands. The republic has not only supplied its own wants but is competing to supply the wants of the world, not only in steel but in the thousand and one articles of which steel is the chief component part. The cheapness with which steel is made is multiplying its uses to such an extent that estimates made of the possible wants of the world in the future can only be the merest guesses. One illustration out of many that could be given is that three years ago there was not a ton of steel used for railway freight cars in this country; to-day a thousand tons of steel per day are used for that purpose alone; indeed, so rapidly is the use of steel extending that it is difficult to see how the world's demands can be filled. At present the mines of ironstone and of coking coal in Britain are worked to their fullest capacity, and yet the output is not greatly increased; it is the same with those of Germany, except that in the latter country there remain some inferior fields capable of development if prices rise, as is probable. Russia so far has not been much of a factor in steel-making; if she is able to supply her own wants by the middle of the century she will be doing well. Except by the United States, Great Britain, and Germany little steel is made, nor is any other country likely to make much. The hopes in regard to China and Japan making steel, the writer believes, are to prove delusive. Great Britain and Germany can not manufacture much beyond what they do now, so that the increased wants of the world can be met only by the United States. The known supply of suitable ironstone here is sufficient to meet all possible demands of the world for at least half of the present century; in the case of coke for the entire century. It is not to be supposed that other deposits will not be discovered before known supplies are exhausted.

A few years hence the exports of iron and steel and manufactures of iron and steel from the republic to many parts of the world, which in 1900 were valued at $129,000,000, promise to be so great as to constitute another chapter in the record-breaking history of steel.

The influence of our steel-making capacity upon development at home must be marvellous, for the nation that makes the cheapest steel has the other nations at its feet so far as manufacturing in most of its branches is concerned. The cheapest steel means the cheapest ships, the cheapest machinery, the cheapest thousand and one articles of which steel is the base. We are on the eve of a development of the manufacturing powers of the republic such as the world has never seen.

The republic's progress and commanding position as a steel-producer are told in a few words: In 1873, only twenty-seven years ago, the United States produced 198,-796 tons of steel, and Great Britain, her chief competitor, 653,500 tons, more than three times as much. Twenty-six years later, in 1899, the republic made more than twice as much as the monarchy, the figures being 10,639,-857 and 5,000,000 tons respectively, an eight-fold increase for Great Britain and fifty-three-fold for the republic, and it made almost 40 per cent. of all the steel made in the world, which was 27,000,000 tons. Industrial history has nothing to show comparable to this.

So much for the past; as for the future, ere the present century runs one-third its course, perchance only one-fourth, the United States is to make more steel than all the rest of the world combined and supply the wants of many lands besides our own.

Farewell, then, Age of Iron; all hail, King Steel, and success to the republic, the future seat and centre of his empire, where he is to sit enthroned and work his wonders upon the earth.

THE COST OF LIVING IN BRITAIN COMPARED WITH THE UNITED STATES

The costs of the necessities of life in England and America. Why the American can enjoy luxuries that are denied the Englishman.

THE COST OF LIVING IN BRITAIN
COMPARED WITH THE
UNITED STATES

IF ASKED upon what subject the general opinion of Britons was farthest astray regarding the United States, one would not be far wrong in answering, As to the comparative cost of living in the old land and in the new.

It will probably prove a work of time and of some difficulty to remove an impression so generally entertained as that which finds expression in the words recently spoken by a high English authority—viz., that "the United States would be a perfect El Dorado for the workingman, if it were not for the high cost of living."

It is easy to show how this impression has arisen. The Briton arrives in New York and hires a carriage, which has been waiting for the steamer several hours; he is charged an exorbitant price; he orders a bottle of imported wine, and finds it much dearer than at home; he learns that the cost of clothing made to order from imported material is also much dearer: and these things strike him deeply, because they are the first impressions received. When asked upon his return upon what data he has reached the conclusion that the cost of living is dearer in the United States than at home, he invariably gives

From *The Contemporary Review*, September, 1894.

these three items, and stops there. But these do not con-
stitute the chief sources of expenditure even to travellers,
much less to residents. Asked how he found the cost of
living at hotels, he remembers that it costs less in the
Republic, where the charge in the best hotels is from fourteen to eighteen shillings ($3.50 to $4.50) per day, the
latter being the extreme rate in New York. For this he
has a comfortable room and all meals—breakfast,
luncheon, dinner and supper. He also remembers that he
could scarcely have such a dinner at the Metropole in
London for the entire eighteen shillings ($4.50) which
pay for all meals and a room at a good hotel in New
York. Asked how he found the cost of travelling, he
figures a little and finds that it is just a little more than
one-half, first-class, even including sleeping cars. The
cheaper cost of railway travel per mile, and of hotels, is
not nearly offset by the extra cost of cabs and foreign
wines. The visitor buys no clothing, and if wise will follow
the American example and use the hotel omnibuses or
electric cars, and rarely, if ever, use cabs, which are not
an American institution. If the visitor wishes, however,
to hire a carriage and pair by the day, week, or month,
or for theatre or reception, he is provided in New York
at prices not beyond those charged in London—forty to
fifty pounds ($200 to $250) per month, according to
circumstances, and twelve shillings ($3.00) per night for
a brougham; for an afternoon in the park the charge for
a carriage and pair is even less in New York. It is undoubtedly a fact that the cost of travel, including all
necessary expenditures per day, over equal distances, is
much dearer in Britain than in America. But this fact
affects only the few travellers, usually persons of means,
and is of little moment. The great point is, as to the

comparative cost of living to the mass of people, the wage-earning class of the two countries.

Let us calmly consider this. The income of the mass of workingmen, skilled and unskilled, is from £60 to £120 sterling (300 to 600 dollars) per year. Now we must first learn the percentage of these earnings spent for each of the principal necessaries of life. According to the Bureau of Labour statistics of Massachusetts, the highest authority, these in England and America are as follows:

Income, $300 (£60) to $450 (£90) per year			Income, $450 (£90) to $600 (£120) per year		
Items	American	English	Items	American	English
Subsistence	64	81	Subsistence	63	78.75
Clothing..	7	7	Clothing..	10.50	10.50
Rent......	20	13	Rent......	15.50	10.37
Fuel......	6	7	Fuel......	6	6
Sundries..	3	3	Sundries..	5	5
Total...	100	110	Total...	100.00	110.62

This shows the increased cost of articles in Britain to be 10 1-2 per cent. But prices in the United States have fallen since this table was made, much more than in Britain. In Charles Booth's valuable work, "Labour and Life of the People" (British), he gives the amount spent for food alone as from 60 to 50 per cent., according to the family revenues. In the broader term "subsistence," not only food, but all that enters the mouth is embraced. Thus "subsistence" is the chief item of cost for the workingman's family. It ranges from 64 per cent. in America to 81 in England. The reason for this difference is obvious. Of course, all food is cheaper in the United States than in Britain. The former exports it to the latter. Tobacco is very much cheaper. America grows tobacco, and only taxes it 3*d* (6 cents) per pound, as against a 3*s*. 6*d*. (84 cents) tax in the Monarchy—fourteen times as great. Of course, what he drinks is cheaper. The duty on whisky is 20*d*. (40 cents) per gallon, as against 11*s*. ($2.64)—six times greater—in Britain, and it is made more cheaply in Kentucky than in Ireland or Scotland. Upon beer the taxation is 4*s*. and 7*s*. (96 cents and $1.75) respectively per barrel. Tea and coffee are free of duty to the American; they are taxed to the Briton. Sugar (raw) is free in both lands, but in the Republic there is a slight tax upon foreign refined. When the masses in Britain realize how heavily they are taxed compared with the workers of the United States, there will probably be a prompt demand for reductions upon articles embraced in the term "Subsistence," and especially for a free breakfast-table.

The low cost of what goes into the mouths of the people throughout the United States would surprise any British investigator who made it a study, but the cost of living in the forty-four States, occupying a continent, is to be determined not only in New York City, and in the cities and towns upon the Atlantic sea-coast, to which products of the great West have to be transported, but also by taking into account cost at the centre of population, which is now near Indianapolis, Indiana, midway between Chicago and St. Louis, eight hundred miles inland from New York.

Having dealt with, say, three-fourths of the total expenditure of the workingman's family—namely, that for "subsistence"—and found that it cannot be otherwise than that the articles consumed must be cheaper in Indianapolis than in Manchester, by at least the cost of

rail and ocean transport and merchants' profits, we come
to the second item, which is "rent," consuming 20 per
cent. of the earnings of the family in America and 13 in
England. The British workman lives in a smaller house.
The better class of American, as a rule, has three or
four rooms; the Briton two. Rent is undoubtedly much
higher in the newer land.

The next item in importance is "clothing," which
represents 7 per cent. of the expenditure in the United
States, and exactly the same percentage in Britain. This
will, no doubt, surprise most readers until the reason
is given, which is, that while clothing made from the
finest imported cloth is very much dearer in America
than in Britain where the cloth is produced, clothing made
from the American cloth is very cheap indeed and serviceable. It is, however, coarse and harsh, and not so
agreeable to wear—harsher even than the Scotch cheviot.
But the mass of the people wear it as they wear woollen
underclothing of the same kind. Hence the masses are
not affected by the duties placed upon the fine woollens,
which are imported only for the rich few. I have before
me advertisements in the American papers of complete
suits of ready-made clothing ranging from two to three
pounds (ten to fifteen dollars)—just the cost in Britain.

Here is a true story bearing upon this subject. A well-
known member of Parliament, addressing his constituents
in the Midlands some time ago, told them that living
for the workingman was much higher in America than in
Britain, and said that the cost of clothing was three times
as great. A copy of this speech was sent to his friend,
one of the best-known men in the United States, whom
the speaker was in the habit of visiting. A short time
after, he visited his friend in the Republic, accompanied

by his wife. One morning the host appeared at breakfast in a new suit which elicited general admiration, the English lady stating that it was "much smarter than the suit worn by her husband." The host then asked his visitor what he supposed the suit cost him; to which the unwary Briton replied, "Well, the suit I am now wearing cost me £7 (35 dollars), and I suppose yours, in this terribly protected country, must have cost £12 (60 dollars)." This was his opinion after having examined the suit. "Well," said his host, "I paid just $4.50 (18s.) for this suit, and I wish you to take it back to England and show it to your constituents and tell them this." Amidst much laughter, this was declined. His host had seen in the village a travelling van from Boston, from which ready-made clothing was being sold, and asked the vendor if he had a suit to fit him; to which he replied "Yes, and if you take a suit you can have it at wholesale price. Retail price is $6 (24 s.)." "Very good: send it to the house." It was promptly sent, with the result stated. Of course it was American material, not as smooth or as fine as the cloth worn by the honourable member; nevertheless, a good, smart suit. The price, however, was so very low that it is fair to record that I should hesitate to say that it was likely to prove serviceable. For £3 ($15.00), however, serviceable suits are easily obtained.

When we look at the amount of the extra fine woollen goods imported by the United States, we see how trifling it is, compared with the total consumption of wool. In 1890 the value of home woollen manufactures was $338,000,000—say sixty-eight millions sterling. The import of the high-priced fine foreign woollens was only $35,500,000—seven and a tenth millions sterling. It is safe to say that the value per yard of the foreign was double that of the domestic; hence the number of yards of foreign woollens used was not much beyond 5 per cent. of the amount consumed, and all by the few wealthy people, who alone use the high-priced foreign articles.

We have the same result with cotton manufactures, the value of the home American product being $268,-000,000—fifty-four millions sterling; the amount imported being $28,000,000, not six millions sterling, which represents not quite 5 per cent. of the total consumption, assuming double value per yard for the foreign. The amount of cotton goods used by a workingman's family is considerable.

In regard to silks we have the following figures for the year 1890: product of American mills, $69,000,000 —thirteen millions eight hundred thousand sterling; the imported manufactured silk, $31,000,000—six millions two hundred thousand sterling. It may safely be assumed that the value of silks imported, per yard, was double that of the domestic, so that more than four yards of American silk were consumed to one of foreign.

While upon the subject of clothing I may note two facts within my own experience. An American family, having numerous servants, resides part of each year in Britain. The servants pass to and fro and thus have opportunities to purchase their clothing, boots and shoes, etc., either in the one land or the other. The menservants continue to purchase clothing in the old land. The women-servants find they can purchase to better advantage in New York. Boots and shoes are purchased by all in New York.

The second instance: A Scotch-American family with five children spends part of almost every year in Scotland.

The able, thrifty mother formerly took the opportunity to supply her own and the children's clothing, etc., in Glasgow. Upon recent visits she has purchased nothing upon this side, and I heard her give as a reason that she found that clothing for herself, and especially for her children, could now be purchased better and cheaper in New York than in Glasgow.

The well-known Free-Trade or tariff-reform writer, Mr. Schoenhof, was deputed by the State Department to report upon cost in the United States and Britain, and reported as follows some years ago:—

"So far as clothing and dry goods in general are concerned, I find that cotton goods are fully as cheap in the United States as here. Shirtings and sheetings, if anything, are superior in quality for the same money with us, so far as I can judge from the articles exposed for sale in the retail stores. Articles of underwear for women, made of muslin, are far superior in workmanship and finish, and cheaper in price, in the United States. Nor can I find that men's shirts, when chiefly of cotton, are any cheaper here. Of boots and shoes, if factory made, the same may be said. In workmanship and finish I find corresponding articles of the wholesale process of manufacture superior in the United States. This is true of clothing as well as of cuffs, collars, and like articles."

Prices of articles other than agricultural have fallen in the United States much more than in Britain since Mr. Schoenhof reported. This fall has been so great as to put the price of Bessemer, pig-iron, and steel billets at Pittsburg lower than at Middlesborough; to enable American carpets to be sold in Britain; to tempt the leading American shipbuilders to ask permission to tender for some of the new British war-ships; the Clyde

Trustees to purchase their new and powerful dredgers in New York. It has also enabled the American manufacturer of agricultural implements to reach the British market, and the quarrymen to send granite from Maine to Aberdeen.

The next item which figures in the expenses of the workingman's family is "fuel." Speaking generally, this is much cheaper in the United States than in Britain. If we compare New York and London, New York receives anthracite coal as cheaply as London receives bituminous coal. The former will, at least, give double service, and it is said to yield three times as much. In the centre of population in the United States the cost of coal does not exceed 8s. (about $2.00) per ton. In the great western Pennsylvania and Ohio districts it is not more than 6s. The American has to use more coal in winter owing to the severe cold, and has more fires going in his larger house. Experts have found that the percentage of their earnings spent by the American and Briton on fuel is equal—viz., 6 per cent.

It has been common in Britain to attribute the supposed higher cost of living in the United States to the effect of the tariff. Now a little consideration will show that this impression is not well founded. The principal highly-taxed articles under the McKinley Bill are five: First, the extra fine silks of France; second, the fine woollens and linens of Britain; third, the extra fine linens of Germany and France; fourth, the high-priced wines of France; and fifth, Havana tobacco and cigars. The duties on all these are very high. Woollens 60 per cent. of their value, silks even higher, champagnes, 32s. per dozen, etc., etc. This is our "Democratic" Budget. There is not a workingman in America who uses any of these articles. It is considered good policy thus to tax heavily the luxuries of the rich, and admit free the tea and coffee and raw sugar used by the masses. It is not probable that this policy will be reversed, or even greatly modified, however much talk there may be of tariff reform. Indeed, the wholesome tendency now seen in Britain to lay the burden of taxation upon the wealthy few who can best afford to bear it is not less strongly marked in the Republic. The necessaries of life used by the workers will probably remain duty free in the Republic and soon become free in the Monarchy, and the luxuries of the rich will continue to be taxed more and more in both lands.

The position of the supposed unfortunate farmer of the United States used to be cited, and the point made, that owing to the tax upon machinery he had to pay more for his agricultural implements than was otherwise necessary, but as the American has now the command of the world for agricultural machinery, and exports it, the farmer is no longer interested in the tax upon foreign machinery.

The appearance of the United States as an exporting country of manufactured articles, owing to reduced costs, is one of the notable events of recent years. Here are a few items: In the year 1893 agricultural implements were exported to many parts of the world to the extent of nearly £1,000,000 (about $5,000,000), manufactures of copper to the extent of £900,000 ($4,500,000); cotton manufactures, £2,400,000 ($12,000,000); iron and steel, and manufactures of these, £6,000,000 ($30,-000,000); carriages, cars, etc., more than £500,000 ($2,500,000); wood, and manufactures of wood, over £5,000,000 sterling ($25,000,000), American furniture being now largely exported.

In the year 1892 the Republic exported as much iron and steel, and manufactures thereof, as she imported—viz., $28,000,000 worth in both cases—five and three-quarter millions sterling.

It is notable that musical instruments, valued at £360,000 ($1,800,000), were exported; glass and glass ware to the extent of £1,600,000 ($8,000,000); leather and manufactures of leather, over £2,000,000 ($10,-000,000); paper and manufactures of paper, to the extent of over £300,000 ($1,500,000) (some English journals are now printed upon American paper); instruments for scientific purposes, £260,000 ($1,300,000); clocks and watches, over £2,000,000 ($1,000,000).

The export of manufactured articles rapidly increases year after year, but, unlike that of Britain, must ever remain totally insignificant as compared with the value of the total home production of manufactures, which was no less in 1890 than £1,750,000,000 ($8,750,000,000). The value of British manufactures in 1888 was not quite half as great, being £820,000,000 ($4,100,000,000).

The prosperity of a new continent like the United States is not to be gauged by its foreign but by its home commerce. As the new land more and more supplies its own wants, her foreign commerce must relatively decline; more of the cotton grown, for instance, being manufactured at home, and less going abroad, and so with all the natural products, as also with many articles now imported, which will be made at home.

In view of the facts here noted, and also the obvious fact, that subsistence must be cheaper in one country than in the other, and that this embraces three-fourths of the total cost of the necessaries of life for a workingman's family, how are we to account for the general impression still lingering in Britain, that the cost of living is higher in the United States? Simply for this reason: that while it is true that a pound sterling in the United States to-day will purchase more of the necessaries of life for the mass of the people than it will in Britain, and while the American workman has great advantages over his fellow British workman in consequence, still it does not follow by any means that the American workman lives as cheaply as the Briton—far from it. He has much higher wages. The report of the Senate Committee recently made shows that the average percentage of American wages obtained by the British workman is only 56 1-2 per cent.—not much more than one half—the principal handicrafts being made the basis of comparison. Having higher revenues, the American is not content to live without what would be considered luxuries in any of the old countries of Europe. He earns more and he spends more. Therefore, in one sense it is true that the cost of living as the American workman lives is greater than that of the Briton as he lives. But it is none the less true that this arises from the fact that he lives in a different manner. For those similar things which are absolutely necessary the cost is much less in the newer land.

The American workman and his family can live very cheaply indeed if so inclined, or they can spend inordinately just as easily as in any other country. We find this proven by the expenditures of foreign workmen, especially Hungarians and Italians, who have in recent years emigrated to the United States in great numbers. The usual price paid by these foreigners to the keeper of the boarding-house is ten cents (5d.) per day for food. They usually sleep in wooden huts erected for them by their employers. In times of unexampled industrial de-

pression, like the present, the ability of the masses of the
people of the United States to live cheaply and yet comfortably is of the greatest moment, for it has shielded
them from much acute suffering which would otherwise
have resulted from the lack of work—an experience new
to this generation of Americans, and likely soon to pass
away, unless the faith of capital in the maintenance of
the gold standard be again shaken. An equivocal note
upon this subject, struck by the Secretary of the Treasury
in May last year, paralyzed the business of the country
for the time—and recovery has been retarded by impending new legislation affecting duties upon imports.

Whether America be the El Dorado of the workingman or not, depends upon the workman himself. He and
his family can now live for less than a family in Britain,
if they will live as frugally. They are in the position of
the old Scotchwoman I knew, who, being asked if she
could live upon a certain sum as an annuity, replied, "Ou
ay, I could live on half o't, but I could spend dooble."
That is to say, a pound sterling in the new land, judi-
ciously spent for the necessaries of life by the workingman and his family, will to-day purchase more of
these in the new than in the old home of our race—a fact
probably fraught with far-reaching consequences upon
both sides of the Atlantic in the not distant future.

THE NATURAL OIL AND GAS WELLS OF WESTERN PENNSYLVANIA

A short history of the discovery of oil and gas. The method of driving wells and the use of the product. The fortunes won on a small capital. The possibilities of its use in the future.

THE NATURAL OIL AND GAS WELLS OF WESTERN PENNSYLVANIA

That the novel fuel which the earth has recently thrown forth for us should attract general attention is not to be wondered at, for certainly nothing like it has hitherto ever been known. Probably the richest district in subterranean treasures upon the face of the earth is Western Pennsylvania, which has for its metropolis the smoky city of Pittsburg. To the southeast of the city lies the famous deposit of coking coal, known and used all over America from the Atlantic seaboard to the silver mines of Colorado. The vein is from seven to nine feet deep, and embraces an area of two hundred square miles. It is so favourably situated for mining, that thousands of tons of coke have been sold for three shillings and six-pence (84 cents per gross ton), loaded upon cars. The growth of this trade has been rapid, even for this country, for the men are still living who built the first coking oven, while there are to-day between nine and ten thousand ovens. It is but twenty years since the coke was first used in the blast furnace. In the year 1882 there were made 138,001,840 bushels.

Directly east of Pittsburg lies the Westmore and gas coal field, from which the eastern cities draw their supplies for gas. The vein of this coal is from five to six feet deep, and so easily mined that the Pennsylvania

From *Macmillan's Magazine,* January, 1885.

Railroad Company obtains coal loaded in the engine tenders for about three shillings (72 cents) per gross ton. The field extends east and southeast of the city, along the banks of the Monongahela and Youghiogheny rivers. It is from mines on their banks that cities, even as far away as New Orleans, are supplied with gas coal. The annual production exceeds 7,000,000 tons.

Turning now from the coking and the gas coal deposits towards the north, and at a distance of a hundred miles from Pittsburg, we reach the oil region. Rapid as has been the development of coke and gas coal, that of petroleum eclipses anything ever known. It is only twenty-two years since I visited, in company with some friends, the then famous oil well of the Storey Farm, upon Oil Creek. The oil was then running from the well into the creek, where a few flat-bottomed scows lay filled with it, ready to be floated down to the Alleghany River upon an agreed-upon day each week, when the creek was flooded by means of a temporary dam. This was the beginning of the natural oil business. We purchased the farm for £8,000 (about $39,000) sterling, and so small was our faith in the ability of the earth to yield for any considerable time the hundred barrels per day which the well was then producing, that we decided to make a pond capable of holding 100,000 barrels of oil, which we estimated would be worth 200,000*l*. (about $975,000) when the supply ceased. Unfortunately for us the pond leaked fearfully; evaporation also caused much loss, but we continued to run oil in to make the losses good day after day until several hundred thousand barrels had gone in this fashion. Our experience with the farm may be worth reciting. Its value rose to 1,000,000*l*. (about $4,870,000) ; that is, the shares of the company sold in the market upon this basis; and one year it paid in cash dividends 200,000*l*. (about $975,000) sterling—rather a good return upon an investment of 8,000*l*. But this is an exceptional result, many thousands of pounds having been lost by investors in oil properties. Only a few years before this, the same oil had been sold at eight shillings (about two dollars) per bottle, as a certain cure for all the known or imagined disorders of man. It was then known as Seneca oil, "the great Indian remedy," because the tribe of Indians of that name, which then inhabited the district, skimmed the oil from the surface of the creek. "The sovereign remedy" now sells for less than three shillings (about seventy-five cents) per barrel, but strange to say the people who eagerly bought it for eight shillings per bottle, and gave testimony to its healing properties, now find that all its virtues have fled since it can be purchased for a half-penny. So much for the mysterious in *materia medica*.

Starting, then, at nothing only about twenty years ago, we find the region now (1885) giving forth 70,000 barrels of oil per day. On the first day of November last there were stored in tanks no less than 38,034,337 barrels, an amount sufficient to meet the wants of the world for some years. Up to January 1st, 1884, this region has yielded 250,000,000 barrels of oil, and still it flows in increasing quantities day after day. To transport this enormous traffic 6,200 miles of iron pipe lines have been laid. The oil is pumped through these from the wells—which number 21,000—to the seaboard, a distance of about 300 miles.

The value of petroleum and its products exported in the year 1877 amounted to $61,789,438, or over 12,-000,000*l*. sterling. In 1883 its exports were only

9,000,000*l*. sterling (about $45,000,000) in value, although the number of gallons (656,363,869) was almost double that exported in the year 1877. The total amount exported up to January 1st, 1884, exceeds in value 125,000,000*l*. (about $625,000,000) sterling. It may confidently be said that the oil wells of Western Pennsylvania bid fair to yield sufficient to pay off the entire national debt before they are exhausted.

We come now to the latest revelation of our subterranean treasures, viz., the natural gas wells, which are rapidly surrounding Pittsburg. Just as the natural oil was seen upon the surface of Oil Creek (hence its name), so throughout the district northeast of Pittsburg, and about fifteen miles distant, small jets of gas have been seen bubbling up through the waters of the creeks. A marsh gas has also been found for many years, at a depth of twenty feet, which the farmers sometimes use for boiling the sap of the maple tree into sugar. The centre of this natural gas district is the village of Murraysville, in Westmoreland County. In the race of a small flour mill at that place, a larger amount of gas than usual had been noticed, and fifteen years ago a party of speculators bored there, hoping to find oil, but after boring to a depth of 900 feet, nothing was found. Seven years later another party concluded to try it again, and decided not to stop boring until a much greater depth had been reached. Their hope, of course, was that oil would be obtained, but when they had bored to a depth of 1,320 feet a tremendous explosion occurred, which drove the drills from the well into the air and broke everything to pieces. The roar of the escaping gas was heard in Monroeville, five miles away. The imprisoned force had found an escape at last, and a new source of wealth was given to Western Pennsylvania, already far too highly favoured, I suppose my readers will be disposed to say. After four pipes, each two inches in diameter, had been laid from the mouth of the well, and the flow directed through them, the gas was ignited, and the whole district was lighted up for miles around. This valuable fuel was permitted to waste for five years, as capitalists could not be found who were willing to risk the 40,000*l.* (about $200,000) for pipes to convey it to the factories and mills where it could be utilized.

I visited this region last week and saw nine wells furnishing gas. The gas from the three largest was still passing into the air. These are wonderful sights indeed. The gas rushes up with such velocity through a six-inch pipe, which extends perhaps twenty feet above the surface, that it does not ignite within six feet of the mouth of the pipe. Looking up into the clear blue sky you see before you a dancing golden fiend without visible connection with the earth, swayed by the wind into fantastic shapes, and whirling in every direction. As the gas from the well strikes the centre of the flame, and passes partly through it, the lower part of the mass curls inward, giving rise to the most beautiful effects, gathered into graceful folds at the bottom, a veritable pillar of fire. There is not a particle of smoke from it.

Already four distinct pipe lines, two of them eight inches in diameter, convey the gas from this district to manufacturing establishments in Pittsburg, and a fifth line conveys it to our Bessemer steel mills, nine and ten miles distant. Another line of ten-inch pipe is being laid.

The cost of piping is now estimated at the present extremely low prices, with right of way, at 1,500*l.* sterling (about $7,500) per mile, so that the cost of a line to

Pittsburg may be said to be about 27,000*l.* sterling (about $135,000). The cost of drilling is about 1,000*l.* (about $5,000), and the mode of procedure as follows: A derrick being first erected, a six-inch wrought iron pipe is driven down through the soft earth till rock is reached, from 75 to 100 feet. Large drills, weighing from three to four thousand pounds, are now brought into use; these rise and fall from four to five feet a stroke. The fuel necessary to run these drills is conveyed by small pipes from adjoining wells. An eight-inch hole having been bored to a depth of about 500 feet, a 5 5-8-inch wrought iron pipe is put down to shut off the water. The hole is then continued six inches in diameter until gas is struck, when a four-inch pipe is then put down. From forty to sixty days are consumed in sinking the well and striking gas. The largest well known is estimated to yield about 30,000,000 cubic feet of gas in twenty-four hours, but half of this may be considered as the product of a good well. The pressure of the gas as it issues from the mouth of the well is nearly or quite 200 pounds per square inch. One of the gauges which I examined showed a pressure of 187 pounds. Even at our works, where we use the gas, nine miles from the well, the pressure is 75 pounds per square inch. At one of the wells, where it was desirable to have a supply of pure water, I found a small engine worked by the direct pressure of the gas as it came from the well, and an excellent supply of water was thus obtained from a spring in the valley.

There are, of course, various theories as to the location and extent of the gas belt. Enough wells have already been bored in the Murraysville district to indicate that it is about half a mile wide, and extends in a southeasterly direction from Murraysville for five or six miles. The wells bored beyond this encountered a flow of salt water in such great quantities as to nearly drown out the gas; for while some gas came to the surface it was not in sufficient quantities to render it valuable, and merely proved its existence. Experts have therefore concluded that while the gas exists in such wells, it is under a basin of salt water. Several wells have been bored in the city of Pittsburg and the vicinity, but the same trouble from salt water has been encountered there. A geological friend informs me that the stratum dips about 6,000 feet near Pittsburg, and his theory is that this depression has been filled with salt water, and hence the attempts in that district have proved unsuccessful. Whether deeper boring or some plan of shutting out the water will overcome this difficulty is yet to be seen. Northwest from Murraysville but little has been done to prove the extent of the gas belt. So much for the Murraysville district, which is to-day furnishing most of the gas consumed in Pittsburg.

If any of my readers will take a map of Western Pennsylvania and follow the Alleghany River some twenty miles from Pittsburg, they will find the town of Tarentum, which is the centre of the second gas district. Several large wells have been found there, and it is quite probable that future developments will reveal a territory somewhat like the Murraysville. A well recently struck compares favourably with those in the latter region. Capitalists have recently arranged to bring this gas in pipes, laid in the bed of the river, to Pittsburg; and I have no doubt that by the end of the year these lines will be in operation, and the Tarentum district giving us a large amount of gas.

I now come to the third district, of which the county town of Washington (Pennsylvania) is the centre, which is situated about twenty-five miles south of Pittsburg. I drove out to this region, stopping over night at a friend's house, twelve miles from the wells. These had been ignited, and the whole sky was brilliantly illuminated by them. It seemed to us, although such a distance away, as if a great conflagration was raging. The next morning we drove to the wells. A pipe line has already been laid, and takes the product of one of these wells to the iron mills along the bank of the Ohio at Pittsburg, and two more pipe lines are already under contract. What we saw here was very similar to that seen in the Murraysville district, except that the gas was led from the mouths of the wells in pipes along the ground, instead of being shot upright into the air. Looking down from the road-side upon the first well we saw in the valley, there appeared to be an immense circus ring, the verdure having been burnt, and the earth baked by the flame. The ring was quite round, as the wind had driven the flame in one direction after another, and the effect of the great golden flame lying prone upon the earth, swaying and swirling with the wind in every direction, was most startling. The great beast Apollyon, minus the smoke, seemed to have come from his lair again.

America is generally supposed to be the land which receives emigrants, but the movement of man to and fro over the whole earth is fast becoming more and more general. The Anglo-Saxon race grows restless everywhere. As I stopped to climb the fence to go down to this fiery monster, my eye caught sight of the following hand bill:

"PUBLIC SALE.

"The undersigned, going to move to Australia, will sell at public sale on Thursday,

SEPTEMBER 25,

at his residence on what is known as the Mrs. Andrew Carlisle farm, one and one-half miles east of Hickory, on the Hickory and Washington road, his entire stock of

Household and Kitchen Furniture,

consisting of Bureaus, Bedsteads, Bedding, Chairs, Tables, Dishes, Cooking Stove, in fact everything I have got. Sale to commence at 1 o'clock, prompt, when terms will be made known.

WILLIAM TIPLADY.

A. W. Cummins, Auctioneer."

Now what on earth takes Mr. Tiplady from this beautiful region, one of the finest agricultural districts in the whole of America—takes him just as unexpected treasures are found to exist below him; which are bound to produce unwonted activity in the district, and give every man a fair opportunity to do more than well? Many reasons were suggested, but the most likely one was that he had kin in Australia, and had determined to end his days among them. The name had never been heard by any of us, but it is similar to many of the compound names which we had been so much struck with in our recent coaching tour through south-western England, so that we thought he must be from the motherland. One brother had probably left the old home for the antipodes, while another sought the shelter of the Republic. Truly our race are the true nomads, and wander over the earth, knowing no rest.

Laying our hands upon the vibrating pipe at the well —and it takes strong nerves to approach so near to the

screaming roar and the swirling flame, and stand there
—we were surprised at its icy coldness. At one well,
where a wooden covering had been placed over the valves,
a beautiful coating of ice, not less than an eighth of an
inch thick, caused by condensation, covered the pipe. New
wells are being put down, and it is evident that Washington County is destined to supply its quota of the gas used
in Pittsburg. Thus, upon three-fourths of a complete
circle surrounding the city of Pittsburg, at a distance of
from fifteen to twenty miles, gas is already proved to
exist in large quantities, only waiting for escape from its
home beneath the sandrock.

Now, as to the commercial aspect of natural gas. The
first question naturally is, How long will it last?

Friends who are best acquainted with the oil territory,
with which natural gas has much in common, assure me
that twenty years will not see the present known territory exhausted. That we have discovered all the gas
territory is not to be believed; on the contrary, it is
highly probable that the break in the belt near Pittsburg
is merely a local fault, and that southwest of Pittsburg
the belt will be found to extend for many miles. It will
probably be the story of the oil region over again. Month
after month the cry has gone forth that the earth cannot
stand this depletion. Not only rivers but seas of oil will
be exhausted when drained at the rate of 70,000 barrels
per day. Speculators step in at intervals, and buy millions of barrels of oil, certain that the supply must
diminish; and yet every successive speculation cripples or
ruins its promoters. Petroleum at 2l. (about $10) per
barrel was considered cheap, then at 1l. ($5.00), and at
4s. ($1.00), it was almost given away; yet to-day (1885)
it can be bought for 2s. 10d. (about seventy cents), and

the supply is greater than ever. It promises to be much the same with natural gas.

In the manufacture of glass, of which there is an immense quantity made in Pittsburg, I am informed that gas is worth much more than the cost of coal and its handling, because it improves the quality of the product. One firm in Pittsburg is already making plate glass of the largest sizes, equal to the best imported French glass, and is enabled to do so by this fuel. In the manufacture of iron, and especially in that of steel, the quality is also improved by the pure new fuel. In our steel rail mills we have not used a pound of coal for more than a year, nor in our iron mills for nearly the same period. The change is a startling one. Where we formerly had ninety firemen at work in one boiler-house, and were using 400 tons of coal per day, a visitor now walks along the long row of boilers and sees but one man in attendance. The house being whitewashed, not a sign of the dirty fuel of former days is to be seen, nor do the stacks emit smoke. In the Union Iron Mills our puddlers have whitewashed the coal-bunkers belonging to their furnaces. Most of the principal iron and glass establishments in the city either are to-day (January, 1885) using this gas as fuel, or are making preparations to do so. The cost of coal is not only saved, but the great cost of firing and handling it; while the repairs to boilers and grate bars are much less.

The following extract from the report of a committee, made to the American Society of Mechanical Engineers at a recent meeting, gives an idea of the value of the new fuel.

"Natural gas, next to hydrogen, is the most powerful of the gaseous fuels, and if properly applied, one of the most economical, as very nearly its theoretical heating power can be utilized in evaporating water. Being so free from all deleterious elements, notably sulphur, it makes better iron, steel and glass than coal fuel. It makes steam more regularly, as there is no opening of doors and no blank spaces are left on the grate bars to let cold air in, and, when properly arranged, regulates the steam pressure, leaving the man in charge nothing to do but to look after the water, and even that could be accomplished if one cared to trust to such a volatile water tender. Boilers will last longer, and there will be fewer explosions from unequal expansion and contraction due to cold drafts of air being let in on hot plates.

*   *   *   *   *   *

"An experiment was made to ascertain the value of gas as a fuel in comparison with coal in generating steam, using a retort or boiler of forty-two inches diameter, ten feet long with four-inch tubes. It was first fired with selected Youghiogheny coal, broken to about four-inch cubes, and the furnace was charged in a manner to obtain the best results possible with the stack that was attached to the boiler. Nine pounds of water evaporated to the pound of coal consumed was the best result obtained. The water was measured by two meters—one in the suction and the other in the discharge. The water was fed into a heater at a temperature of from 60° to 62°; the heater was placed in the flue leading from the boiler to the stack in both gas and coal experiments. In making the calculations the standard seventy-six pound bushel of the Pittsburg district was used. Six hundred and eighty-four pounds of water were evaporated per bushel which was 60.9 per cent. of the theoretical value of the coal.

Where gas was burned under the same boiler, but with a different furnace, and taking one pound of gas to the 23.5 cubic feet, the water evaporated was found to be 20.31 pounds or 83.4 per cent. of the theoretical heat units were utilized. The steam was under the atmospheric pressure, there being a large enough opening to prevent any back pressure; the combustion of both gas and coal was not hurried. It was found that the lower row of tubes could be plugged, and the same amount of water could be evaporated with the coal; but with gas, by closing all the tubes (on the end next the stack), except enough to get rid of the products of combustion, when the pressure on the walls of the furnace was three ounces, and the fire forced to its best, it was found that very nearly the same results could be obtained. Hence it was concluded that the most of the work was done on the shell of the boiler."

The only analyses of this natural fuel which have yet been made or published are those by our chief chemist, Mr. Ford. These are from samples of the gas taken from the pipe as it enters our steel rail mills, after it has travelled nine miles from the wells.

Mr. Ford writes me as follows:

"Enclosed find four of my latest analyses, which were made the same day the samples were procured. At present these investigations are but in embryo. I wish whenever I can do so without interfering with the work at the laboratory of the steel works, to take samples from different gas wells, and make a collection of their salts. I think I have discovered some very interesting facts in regard to these salts, but it would be most unwise at the present time to give expression to my opinions upon this subject, since as yet I have had no time or opportunity to go to the different wells and make a collection of their salts, and by that means confirm my first impression.

"My discovery of the fact that natural gas varies in its chemical composition from time to time will be rather startling to some, and it will open a new field for thought. I wished before these results were made public to ascertain whether the gas from other wells changed as does this from the Murraysville, and should the gas from some wells vary whilst that of others remains constant, the question naturally arises which class of well will prove the more lasting. This fact of the variation of the gas from the same well will certainly throw some new light upon the subject of the generation of this material, and if I may dare say it, possibly some additional light as well upon the subject of petroleum. Having had all the points in view, I have refrained from publishing my results until I should have my opinions confirmed and reconfirmed by numerous analyses. Hoping that these analyses will be of use to you.

"I am, &c.,

"S. A. FORD."

ANALYSES OF NATURAL GAS

	Gas of $\frac{9}{8}$	Gas of $1\frac{9}{2}$	Gas of $1\frac{9}{8}$	Gas of $2\frac{9}{2}$	Gas of $\frac{9}{1}$
	Per cent.	Per cent.	Per cent.	Per cent.	Per cent.
Carbolic Acid......	*Nil.*	.61	.81	*Nil.*	.67
Oxygen............	2.60	.40	.61	.61	2.90
Olefiant Gas.......	.80	.61	.81	.61	2.45
Carbonic Oxide.....	.40	.61	.81	.40	3.12
Hydrogen..........	3.51	29.75	2.94	19.67	31.52
Marsh Gas.........	88.40	68.01	94.02	78.72	39.97
Nitrogen...........	4.29	*Nil.*	*Nil.*	*Nil.*	19.35

Mr. Ford's investigations are the only ones made so far as I know, and my readers have in them all that is yet determined about natural gas.

How, where and upon what scale natural gas is generated in the regions below must be a matter for conjecture. This much is clearly proved, that the gas is found in every direction around Pittsburg except the north-west, that the gas belt is about half a mile wide near Murraysville; but this is not to be assumed as the true limits of the supply, for even as I write news comes of a large well having been struck at Canonsburgh, which is about eight miles from the wells which I visited in Washington County; and besides this a new region west of Canonsburgh has been recently proved, the gas from which is now used in the manufacturing establishments at Beaver Falls, Pa., twenty-five miles west of Pittsburg.

We may, therefore, reasonably conclude that Pittsburg is the centre of a gas supply covering many square miles, and capable of producing all the gas that can be used within her limits during the present generation, both for manufacturing and domestic uses. By the end of this year eight pipe lines will be conveying it to the city, and still the supply of gas already obtained and now going to waste will exceed the capacity of these lines. Two of these have pipes 5 5-8 inches in diameter, four are of 8-inch, one is of 10-inch, and another of 12 inches in diameter.

Many theories are advanced to account for the existence of this fuel, but the most reasonable one is that given me by Prof. Dewar, of Cambridge, who recently visited us, and who was deeply impressed by what he saw of this new mine of wealth. He holds that the gas is being constantly distilled from the oil, or from immense beds of matter which are slowly being changed to oil, and, therefore, that long after the oil region has ceased to give oil in paying quantities, we shall still have an abundant supply of gas; for the shallower the deposit of oil, the more favourable will be the conditions for rapid distillation. Instead of occupying the bad eminence, therefore, of being by far the dirtiest city in the world, which it undoubtedly is to-day, it is probable that the

other extreme may be reached, and that we may be able
to claim for smoky Pittsburg that it is the cleanest city.
However this may be, I think that few will be disposed
to dispute that, surrounded by such resources as I have
attempted to describe, Pittsburg is to-day, as far as subterranean treasures are concerned, the metropolis of the
richest district in the known world.

NOTE.—So prodigal has been the use and so great the waste of this
natural fuel (since this article was written) that even the apparently
inexhaustible has become precious because of its scarcity, and the gas
that flared through the waste pipes and lighted the streets of the little
towns with flames five feet high is now measured by meter; doled out by
the thousand cubic feet.

THE THREE-LEGGED STOOL

SCHEME OF THE WORLD'S WORK

The triple alliance of labour, capital and business ability is necessary to produce successfully. Each dependent on the others—combined, invincible.

THE THREE-LEGGED STOOL

Scheme of the World's Work

THERE is a partnership of three in the industrial world when an enterprise is planned. The first of these, not in importance but in time, is Capital. Without it nothing costly can be built. From it comes the first breath of life into matter, previously inert.

The structures reared, equipped and ready to begin in any line of industrial activity, the second partner comes into operation. That is Business Ability. Capital has done its part. It has provided all the instrumentalities of production; but unless it can command the services of able men to manage the business, all that Capital has done crumbles into ruin.

Then comes the third partner, last in order of time but not least, Labour. If it fails to perform its part, nothing can be accomplished. Capital and Business Ability, without it brought into play, are dead. The wheels cannot revolve unless the hand of Labour starts them.

Now, volumes can be written as to which one of the three partners is first, second or third in importance, and the subject will remain just as it was before. Political economists, speculative philosophers and preachers have been giving their views on the subject for hundreds of years, but the answer has not yet been found, nor can it

From *The New York Journal,* 1900.

ever be, because each of the three is all-important, and
every one is equally essential to the other two. There is
no first, second or last. Thre is no precedence! They
are equal members of the great triple alliance which
moves the industrial world. As a matter of history
Labour existed before Capital or Business Ability, for
when "Adam digged and Eve span" Adam had no capital
and if one may judge from the sequel neither of the two
was inordinately blessed with business ability, but this
was before the reign of Industrialism began and huge
investments of Capital were necessary.

In our day, Capital, Business Ability, Manual Labour
are the legs of a three-legged stool. While the three legs
stand sound and firm, the stool stands; but let any one
of the three weaken and break, let it be pulled out or
struck out, down goes the stool to the ground. And the
stool is of no use until the third leg is restored.

Now, the capitalist is wrong who thinks that Capital
is more important than either of the other two legs. Their
support is essential to him. Without them, or with only
one of them, he topples over.

Business Ability is wrong when it thinks that the leg
which it represents is the most important. Without the
legs of Capital and Labour it is useless.

And last, let it not be forgotten that Labour also is
wrong, wildly wrong, when it assumes that it is of more
importance than either of the other two legs. That idea
has been in the past the source of many sad mistakes.

The three are equal partners of a grand whole. Combined they work wonders; separate, neither is of much
account. Thus far, notwithstanding the differences that
from time to time have unfortunately rent them apart,
they have made the closing century the most beneficent

of all that have preceded it. Humanity, the world over, is better than it has ever been, materially and morally, and I have the faith that it is destined to reach still higher and loftier planes than even the most sanguine have imagined.

Capital, Business Ability and Labour must be united. He is an enemy to all three who seeks to sow seeds of disunion among them.

[First spoken as part of an address to the men at Homestead upon the opening of the Library Hall and Workingmen's Club presented to the employees there by Mr. Carnegie.]

RAILROADS PAST AND PRESENT

Railroading in the seventies; rails, systems, speeds, salaries and methods. Railroading in the future. The needs of the railroad man and his responsibilities.

RAILROADS PAST AND PRESENT

IT IS a matter of great satisfaction and some pride to me that I began in the railroad service as telegraph operator and rose to the position of superintendent of the Pittsburg Division of the Pennsylvania Railroad. Perhaps it would be interesting to contrast in a few particulars the condition of affairs in the railroad world then and now. We are always urged to look well ahead in railroading. It is one of the chief rules, but it is also well to cast a look back and see the progress that has been made.

When I had the honour to become a railroad man, the Pennsylvania Railroad was not yet finished to Pittsburg. By means of some miles of staging between two points, and a climb over the mountains by means of ten inclined planes, the passenger was enabled to reach Philadelphia by rail. The rails on the mountains were iron, fourteen-feet lengths, imported from England, lying on huge hewn blocks of stone, although the line passed through woods and ties would have cost little. The company had no telegraph line and was dependent upon the use of the Western Union wire. Mr. Scott, the superintendent, the celebrated Thomas A. Scott who was afterward president, often came to the telegraph office in Pittsburg to talk to his superior in Altoona, the General

From a Speech delivered to a gathering of Railroad Men in New York, January, 1902.

Superintendent. I was then a young operator and made his acquaintance by doing this telegraphing for him.

I was receiving the enormous salary of twenty-five dollars per month then, and he offered me thirty-five to become his secretary and telegrapher, which meant fortune. Let me congratulate you upon the great advance in your own wages and salaries since then. Mr. Scott received $125 a month—$1,500 a year, and my wonder was what a man could do with that amount of money. I hadn't thought then of one use—he might succeed by giving part of it away. What are the advantages a man receives from wealth is often discussed, but the best of wealth is not what it does for the owner but what it enables him to do for others. I served for some time before I received an advance of salary of ten dollars per month. That gave me an enormous revenue compared with the $1.20 a week at which I started in the cotton factory.

It is one of the most cheering facts of our day that under present conditions the wages of labour tend to rise, and the prices of the necessaries of life tend to fall. There never was a nation so splendidly situated as ours is at this moment in regard to labour. Every sober, capable and willing man finds employment at wages which with thrift and a good wife to manage will enable him to go far toward laying up a competence for old age. Those so fortunate as to be married know how much depends upon a wife who can manage your household affairs and those who are not yet married will find that out. There is nothing that the success and happiness of a workingman so much depends upon, next to his own good conduct, as a good managing wife. And here let one who has, almost without intention or desire, had himself loaded with somewhat more than a competence tell soberly that what one has beyond this brings little with it, and sometimes nothing desirable with it; what all should strive for is a competence, without which Junius has wisely said no man could be happy. No man *should* be happy without it, if it be within reach, and I urge everyone to save part of their earnings these prosperous days and put in savings bank at interest, or better still, buy a home with it.

But to revert to railroading. President Thomson one day amazed the community of Pittsburg by stating that on some future day the Pennsylvania Railroad would transport 100 cars a day over it. Cars then carried eight tons net. We had small locomotives and the roadbed was something to frighten one. It was laid with light rails and cast-iron joints were used. I have known 47 broken joints found one morning in winter on my division, and it was over such a line that we ran our trains. It is no wonder that breakdowns were frequent. We had no cabooses on freight trains. Trainmen had to be out in all weathers. It was single track, and not having a telegraph line, in case of delays trains ran curves; that is, a flagman went ahead and the train followed and met when they could, and sometimes met with considerable force, on the sharp curves. There is nothing apparently takes so long to learn by the average railroad man as this proposition, that two trains cannot pass each other successfully on a single track. We never did quite learn that lesson, even on the Pittsburg Division.

Being a telegrapher I took charge of our own railroad telegraph wire when it was constructed, and I believe that I placed the first young woman telegraph student at work on a railroad; so I see it stated. In those days the superintendent had to do everything; there was no division of responsibilities. It was supposed that no subordinate could be trusted to run trains by telegraph or attend to a wreck, and Mr. Scott and I, his successor, were two of the most foolish men I have ever known in this respect. We went out to every wreck, worked all night; often I was not at home for a week at a time, scarcely ever sleeping, except a few snatches, lying down in a freight car. I now look back and see what poor superintendents we were; but I had a great example in Mr. Scott. It took me some time to learn, but I did learn, that the supremely great managers, such as you have these days, never do any work themselves worth speaking about; their point is to make others work while they think. I applied this lesson in after life, so that business with me has never been a care. My young partners did the work and I did the laughing, and I commend to all the thought that there is very little success where there is little laughter. The workman who rejoices in his work and laughs away its discomforts is the man sure to rise, for it is what we do easily, and what we like to do, that we do well. When you see a president or superintendent or a treasurer loaded down with his duties, oppressed with care, with a countenance as serious as a judge uttering a death sentence, be sure that he has more responsibility than he is fit for and should get relief.

Compare the speed of trains for instance. On the great Pennsylvania Railroad we thought that we had reached perfection when a passenger train was put on which ran between Pittsburg and Philadelphia in 13 hours, about 27 miles an hour. It was christened the "Lightning Express." That was not because we thought the lightning was so slow, but because we thought the train was so terrifically fast. To-day the Empire State Express is run at double this speed, which holds the world's record. But do not let us make the mistake again of thinking that we have reached perfection. The next generation will run trains at a hundred miles an hour, double the present speed, just as trains are run at double the speed of 30 years ago. The line will be straight. In the language of Scripture, "the crooked places," that is the curves, "shall be made straight."

In the improvements made to-day on the various lines I don't think many managers look far enough ahead. They are spending on some parts perhaps half a million dollars where they ought to spend double, and easing the curves which they should abolish, and some future president is to say that they wasted a good deal of money. Nothing but a straight line will be up to date in 1950, or before that.

But there is another department in which progress has been as great, and even of greater importance than in that which has been referred to. It is in the care of railroad employes, their position, their advantages, their earnings, and in the pension system which the leading railroads of this country feel themselves obligated to establish, that those who labour year after year at stated salaries and have no prospect of making great gains should at least have this consolation in view, that in their old age they will be able to live in comfortable independence, not as a matter of charity, but by virtue of their own exertions, and what they are entitled to as a bonus for faithful service rendered. I know of nothing which lifts and improves the service of a great line and adds so much to its safety as a staff which can rest in the knowledge that after they have grown old in the service their old age is made comfortable through the system of pensions. Before long no line will rank as in the front rank which has not this invaluable, I might almost say necessary, element in securing a staff of trustworthy, intelligent, and loyal men filled with *esprit de corps* for the company they serve. In the buildings now being provided at transfer stations, in the reading rooms and libraries, and in some cases, especially on the Santa Fé, I learn billiard tables and other means of harmless and needful entertainment are provided. Last, but not least, in such buildings and societies which draw men together for their good, in all these improvements, and in many other ways we have evidence that employers are recognizing their duties to the employed more clearly than in the past.

The railroad man is to be congratulated also upon this fact, that wherever improving agencies have been established the men have endeavoured to show their appreciation by using them to the fullest extent. Railway companies can make no better use of money than in establishing additional institutions of this kind and enlarging those which already exist and are crowded. It will be that company which does most for its men in the direction indicated which will do best for its shareholders, and on the other hand it will be upon that line the workingman will feel most at home, and in which they will take the greatest pride, and for which they will be most willing to incur the exhausting labour and danger incident to the railroad man's calling, thus giving another proof that their interest and the interest of those whose capital is invested are not antagonistic, but mutual. It is a great delusion to say that labour and capital are foes, they must be allies, or neither succeeds. I have before used the simile of likening Capital, Business Ability and Labour to the legs of a three-legged stool; the stool will not stand up without the support of all these three legs, and to dispute as to which of these three is most important is useless. It can never be determined, and if determined it would be of little consequence, since the great fact remains that they are all absolutely necessary for such success as we see on the great transportation lines of our country.

The men of the railroad world are to be congratulated on occupying the proud position, as I believe, of the most temperate body of employes in the world. They are an example to the workingman in other branches of the outspreading tree of labour, and their influence cannot fail to prove of incalculable benefit. No rule that a man can adopt will bring greater reward than this, to abstain from the use of alcohol as a beverage. A drinking man has no place in the railway system. Indeed he should have no place anywhere.

The satisfactory relations which exist upon the whole between the railroads and their men should be gratifying to them both. It is always sure to be created and to exist where the officers are intelligent and sympathetic, and feel themselves part of the one organization which manages the line, comprising all employes from the track labourer to the locomotive engineer and up through all grades to the president himself, every one a N. Y. C., or a P. R. R., or a C., B. & Q., or a D., L. & W. man.

There is no room for antagonism upon a railroad between employer and employe, for the president and superintendent do not own the property any more than the employes do, therefore, all are as just said members of the same corps; all are equally the servants of the company. The official, therefore, recognizes in the train man, the road man, or the engineer, employes like himself to whom he must naturally feel the glow of comradeship, while they cannot but regard the officials as their fellow members and feel that in all matters of compensation or discipline, what their fellow members in office prescribe has not for its end their own self-aggrandizement, but the successful operation of the line.

There is another feature of cheering import. The road to promotion is clear and direct. All can certify to that; for, I doubt not, many of those now in authority began in subordinate positions and have won their way by merit, not by favour. Every man in the Railway Industrial Army, as Napoleon said of his army, carries a marshal's baton in his knapsack. Upon railroaders there rest grave responsibilities; they have in their keeping the lives of the public, I need not say the travelling public, for with us all travel. Strict sobriety, unceasing vigilance, staunch courage, faithfulness to duty, are demanded of them, and that these are characteristic of the force is testified at recurring intervals and by the position they have reached and occupy in the estimation of their grateful fellow citizens.

IRON AND STEEL AT HOME AND ABROAD

Conditions of the iron and steel trade in the United States and abroad compared. The future of these metals.

IRON AND STEEL AT HOME AND ABROAD

Britain, hitherto, has been able to make and market steel cheaper than Germany (Germany now leads Britain 6,000,000 tons to 5,000,000); therefore, she had the lead in Europe. She had the lead in the world. But her position has become artificial. She cannot make coke under $2.50 a ton. It costs about $3.00 a ton at the steel works. She cannot maintain even her present supply of ore. It is becoming more and more costly to get. She has depended largely on the Bilbao mines of Spain, but that ore has deteriorated in value, and the owners will no longer guarantee the quality. British manufacturers must take it as it comes, and year after year it is bound to get scarcer. In this condition of affairs it is not possible for Britain to make steel as cheap as we can make it in Pittsburg and send it to Britain. Besides, Britain and other foreign nations have become our dumping ground for surplus, which means more than the uninitiated would suspect. The Carnegie Steel Company are making over 200,000 tons of steel a month, and President Schwab said to me the other day that he believed in a short time a third of it would go abroad.

The position of Germany is also largely artificial. Of course, they have a high protective duty. The manufacturers are able, therefore, by combinations to get a big price in the home market. This enables them to ship

From *The Iron Age,* 1898.

257

abroad and sell very cheaply. They, too, are trying to make the world their dumping ground. But there is this difference: The prices charged to the consumer in Germany limit the consumption. The extraordinarily cheap prices prevailing here—3 pounds of steel for 2 cents—increase consumption. Germany's foundation is on sand. I am a staunch protectionist, but only when we have reason to believe that by temporary protection we can furnish the consumer the supply of any given article better and cheaper than he has ever been able to purchase it abroad. If we cannot do that I do not believe in protecting. If we can do it I do believe in protecting. Germany abandons that sound economic doctrine, and is protecting for the sake of protection, and the German consumer gets no benefit. This is false political economy.

There is only one thing needed to further expand our export trade in iron and steel and that is regular lines of steamships to the various parts of the world. We can never hope to have such facilities as Britain, because Britain imports so much of bulky goods from various parts of the world which we fortunately grow at home. Therefore, Britain's ships get return cargoes, and the rates will be cheaper. But even this disadvantage we can overcome in the lower cost of our manufactures. If we could restore to the United States its rightful position as the shipbuilder of the world our attention would soon be directed to the establishing of regular steamship lines, and this obstacle would fade away. Even now the export trade is becoming of such magnitude as to justify several new steamship lines, as you see, and we will conquer by and by. I have been urging the importance of a shipbuilding yard in New York, and it is bound to come. Capital will see that there is a good chance for it, since steel and wood work are both cheaper in New York than in Belfast and on the Clyde. It will not take long before capital is attracted.

Our present shipyards being prosperous will extend, but there is plenty of room for a good shipyard in New York. It is rather humiliating to see the *St. Paul* and the *St. Louis,* the *New York* and the *Paris* following each other to Southampton to be docked there, there being no dock in the great port of New York capable of holding these small ships. Yes, small ships. I came over in the *Kaiser Friedrich,* made in Germany. After you travel on a ship like that you can never think of anything else. We had a rough passage, the roughest I have ever known, and yet the most comfortable.

The consolidation of the iron and steel interests is a natural evolution. If we are going to sell 3 pounds of steel for 2 cents, it must be made by the millions of tons. It is a tight race for the best of concerns. Review the record during the past few years of every one of the large steel companies the results of whose business have become public property through their annual reports, or whose properties have been in the hands of a receiver. The result will show that selling 3 pounds of steel for 2 cents troubles the best of them. Therefore, concerns that are losing money seek consolation somewhere, and consolidation is something like Mesopotamia, a very comforting word. Do not understand me as reflecting on the management of these concerns. Very far from it. It is not the management but the situation. Steel cannot be made and sold as low as it has been ruling without involving loss to all these concerns.

Consolidation is wise and necessary. It is a step in the right direction. The steel manufacturer must reconcile himself to making a very small shaving of profit per ton. When a concern makes 2,500,000 tons per annum it does not need much per ton to keep the wolf from the door, especially if it has no bonded debt.

While the consumption of iron and steel is enormous, yet prices do not rise. I do not believe that we can increase consumption, therefore I argue that the capacity to manufacture is beyond our legitimate requirements. If it had been otherwise we would have seen a great boom in prices, which, however, remain low. Indeed, too low for our friends to make even a fair return.

Railroads are exceedingly prosperous, especially in the West. There is little fear that all the rails that can be made will find a market. Another thing, the use of beams will grow in this country if the price is kept down to the present rate. At the present time a little country like Germany uses three times the amount of beams that the United States does. In Germany no one thinks of building an ordinary house without making it fireproof. Here the millionnaire builds his house fireproof, although I know of several millionnaires who have recently erected fire traps. No, the ordinary house in the United States will in the near future be made fireproof, as it is in Germany. At the present time, however, the whole amount of structural material consumed in the United States could be made by the Carnegie Steel Company. It is a very trifling business, but it is an index to the possibilities of the greater uses and increased consumption of steel and iron.

THE MANCHESTER SCHOOL AND TO-DAY

The British contention that each nation is specially qualified for but one general branch of industry discussed and combatted.

THE MANCHESTER SCHOOL AND TO-DAY

WHILE Ex-Premier Rosebery was recently lauding the triumphs of the Free Trade Manchester School at Manchester, Foreign Minister Goluchowski, in Vienna, was beseeching the nations of Europe to combine against the destructive competition with Trans-Oceanic countries: "We must fight shoulder to shoulder against the common danger," he exclaims, "and arm ourselves for the struggle with all the means at our disposal." "European nations must close ranks in order successfully to defend their existence."

Thus do extremes meet, and we see once more how much depends upon the point of view. Had the predictions of the Manchester School been realized, cheaper goods from across the seas would be hailed as an economic gain, and a blessing to the recipients, instead of being considered a menace to their existence. Every port would be open to this influx of goods, and the new countries which supplied them hailed as benefactors, for "Free exchange of commodities" was the watchword, but it was un-dreamt of then that the commodities of the new lands sent to the old might take the form of competing manufactured articles, which makes all the difference.

From *The Nineteenth Century,* February, 1898.

Sixty years ago steam upon land and upon sea—the steamship and the railway train—began their revolutionary work, Britain, their creator, situated upon beds of coal and ironstone, being naturally the scene of their development. The world was a mere looker-on while she harnessed steam and began to change it. If any other country wished to avail itself of the advantages of the new inventions, to Britain it must go for everything connected therewith. Britain had realized her destiny, and was soon to become the workshop of the world.

There appeared upon the scene the Manchester School —Villiers, Cobden, Bright, and their colleagues—demanding on behalf of the masses that the taxes upon food should be repealed. The repeal of these taxes which passed under the name of "Free Trade" in Britain, in contradistinction to "Protection," has little to do with the modern doctrine of Protection, as it is now known in other countries. Such taxes could never have been defended by the Protectionist of to-day, because it was impossible that the amount of food-products could thereby be considerably increased. The only sound defence for a protective duty, according to the cosmopolitan protectionist, is when it can be justly claimed that to levy it for a time will so stimulate home production of the article taxed as to supply the wants of the nation; and, further, that home competition will then soon result in the nation obtaining a surer, cheaper, and better supply from within its own domain than it ever did or could do from foreign sources.

A tax levied under these conditions is endorsed by John Stuart Mill's celebrated paragraph, which John Bright once said to the writer "would cause hereafter more

injury to the world than all his writings would do good,"
and is also recognized as sound or unsound by Marshall,
according to circumstances, and is what is meant in our
day by "Protection" outside of Britain.

Conditions connected with this tax have in no wise
changed, and therefore the work of the Manchester
School stands. Such a tax imposed upon food to-day
would operate precisely as it did before, unless by some
marvellous discovery the soil of Britain can be made to
grow an abundance of food for the wants of its in-
habitants. A temporary tax then, if necessary, to induce
capital to develop the new process would be justifiable.

For the reason stated, the modern advocate of Protection denounces as strenuously as any Corn Law Re-
pealer the tax upon food in Britain.

The wonderful success of these British inventions, the
steamship and the train, and the profits resulting from
the command of the world's manufacturing which these
inventions gave, coupled with the undoubted advantages
flowing from the free importation of food products, had
the natural result of creating the most sanguine views
of the future position and prosperity of the United Kingdom, and the successful apostles of the Manchester
School were above all men justifiably the most sanguine,
and this was the lesson they drew from the then existing
conditions:

Nature has decreed, and wisely so, that all nations of the earth
shall be interdependent, each with a mission. To one is given
fertile soil, to another rich mines, to a third great forests; to one
sunshine and heat, to another temperate zone, and to another
colder clime; one nation shall perform this service, another that,
and a third shall do something else; all co-operating, each furnishing its natural product, forming one grand harmonious whole.

How beautiful the picture! Then followed the second postulate:

It is clearly seen that to our beloved land, Great Britain, has been assigned the high mission of manufacturing for her sister nations. Our kin beyond the sea shall send to us in our ships their cotton from the Mississippi valley; India shall contribute its jute, Russia its hemp and its flax, Australia its finer wools, and we, with our supplies of coal and ironstone for our factories and workshops, our skilled mechanics and artificers, and our vast capital, shall invent and construct the necessary machinery, and weave these materials into fine cloth for the nations; all shall be fashioned by us and made fit for the use of men. Our ships which reach us laden with raw materials shall return to all parts of the earth laden with these our higher products made from the crude. This exchange of raw for finished products under the decrees of nature makes each nation the servant of the other, and proclaims the brotherhood of man. Peace and goodwill shall reign upon the earth, one nation after another must follow our example, and free exchange of commodities shall everywhere prevail. Their ports shall open wide for the reception of our finished products, as ours are open for their raw materials.

Such the beliefs, the hopes—the not unreasonable hopes, judging from their premises—of the Manchester School; for let it be said, in justice to these good and great men, that the picture they drew, and which we have endeavoured to portray, was realized, Great Britain did become the workshop of the world, and each of the great nations played the *role* prescribed and performed the services indicated. No nation, not even the American, ever made such progress or accumulated such wealth upon products manufactured as Britain did in this stage of her history. The prospectus of the Barrow Steel Company stated that profits had been 30 and 40 per cent. per annum, and in one year they had reached the incredible rate of 60 per cent. upon the entire capital. This is only straw showing the unheard-of returns made by the manufacturers of Britain when the world was at its feet, and before strenuous competition had reduced, and in many cases banished, profits. And well deserved was the reward reaped by the nation, great as it was, which had given steam to the world, inaugurated the age of machinery, and made the world its debtor for all time.

The law of Nature as interpreted by the Manchester School was revealed in the supposed facts that the resources of the various countries of the earth greatly differed, the capabilities of the men and women thereof not less so, and that manufacturing could be successfully conducted only in Great Britain. That tool-steel, or indeed any kind of steel, much less fine machinery, could be made except there—that the finest woollen, linen, and cotton cloth could be produced successfully in new lands —were suggestions which at that day were not even hinted, but which, if they had been made, would have been greeted with derision.

It is unreasonable to suppose that these able men of the Manchester School would ever have assumed that the principal nations of the earth, or those aspiring to become such, would contentedly play the subordinate part assigned them had the manufacturing field been open to them. The very keynote of the Manchester structure was necessarily that the various nations were restricted by nature to play the *role* of growers of raw materials, no other being possible. We find to-day, on the contrary, after a period of enforced acquiescence, that nations with rare unanimity have aspired to share the higher task of fashioning their raw materials into finished products for themselves, and neither British capital nor skill has been wanting to insure their success. Indeed, it is chiefly owing to these that competition with their own country has been rendered possible in the Far East. So far from the resources of nations being generally meagre and unsuitable for manufacturing, or their people incapable, as the Manchester School assumed, the success of their manufacturing efforts, generally speaking, has been surprising. Germany has become one of the largest manufacturing countries. France and Switzerland have almost monopolized the silk manufacture in Europe. Russia is engaged in building steel and engineering works under the supervision of the most skilled American constructors; two of these establishments, now well forward, rival the best works of America, after which they are copied. Japan and China are building factories of the latest and most approved character, always with British machinery and generally under British direction. Mexico is weaving cotton cloth, manufacturing paper, and two bicycle factories are now under construction there. The jute and cotton mills of India are numerous and increasing, and Bombay is establishing an Engineering Works. It is stated that one British manufacturing concern sends abroad the complete machinery for a new mill every week. Of America it is unnecessary to speak.

Thus every nation of the first rank, or which has the elements of future rank, has rejected the *role* which the Manchester School assigned it, and aspires to manufacture for itself. Political Economy now points out that it is for the benefit of mankind that the transportation charges incurred by distance between producer and manufacturer should be saved. Attempts to manufacture by some small populations in certain directions will no doubt fail and be abandoned, but success in the main seems assured.

Some lands, notably Germany and America, not content to supply their own wants, now appear as exporters of many competing articles to other countries, several of which reach the United Kingdom, and the experience which the men of other nations have long had of innumerable articles "made in Britain" is now being brought home to the Briton, and it is found that there is "a good deal of human nature in him" not differing from that of other lands. A score of articles "made in Germany" cause him irritation; contracts given to American manufacturers for engines in London, Dublin, and Edinburg are not approved. Glasgow rejects an American bid for waterpipes, and gives it to Glasgow manufacturers at a higher price. When a great show of bicycles takes place in London, no room can be found for the American. Government contracts, even including stationery, must be filled by home-made articles. Although free entrance for importations is not denied, yet when purchases are to be made—no foreigner need apply. The mails must go by slow home-made ships, even if thereby delayed. All this is only what we should expect and excuse. He is a poor citizen who does not prefer and patronize his own country rather than foreign lands, but the Briton should expect the American, and German, and others to be equally patriotic. With the same feelings with which he regards competing articles "made in Germany" or America invading his own country, let him realize that the patriotic German and American naturally regard competing articles "made in Britain" which invade theirs.

To-day it is seen that Nature has distributed more generously than was imagined the indispensable minerals, coal, lime, and ironstone, as it was known before that it had widely distributed the ability to grow raw materials; and that it has endowed the man and woman of most countries with latent ability, sufficient under the new conditions to manufacture their own raw materials, in most cases not so well, in one or two special lines perhaps as well, as the Briton or American, and that hence there is not to be only one or two but many principal manufacturing countries.

The wonderful machinery, mostly of British invention, especially in iron and steel, and in textile manufactures, enables the Hindoo of India, the Pæon of Mexico, the negro of America, the Chinaman and the man of Japan, to manufacture with the more carefully educated workman of Britain and America. The mechanical skill of old is not now generally required, but, where necessary for a few positions in each huge factory, is readily obtained from the older manufacturing lands.

Automatic machinery is to be credited as the most potent factor in rendering non-essential to successful manufacturing a mass of educated mechanical labour such as that of Britain or America, and thus making it possible to create manufacturing centres in lands which, until recent years, seemed destined to remain only producers of raw materials. We are everywhere to-day the influence of this new machinery. It can be accepted as an axiom that raw materials have now power to attract capital, and also to attract and develop labour for their manufacture in close proximity, and that skilled labour is losing the power it once had to attract raw materials to it from afar.

This is not change; it is revolution.

The ablest and best citizens of every country are in-

spired to favour the development of its resources. They
cannot consider it right to hide the talents given them,
and are now enabled to see clearly that the evident law
of Nature is that there shall be given to many nations
the blessings of diversified industries, in the pursuit of
which the various aptitudes and talents of their people
shall find scope.

All this the Manchester School could by no possibility
have foreseen.

It is delightful to survey the movement of the nations
in the march of industrial progress under the new conditions. Had one or two become the chief manufacturers
for all, the genius of their people alone would have been
enlisted in the work of improvement and invention. To-
day we have the genius of many nations already at work,
with more to come. It is pleasing also to note how the
genius of each tends to excel in a different line. Thus
France has almost monopolized the superfine in textiles,
as it has long enjoyed supremacy in the department of
women's rich apparel. Britain holds supremacy in machinery for textiles. The inventor of the iron and steel
industry, she is also leading the world to-day in successfully developing a collateral branch, the by-product coke
oven, in which even the American has so far failed.
America leads in electrical appliances and machine tools.
Germany is supreme in chemical dyes, and has recently
invented a condenser for steam which is showing great
results, as well as a remarkable new process for the making of armour. The cause of progress in things material
is thus advanced by the contributions of many minds of
various nationalities.

The stirring competition which has begun among the
nations, and which we may expect to see still more

strenuously pushed, is the true agency for producing the best results, and is to be welcomed and encouraged by those who can lift themselves above the narrow view of what is seemingly best for any one or two of the geographical divisions of the world, and regard what is best for the race as a whole.

The development of the industrial world is taking a different line from that predicted, but the great work accomplished by the Manchester School is neither to be belittled nor forgotten. Villiers, Cobden, Bright, and their compeers, in the repeal of the taxes upon food imports, did their country a service for which it can never be too grateful. Their devotion to the cause of peace, and to all that tended, as they thought, to create the brotherhood of nations, gives the leaders of the movement a secure place in the history of beneficent deeds, and as advocates of noble ends. That some of their predictions are nullified or reversed by forces which have come into play since their day, neither reflects upon their sagacity nor detracts from their services.

The "Free Trade" which Manchester saw, and for which it predicted universal acceptance, was the exchange of different and non-competing articles, and of raw materials for manufactured goods; for nations had not then begun to compete seriously with each other in the same manufactured articles. If this is not to be realized, since the principal nations are to-day becoming manufacturers of their raw material, and supplying their own needs, and competing with each other in the world's market for similar things, yet we may congratulate ourselves that something better even than the Manchester ideal for the progress of the world is rapidly being evolved.

What the effect of this change is to be upon the relative positions of nations in the future it were useless to consider, since conditions might be transformed in a day; a chemical discovery, an electrical invention, the properties of a plant utilized—any one of such, or of other not improbable surprises upon which we seem to be sometimes on the very threshold, might work an entire change. The substitution of beet for cane sugar has just blighted the West Indies, which seemed to possess almost a monopoly. The discovery of the Mesaba Iron Mines, improved transport, and a few other minor causes have just made America the cheapest manufacturer of steel, while until recently she was the dearest. The basic process has made Germany a leading steel producer, when otherwise she seemed destined to be excluded, and promises to tell scarcely less heavily for Britain. The discovery of mines and the extension of its railway system are soon to make Russia an important manufacturing country, in which she has hitherto failed. The utilization of waterfalls for electricity, displacing coal, is already changing some centres of manufacture. All these changes are of yesterday.

It is not wise, therefore, for any nation to plume itself unduly upon present resources or prospects, neither for any to despond. "We know not what a day may bring forth."

WHAT WOULD I DO WITH THE TARIFF IF I WERE CZAR?

The advantage of taxing the imported luxuries heavily and reducing the tax on raw materials and necessities. A few striking examples of correct and misapplied tariffs.

WHAT WOULD I DO WITH THE TARIFF
IF I WERE CZAR?

I RATHER like the swing of the question, and I proceed to reply. The estimated expenditure of the National Government according to Secretary Carlisle's report for the present fiscal year (1895) is $424,000,000, and the estimated receipts $404,000,000, leaving a deficit of $20,-000,000. He estimates that next year there will be a surplus of $30,000,000, assuming the expenditure to be the same.*

The decrease in the cost of pensions this fiscal year over last is no less than $18,000,000, and very soon every year the percentage of decrease must become greater. The navy will require less expenditure upon it than in future years, and the increase in population and wealth will give increased revenues of themselves, so that there is no cause for alarm in regard to the expenditures and revenues of the Government after the next year, although the Secretary is probably much oversanguine as to receipts under present laws for this year.

Of Government revenues, the tariff is estimated to yield $160,000,000 this year, and is estimated to yield

*The following may be interesting as a comparison: In 1901 the total revenue was $587,685,338 and the total ordinary expenditures $509,967,353, leaving an excess of revenue over ordinary expenses of $77,717,985.

From *The Forum*, March, 1895.

$190,000,000 next year; and the question is, What would I do about the tariff if I had supreme power?

First, my aim would be to keep free of duty the necessaries of life used by the many, and to tax highly the luxuries of the few. The masses who wear and consume home products I should not tax, but the luxurious man and woman of fashion who will wear at whatever cost the fine woollens and the exquisitely fine silks and the delicately fine linens of Europe should pay the tariff duties. This small rich class under the new tariff would be made much more fashionable by paying perhaps double the present duties. The American masses who use American tobacco and cigars should find no higher tax upon these than at present; but the rich and luxurious gentlemen whose delicate nostrils require the perfume of the Havana, should become more profitable to the State by paying at least double the present duty. The champagne and rare old wine drinkers and purchasers of rare old or rare new foreign china and glass, perfumeries, and similar articles *de luxe* should be able to boast with perfect truth of their enhanced value. It should never be forgotten that imported articles are used by the rich few, and home products by the masses.

The increased duties proposed upon foreign articles *de luxe* would not be levied with a view of protection, but purely for revenue. That incidentally this policy might slightly benefit the manufacturers at home would not be considered an objection; but this advantage, if any, could be but slight, since the super-fine qualities of wool, silk, and linen goods are not made here, nor are the high-priced wines, cigars, and hundreds of fancy articles. Home manufacturers, however, almost completely control the market for goods of ordinary quality, which are those used by the masses.

The reverse of this has hitherto been the policy adopted. A page could be filled with a list of the luxuries of the rich upon which the taxes have been reduced by the new tariff. Here are a few reductions: china reduced 50 per cent., glass-plate and stained glass 40, gold pens 16, clocks 28, hats 72, knit fabrics 72, flannel 68, silk umbrellas 18, brandy and cordials 28, silks 40, gloves 30, comfits, jellies, etc., laces, embroideries, etc., 16, woollens and silks 10 to 20, owing to *ad valorem* instead of specific duties. Under the present tariff the rich man of fashion wears his superfine foreign broadcloth, superfine linen, silk hat, kid gloves, fine silk umbrella, sips his costly glass of rare old wine, from 20 to 70 per cent. less than the former duty upon these superfluous luxuries. His grand dame plays her fan, flourishes her embroidered handkerchief, displays her exquisite laces, and arrays herself in superb silks at equal reductions, with many smiles and thanks to the newly arisen friend of the people, the charming and brilliant young West Virginian, who apologizes for his failure to reduce the duties upon the champagne she offers him, explaining that this was not his fault as his bill originally provided for its reduction also. Hundreds of fancy articles made of wool, silk and linen are now under reduced duties. These reductions, as we shall see later, embrace articles *de luxe* which furnish two-thirds of the entire revenue from the tariff. Not one workingman in the whole land uses these luxuries. Such is "tariff reform" up to date, and thus is the "burden of taxation removed from the masses of the people." Strange delusion! The taxes are removed only from the rich.

This is not a party question, for neither party has

made the primary object of the tariff the collection of the revenue from the luxuries of the rich regardless of either free trade or protection. A proper tariff would replace the burden upon the shoulders of those best able to bear it, and much higher rates would be imposed upon these articles than have ever yet been charged.

It is a mistake to assume that the use of luxuries would be seriously lessened owing to higher rates of duties. On the contrary, one element of fashionable use is great cost. The imports would be lessened if duties were raised upon articles of general consumption used by the masses, because one article could be substituted for another and the cost is always carefully considered. But this does not apply strongly to luxuries, which are chiefly matters of taste and fashion and are purchased solely by the rich, to whom price is not the first consideration. To double the tax upon champagne, for instance, or upon fine foreign china, woollens, silks, linens, laces, embroideries, etc., would not greatly deter the rich class from purchasing. The reduction in the amount consumed would probably not much more than equal the ordinary increase arising from the increase of population and wealth. The amount of additional duty received, therefore, would soon be substantially the amount imposed. But even if the higher taxes reduced the use of the foreign products one-fourth for a time, the revenues would still be one-fourth more were the taxes doubled. Should, however, a considerable reduction in consumption take place, so much the better. There is a silver lining to that cloud, for so much more of the wealth of the country would be used for the purchase of home products, or, at least, not spent in luxurious living. It might be claimed that the home manufacturer would finally produce the finest qualities of textile goods if the foreign goods were highly taxed. So be it, and so much the better for the country if he did; but it would take years before he could do so, and long before this, the natural increase of the revenues from increased population and wealth would meet any reduction of imports. In a few years the decrease in pensions—the great drain at present—will relieve the Government from the necessity to collect as much revenue.

Tariff duties as follows were collected in 1892 on foreign importations of the luxuries of the rich:

Wool manufactures	$32,293,609
Silk manufactures	16,965,637
Cotton manufactures	16,436,733
Flax manufactures	10,066,636
Glass and china	10,339,000
Wines, liquors, etc.	8,935,000
Tobacco and cigars	11,882,557

Here are $106,000,000 of revenue from seven classes of luxuries, and here are a few others which netted more than $8,000,000 additional—jewellery, carriages, artificial flowers, clocks, brushes, paper, perfumeries, musical instruments—making $114,000,000 revenue collected from imports out of the total of $177,000,000. To reduce duties upon articles which are all luxuries of the rich, furnishing two-thirds of the whole tariff revenue, is the chief result of the Wilson act.

The statement cannot be disputed that these articles were not imported for the use of the masses of the people. With woollen manufactures, as those of silk, the masses of the people of the United States are supplied by the home manufacturer almost exclusively. The only class which uses imported cloths, and foreign glass and china, and foreign wines and tobacco, is the rich. To prevent the charge being made that the articles used to any extent by the masses might be made dearer by the increased duties, the bill should provide that woollen, silk and linen cloths of common grades should be exempt from the higher duties. Substantially none but the high grades is imported, but this clause would disarm criticism. Had even the duties of 1892 been retained upon these luxuries of the few, the present deficiency in the revenues would have been much less than now disturbs the national exchequer. We have here a rich mine, indeed, which should be drawn from when the next tariff legislation is undertaken. Were the duties upon these luxuries doubled, and another $114,000,000 collected, or if the increased taxes diminished consumption by one-fourth and the Government obtained but half the increase, as it still would in that extreme case, then we would have taken, say, $57,000,000 of taxation from the shoulders of the toiling masses and placed it upon those of the luxurious, pleasure-loving, extravagant class who can be made to pay for their extravagance with benefit to themselves and to the nation. If 50 per cent. additional duty were tried, the revenues would soon be increased to almost the whole of the extra tax. This is neither protection nor free trade, and has nothing to do with either. It is simply a question of revenue. And it is submitted that in no way can the necessary revenue be so wisely obtained as from foreign luxuries consumed only by the rich and most extravagant class of the people. My tariff would about double present duties upon all these luxuries.

When brought face to face with the fact that the principal change produced by the Wilson bill was thus to reduce duties upon two-thirds of the total tariff revenues exclusively for the benefit of the rich, who alone use imported goods, one asks how so able, honest, zealous, and pure a man as Mr. Wilson could represent himself as "lifting the unnecessary burden of onerous tariff taxation from the masses of the people"—the explanation is easy: he was inexperienced. He had not studied the question. I very much doubt whether he would to-day produce a measure so foreign to his published intentions. It is a matter of serious import that such a man as he is relegated to private life simply because one district votes for another. Our custom of choosing only Representatives resident in the district loses us many invaluable men. Mr. Wilson is to-day capable of performing work of the best character, because he has now the only quality he lacked before—knowledge of affairs. We need just such men as he in public life, and I for one hope for his speedy return to it. Some day he will advocate a tariff, I believe, upon the floor of the House, which will tax higher the luxuries of the few, not reduce duties—solely for their benefit.

Few perhaps understand to what extent foreign textile articles are for the rich only. Take woollen goods, for instance: in 1890 the value of the home-manufactured product was $338,000,000. The high-priced foreign fine woollens were imported to the value of only $35,500,000. Their value per yard was much greater than that of the ordinary qualities produced at home, so that the number of yards probably was not more than 6 or 7 per cent. of the total consumption. We have a similar result with cotton: the value of the home-manufactured product in 1890 was $268,000,000 and the total amount imported was valued at only $28,000,000. Even in regard to silks imported, the manufactured product of American mills in 1890 was valued at $69,000,000, the total imported silk manufactures $31,000,000 only. These also are of much higher value per yard than the home product. Since 1890 the silk manufacturers of America have gained greatly, and are constantly filling the home demands more completely.

If the foreign woollens, silks, and linens were classified as to fineness and value, it would be seen that goods of common grades, such as the people generally use, are no longer imported. Nor can they be to any considerable extent even under the present act. So far has the American manufacturer conquered his own market. There is another point bearing upon this matter: a very great proportion of all textile importations consist not of cloth in the yard, but of special fancy textile articles,—braids, laces, trimmings, embroideries,—which are not manufactured at all at home.

In regard to coal and iron ore, so-called raw materials, the new tariff should make no further reductions, because a reduction of nearly one-half of the duty at one time, just made, is serious, and time is needed before any industry can adjust itself to so great a change. Besides, the tax of forty cents per ton upon ore and thirty cents per ton upon coal is comparatively trifling. This applies to iron and steel generally, which have suffered two reductions recently; for the McKinley act reduced these as much as the Wilson act did—about 30 per cent. in each case. Making cotton-ties free of duty when all other forms of steel were left dutiable is the greatest blot upon the present tariff—a piece of pure sectionalism, the bane of the Federal system. One-half of the former duty should be restored.

Works of art should remain free of duty, and the frames of pictures, now dutiable, should also be made

free. The trifling sums levied upon these at present are
nothing; but the trouble and delay caused by assessing
the value of each frame will tend to discourage importations of art treasures, almost all of which find their permanent resting-place sooner or later in public galleries,
and thus become the precious possessions of the people.

One important point in the tariff receives not one tithe
of the attention it deserves—that paragraph which per-
mits all parties to import materials and to use them in
making any article for export. Ninety-nine per cent. of
all duties are in this case remitted. This is statesmanship
and deserves to rank with reciprocity as a valuable step
toward securing extended trade for the Republic. This
should be incorporated in my supposed tariff, except that
I should remit the remaining 1 per cent. also, so that the
American manufacturer would stand free to avail himself
of the markets of the world, for what he purchases for
export, upon free-trade terms, and thus come into the
world's markets with what he has to sell upon equal terms
in competition with the manufacturers of Europe. When
writers and speakers descant upon the exclusion of the
American manufacturer from the markets of the world
owing to protective duties, they are probably ignorant
of the fact that at present he is under free-trade conditions as to his materials, minus 1 per cent. of the duties
which the Government withholds to pay the cost of
accounting. The new tariff would disarm criticism upon
this point by omitting also the trifling 1 per cent. American manufacturers would then have every advantage of
free trade in struggling for the markets of the world.

Such qualities of foreign wool as cannot be produced
in our country, owing to climatic causes, and yet are

valuable for mixtures with our home product, would remain free of duty.

There would be no income tax. I know of no statesman or authority who does not denounce an income tax as the most objectionable of all taxes. Mr. Gladstone once appealed to the country upon this subject alone, denouncing it as tending to make a nation of liars. While it is in theory a just tax, in practice it is the source of such demoralization as renders it perhaps the most pernicious form of taxation which has ever been conceived since human society has settled into peaceful government. Any measure is justifiable in time of war, but the only excuse for an income tax is imperative necessity. There is at present no such necessity. The Government revenues must soon produce a surplus over expenditures, if from no other cause than the increase of population and wealth, and they can be made to do so now, as previously pointed out, by taxing higher only the extravagances of the few.

The question of sugar is important. Raw sugar, molasses, etc., would be taxed, subject, however, to admitting these free from such countries as give us satisfactory advantages in return, which would practically make them all free. The United States holds an immense power in her use of $120,000,000 worth of these articles annually, purchased chiefly from our sister Republics of South America, and from Cuba. It should be wisely used to give her access to their markets in return upon better terms than other nations. A bounty upon home-grown sugar would be given for the present by the new tariff in the hope that this country might ultimately succeed in producing its own supply. The beet-root and sorghum experiment should not yet be abandoned.

The policy of reciprocity would be restored to the fullest extent. The increase in our exports of articles to countries under reciprocity treaties proves that Mr. Blaine was correct in his belief that by means of this system, ably managed, we have taken the best step that can be taken to give our country foreign trade which it cannot otherwise secure. I believe in getting something in return from countries to which we open our markets to sugar, molasses, and tobacco, because we have proved that it can be obtained.

Although I am opposed to taxing the food and the necessaries of the people, I should make an exception in regard to products of Canada, and this without regard to the doctrines of either free-trade or protection, but as a matter of high politics. I think we betray a lack of statesmanship in allowing commercial advantages to a country which owes allegiance to a foreign power founded upon monarchical institutions which may always be trusted at heart to detest the Republican idea. If Canada were free and independent and threw in her lot with this continent, it would be a different matter. So long as she remains upon our flank a possible foe, not upon her own account, but subject to the orders of a European Power, and ready to be called by that Power to exert her forces against us even upon issues that may not concern Canada, I should let her distinctly understand that we view her as a menace to the peace and security of our country, and I should treat her accordingly. She should not be in the Union and out of the Union at the same time, if I could prevent it. Therefore, I should tax highly all her products entering the United States; and this I should do, not in dislike for Canada but for love of her, in the hope that it would cause her to realize that the nations upon this Continent are expected to be American nations, and, I trust, finally one nation so far as the English-speaking portion is concerned. I should use the rod not in anger but in love; but I should use it. She should be either a member of the Republic, or she should stand for her own self, responsible for her conduct in peace and in war, as other nations are responsible, and she should not shield herself by calling to her aid a foreign Power. This is, as I have said, neither free-trade nor protection, but it does bear upon the subject of the tariff. I would tax Canadian articles as long as Canada continued the subordinate of a European Power.

The new tariff bill should provide that it is passed with the understanding and consent of both political parties that no further tariff legislation should be undertaken for ten years. Just as we take a census every ten years, we should revise the tariff, say the second year after the census is taken, because we could then act understandingly. If, for instance, the imports of any article not exclusively used by the rich few, but of general consumption, compared with the amount of that article made at home, proved that the home manufacturer had almost completely driven the foreign manufacturer out of our market, the duty upon that article could be reduced. If, on the other hand, the statistics proved that the imports of an article had remained as before or had increased in comparison with the amount of the production at home, the duties upon that article could be increased. It would be impossible for the home manufacturer or the foreign importer to influence the decision, because we should have the figures which proved the situation. No one could gainsay them. Of course the question would be considered whether the home producer had shown that it was finally possible to produce the article in question at home so that it could ultimately be obtained by consumers upon favourable terms as compared with those obtainable from foreign sources. If a committee, appointed for the purpose of tariff revision, were satisfied that the manufacture of the article in question was proved not suitable for this part of the world, it would then be wise to "protect" it no longer and to make the article free of duty, or to tax it for revenue only.

The attitude in which the committee should approach the subject of revision should be that in which a lover of the country approaches the question of felling a tree. It should consider always, as I know the lover of the country considers, how easy it is to cut down the noble tree he loves, how impossible to restore it. It matters comparatively little to the country whether there be 5 or 10 per cent. more duty upon a foreign article for a few years than required. But it makes all the difference whether there be 5 or 10 per cent. less than is necessary to enable the struggling home manufacturer to continue the contest which may ultimately result in victory. In tariff legislation, the rule should be, in all cases of doubt, to take the safe side. In a committee devoted to this duty there would seem to be little play for partisanship, as its functions would partake of a judicial character. The end aimed at by all would be to obtain a home supply of such articles of general consumption as can finally be produced under the flag, through temporary protection, so successfully as to supply the consumer upon terms as favourable as could be obtained if dependent upon a supply from any other part of the world. Wherever it is demonstrated that the United States cannot produce this result in regard to any article, then, but not till then, should protection be abandoned, and revenue only considered. With articles, however, which are the luxuries of the few, upon which the Wilson bill has greatly reduced duties, I hold that neither free-trade nor protection should have anything to do. Upon these the tax should be excessively high, solely for revenue—high to the point of almost lessening the aggregate revenue collectible upon them; and no other consideration should have weight in levying the duties, for revenue is the end desired.

I am confident that this point will not be reached before the present tariff rates are doubled on those things which have been enumerated as luxuries, which yield two-thirds of all tariff revenue; and I am equally certain that Secretary Carlisle's belief that the lower duties of the Wilson act upon these articles for the few will greatly increase their use is a mistake. The consumption of the luxuries of the rich can be increased or diminished by any change of duties only to a degree so slight as to surprise theorists, because their cost is not the first consideration.

To sum up—

First: Duties should be collected chiefly from foreign luxuries used by the extravagant rich class without regard to free trade or protection, but primarily for revenue. These luxuries embrace two-thirds of all tariff revenue.

Second: There should be no income tax in a time of peace.

Third: Established industries should not be subjected frequently to violent changes but should be given time to adjust themselves to new conditions. A reduction of more than one-half of the duty at one time upon an article is inexpedient and even dangerous.

Fourth: Reciprocity, judging from what has already

been done, is the best step that can be taken to extend our foreign trade, and the policy should be restored.

Fifth: The bounty upon home-grown sugar should not yet be abandoned, for it is not yet proved conclusively that the growth of beet and sorghum sugar cannot finally be developed sufficiently to give us a home supply upon favourable terms.

Sixth: Such wool as we cannot produce at home and yet is required for mixture, should be free of duty.

Seventh: Art of all kinds should be free, because art treasures inevitably flow into public institutions sooner or later.

Eighth: The tariff once settled, there should be tariff legislation only in the second year after each census, except in an emergency like the present, when a deficiency in the national revenue and sound policy require additional sums to be collected from such imports as are luxuries of the extravagant rich, and not the necessaries of life of the frugal poor.

Such would be a tariff in favour of the toiling masses, and for those who live frugal and unostentatious lives. Neither protectionist nor free trader, as such, could claim it, because it would be framed in the interest of neither idea, but primarily with a view to revenue, and upon the theory that to raise this from the foreign luxuries of the extravagant rich class is best for the people in general. Under such a policy, the tariff would be substantially taken out of politics and treated as a business question, and if periods of ten years' rest from tariff legislation are permitted, I believe the country would soon rally and begin its march toward the state of prosperity—as far as tariff policy can be made to accelerate that longed-for march—which characterized the decade between 1880 and 1890, during which its most marvellous development took place,—a decade which is probably to rank as the Golden Age of the Republic, as far as material prosperity is concerned.

THE END

Ability, business men always on the lookout for, 11, 71, 94; the partnership of capital, business ability and labour in industry, 241–243.

Adam and Eve, 242.

Agamemnon, 64.

Agricultural machinery, America's predominance in the manufacture of, 216.

Agriculture, *see* Farmers.

Alabama, the, 146.

Alleghany River, the, 224.

Allegheny County, Pa., production of pig iron and steel in 1899, 199.

American Society of Mechanical Engineers, report on the value of natural gas, 233–235.

Amusements, the importance of, 70–71.

Anderson, Col., of Allegheny City, Pa., 63.

Argentine Republic, depreciated state of its silver coinage, 53.

Artistic career, an, compared with a business career, 181–182.

Associations as a business qualification, 11.

Australia, about to assume self-government, 153.

Austria-Hungary, practical cessation of silver coinage by, 32.

Avarice, 79, 80.

Baltimore, as a shipping point for steel, 200.

Bank cheques, proportion of the business of the United States handled through, 28.

Bannockburn, battle of, 180.

Barrooms to be avoided, 3.

Barrow Steel Company, England, 186, 266–267.

Barter, the exchange of one commodity for another, 18–20.

Beaver Falls, Pa., 237.

Beet sugar, 273, 286.

Behring Sea tribunal at Paris, the, 115.

Belgium, closes her mints to silver, 32.

Bessemer, Sir Henry, 196.

Bessemer process in steel manufacture, 195, 196, 198.

Bessemer works, the success that has attended their development, 66.

Bethlehem Steel Company, 118, 199.

Bilbao, Spain, iron mines of, 257.

Blaine, James G., 118; and reciprocity, 287.

Bombay, engineering works in, 268.

Bookkeepers, the supply of capable, first-class men never equal to the demand, 10.

Booth, Charles, "Labour and Life of the People" by, 209.

Braddock, Pa., Carnegie Library at, 57, 62.

Brains and business ability, always a market for, in the business world, 11.

Bright, John, quoted on the value of a taste for reading, 63; and the Manchester School, 264, 272.

Buffalo, steel works at, 199, 200.

Burns, Robert, 169; his advice to a young man quoted, 78.

Business, the risks of, 112–113; definition of, 159–160; concentration on one line of business, 160–161; choice of a career, 160–162; the start in life and qualities that make it easy, 162–163; the road to success through zeal and ability, the rendering of exceptional service and genuine interest in the business, 163–168; the question of honesty a crucial one, 168–169; intelligence and judgment essential, 169; the difficulty of becoming an owner in business under the system of large corporations, 169–170; where to look for opportunities, 170–172; no line of business in which success is not attainable, 172; honest work, ability, and concentration the secret of success, 172–173; the value of prestige, 173; college graduates in business and their problems, 173–175; speculation to counterfeit of business, 175; percentage of business failures, 176; the young man who is determined to be a business man will not be thwarted, 176; stories illustrative of success, 177–181; value of a business career as compared with other pursuits, 181–185; the romantic side of, 185–186; the vanished prejudice against trade, 185–188; rewards of a business career, 188–189.

Business life, impracticality of a college education for, 64–65, 90–91, 93; the new idea of a practical education for, 65–70.

Business success, the road to: advantage of starting in the most subordinate positions, 1–2; importance of aiming high, 2; honesty, truthfulness, fair-dealing, and a clean life essential to genuine success, 2–3; indulgence in liquor the greatest danger to young men, 3, 98; the folly of speculation, 4–5, 98–99; the perilous habit of indorsing and the only conditions under which it should be done, 5–6, 99; doing not only what your job requires of you, but seizing opportunities to render services that attract attention to you and demonstrate capacity for higher positions, 7–8; making the firm's interest yours, 7–9; acting on your own initiative and breaking orders when you are sure of your ground, 8–9; you should know your own department better than the owner possibly can, 9; value of independence and making plain to the employer that you know your business, 9; saving money and the careful investment of it, 9–10; always room at the top for able and energetic young men, 10; the needlessness and the causes of failure, 10–11; the tests that a young man must pass in the minds of his superiors, 10–11; business men always on the lookout for ability and brains, 11, 71, 94; any legitimate business can be made a success of in the long run, 11–12, 172; the great secret of success is the exclusive concentration of your energy, thought and capital on the business in which you are engaged, 12, 100, 160–161; summary of the conditions of success, 12–13; the handicap of the young man born to riches, 13, 105–108; prospects of the young men of today to rise beyond the position of employes upon salaries, 87 ff.; a list of men who, starting as poor boys, rose to be the heads of manufacturing, business and financial houses of world-wide reputation, 88–89; avenues to success greater in number and easier of access today than ever before, 100.

Canada, trade of, with the United States, 151; self-government of, 153; treatment to be accorded her products in tariff legislation, 287–288.

Canonsburgh, Pa., natural gas at, 237.

Capital, impossibility of employers having personal acquaintance with employes under present-day industrial conditions and the consequent misunderstandings and lack of sympathy, 57–59; what the employer and employes can do to offset this, 59; interest of, and those of labour the same, 60; friction with labour over wages caused by their non-adjustment to selling prices and cost of materials, 60–61; this may be overcome by a sliding scale of wages, 61–62; more knowledge on the part of employers of conditions and qualities of employes would lessen the difficulties between the two, 70; its earnings at their lowest point, 73, 113; the small savings of millions of people, combined as bank deposits, a source of capital for financing great enterprises, 77–78; the partnership of capital with business ability and labour in industry, 241–243; see also Labour.

Career, the choice of a, 108–109, 160–162.

Carlisle, Secretary John G., 277, 290.

Carlyle, 108.

Carnegie, Andrew, sliding scale of wages introduced by, 73, footnote.

Carnegie Library at Braddock, Pa., 57, 62.

Carnegie, Phipps & Co., 198.

Carnegie Steel Company, the, 257, 260.

Carter, James C., description of the millionnaire by, 115.

Century Dictionary, definition of "business," 159.

Chamberlain, Joseph, 147.

Cheques, see Bank cheques.

Chemistry, value of a knowledge of, in business, 65.

Chicago, steel manufacturing in, 199.

Chicago University, 189.

China, shavings and chips from bar silver used as change in, 22; adoption of the silver standard by, 30; development of a capacity for manufacturing in, 149; growth of manufacturing in, 268.

Civilization, its material advantages primarily due to thrift, 77.

Clergymen, broadening of their field, 182.

Cleveland, President Grover, 123; views on the silver question, 52.

Cleveland, Ohio, 199.

Clothing, comparative cost of, in the United States and Great Britain, 211–214.

Coal, discovery of its value as fuel, 110; comparative cost of, in the United States and Great Britain, 215.

Coal fields of western Pennsylvania, 223–224.

Cobden, Richard, 264, 272.

Coinage, the "debasing" of, by governments, ancient and modern, 25–26.

Coining of metals into "money," origin of, 22–23.

Coins, edges of, milled to prevent swindling, 23; the reason for the use of copper and nickel for the smaller denominations, 24–25.

Coke, its production in western Pennsylvania, 223; the by-product coke oven in England, 271.

Coleman, William, early steel manufacturer, 193, 194.

College education, its unpracticality for a business life, 64–65, 90–91, 93; the true domain of a college education is apart from a business career, 93–94.

College graduates in business and their problems, 173–175.

Colorado, steel manufacturing in, 199.

Competition, freedom of, as it affects trusts, 135–136, 137, 140–141.

Concentration on your own business exclusively, the prime condition of success, 12, 100, 160–161.

Confederate States, worthlessness of bonds issued by, 27.

Confucius, 124.

Conneaut, Ohio, a shipping point of steel, 200.

Consolidations, the age of, 129.

Contemporary Review, the, 207, footnote.

Cooper, Peter, and the Cooper Institute in New York, 120.

Cooper, Hewitt & Co., steel manufacturers, 197.

Co-operative stores, 59.

Copper, its use in coins of the smaller denominations, 24–25.

Copper Trust, the, 132, 137.

Copyright law, the, 37–38.

Cornell, Ezra, 116.

Cornell University, 159, footnote, 189.

Corporations, disadvantages in their operation as compared with partnerships and the possibility of their disappearance, 94–95,

171–172; the good results that come of investment by its workmen in the shares of a corporation, 96–97.

Cost of living, at its low point, 73; in America and Great Britain compared, 207–219; the tariff and, 215–216.

Cotton manufactures, domestic and imported, in the United States, 213.

"Cowries" or shell money of Siam, 22.

Cromwell, Thomas, 189.

Curry Commercial College, Pittsburg, 1, footnote.

Dana, Charles A., estimate of rich men by, 115–116.

"Debasing" of a coinage by governments, 25–26.

Denmark, placed on the gold basis, 32.

Devonshire, the Duke of, 186.

Dewar, Professor, of Cambridge, theory of natural gas, 237–238.

Dickens, 68.

Disposition, as a business qualification, 11.

Docks, lack of adequate, in the United States, 259.

Dollar, the silver, a "debased" coin, 26.

"Don't put all your eggs in one basket," fallacy of the axiom, 12, 100, 160.

Dry-goods houses, the great, most successful when conducted by owners rather than salaried men, 95.

Economic questions, value of a study of, 67.

Economic world, unchanging laws of the, 129.

Edgar Thomson Steel Works, Braddock, Pa., 92.

Edison, Thomas A., 89.

Education, for the masses of the people, 64, 70; the impracticality of a collegiate, for business life, 64–65, 90–91, 93; the new idea of a practical education, 65; lack of, has prevented the recognition of labour, 65–66; technical schools and the specialist, 66–67; the workman who studies and observes has the greatest opportunity for promotion, 68–69; fruits of the polytechnic and scientific school in the manufacturing field, 91–92; must be adapted to the career in view, 92; the true domain of a college education is apart from a business career, 93–94; true education can be obtained outside of schools, 94.

Eliot, George, 68; quoted on how to get on in business, 97.

Emerson, Ralph Waldo, 13, 125.

Empire State Express, the, 111, 251.

Employers and employes, see Capital and Labour.

England, "debasing" of her coinage in the year 1300, 26; see also Great Britain.

Erie Canal, the, 200, 201.

Evarts, William M., 117.

Failure in business life, the needlessness and the causes of, 10–11.

Failures, business, percentage of, 176.

Fair-dealing, essential to business success, 2.

Farmers, interest of, in the maintenance of the fixity of value of money, 23–24; what the results of free coinage of silver would be to, 45–46, 50; further distribution of land among, and reduction in the size of farms, 85; importance of the fact that the small proprietor is triumphing over the large proprietor, 85–86; independence of, and freedom from fear of capital, 87.

Farmers' Alliance, the, favored free coinage of silver, 45.

"Fiat" money, 39.

Fiction, benefits from the reading of, 68.

Fireproofing of houses, 260.

Fitzjames, 176.

"Fixed charges," 58, 130.

Food, comparative cost of, in the United States and Great Britain, 209–210.

Ford, S. A., chemist, 235–236.

Foreign trade of nations, the future for, 150.

Forum, the, 277, footnote.

France, "debasing" of the coinage of, 26; repudiation of bonds issued during the Revolution, 27; closes her mints to silver, 32; amount of silver held by, 33–34; cheques and drafts less used in, than other countries, 48; number of millionnaires in, 116–117; silk manufacture in, 268; the leader in superfine textiles and women's apparel, 271.

Franklin, Benjamin, 123.

"Free coinage" of silver, see Silver question, the.

Free Trade, versus Protection, 145; the Manchester School and, 263, 264.

Freight cars, the use of steel for, 202.

Fuel, comparative cost of, in the United States and Great Britain, 215.

Garfield, James A., his doctrine that poverty is the richest heritage, 105.

Gas, natural, its discovery in western Pennsylvania, 226–227; the wells and the use of the gas, 227–233; theories regarding the distribution and generation of, 228–229, 236–238; question of the quantity of the supply, 232–233; value as a fuel, 233–235; analysis of, 235–236; waste of, 238, footnote.

General store, the earliest, 18–20.

Genius, 94.

George, Henry, "Progress and Poverty" by, and its fallacies, 85.

Germany, "debasing" of the coinage of, 26; only two millionaires in, 116; as a factor in the steel industry, 202, 257, 258, 273; fireproofing of houses in, 260; growth of manufacturing in, 268; the leader in chemical dyes, 271.

Girard College, 189.

Gladstone, quoted on wealth, 105; denunciation of an income tax, 286.

Glass, use of natural gas as fuel in the manufacture of, 233.

Gold, its use for many purposes, 21; limits to size of coins of, 24; confidence in the stability of its value the basis of the banking system and credit, 27–29; results of undermining confidence in the money basis of the nation, 29–30; the gold standard adopted by the principal nations of Europe and by the United States, 30–31; the "silver question" raised by the decline in value of silver while gold remained at about the same value, 31; European countries tighten their stand on the gold basis, 32–33; would be driven out of circulation by an unlimited coinage of silver, 41–42; foreign countries would drain the United States of its gold supply under free coinage of silver, 43–44, 46; arguments of the silver advo-

cates for its equality with gold and the reply to them, 46–50; prosperity of the United States under the gold standard, 50–51; the steady unchanging value of, 54; see also Silver question, the.

Goluchowsky, Austro - Hungarian foreign minister, 263.

Government bonds, instances of the repudiation of, 27.

Grant, Ulysses S., 123.

Great Britain, her reserve entirely in gold and her attitude towards silver, 33–35; recoinage of worn gold coins by, 43; tillers of small farms in, pass through agricultural depression better than proprietors of large farms, 85; increase of small incomes in, 113–114; millionnaires in, 117; policy regarding railways and other transportation routes, 139; railway freight charge in, compared with America, 140; American trade relations with, 145–155; protection in, 145; protection in the colonies, 148; her true interest in brotherly relations with America, 151, 152–155; the policy that holds the British Empire together, 154; the vanished prejudice against trade, 186; as a factor in the steel industry, 202, 203, 257, 258, 273; the cost of living in, compared with the United States, 207–219; income of workingmen, 209; wages in, compared with the United States, 218; her lead in ships and docking facilities, 258–259; her success in gaining command of the world's manufacturing and her profits, 264–267; repeal of the taxes on food in, 264, 265, 272; her monopoly of manufacturing being dissipated among the other nations, 267–273; antagonism raised by articles of foreign manufacture in, 269; the leader in machinery for textiles, 271.

Great Lakes, the, water transport on, for heavy materials, 201.

Greece, closes her mints to silver, 32.

Greek and Latin languages, knowledge of, of no practical use, 64.

Greeks, ancient, "debasing" of their coinage by, 26.

Greenbacks, 27.

Habits as a business qualification, 11.

Halifax, Chamber of Commerce, 145, footnote.

Harrisburg, Pa., 63; steel industry at, 200.

Harrison, President Benjamin, 123; views on the silver question, 51–52.

Harvard University, 189.

Hawthorne, 68.

Hector, 64.

Hoarding of wealth, 79, 80.

Holland, placed practically on the gold basis, 32.

Home, the desirableness of owning a, 112, 249.

Homestead, Pa., 198; Library Hall and Workingmen's Club at, presented by Mr. Carnegie, 243, footnote.

Homestead Steel Works, the, 92.

Honesty, essential to business success, 2, 11, 168–169.

Hotel rates, less in the United States than in Great Britain, 208.

Hotels, our great, most successful when conducted by owners rather than salaried men, 95.

Hudibras, 113.

Hussey, Wells & Co., early steel manufacturers, 194.

Illinois Steel Company, Chicago, 92.

Income tax, objections to an, 286.

Independence, personal, thrift a condition of, 79.

India, adoption of the silver standard by, 30; financial confusion in, caused by the decline in the value of silver, 31; development of a capacity for manufacturing in, 149; growth of manufacturing in, 268.

Indorsing, a perilous practice, 5–6, 99; the only conditions under which it is permissible, 6.

Industry, the change from small shops to great corporations and huge manufactories, 57–58, 117–118; the resultant loss of personal contact between employer and employe, 57–59; the partnership of capital, business ability and labour in, 241–243.

Initiative and independence, the value of, in business, 8–9.

Institutions, some ill results of the bequeathing of fortunes to, 119–120.

Intelligence necessary to business success, 169.

Intoxicants, see Liquor.

Inventions, suggested by workmen, indebtedness of manufacturing to, 68, 98; useless, the number of, 69.

Inventions and discoveries, passing of the day of the production of new wealth by, 111.

Investments, making secure, 9.

Ireland, "debasing" of the coinage in past times, 26.

Iron, see Steel.

Iron Age, the, 257, footnote.

Italy, closes her mints to silver, 32.

Japan, adoption of the silver standard by, 30; development of a capacity for manufacturing in, 149; growth of manufacturing in, 268.

Johnstown, Pa., 63.
Jones, Captain, 66.
Jones, Isaac, early steel manufacturer, 193, 194.
Judgment, an essential in business 169.
Junius, 249.

Krupps of Germany, the, 186–187.

Labour, the lack of personal contact between employer and employés because of changed industrial conditions, and the consequent misunderstandings and absence of sympathy, 57–59; what the employers and employés can do to offset the results of this, 59; interests of, one with those of capital, 60; friction with capital over wages occasioned by the difficulty of adjusting them to selling prices and cost of materials, 60–61; a sliding scale of wages to obviate this, 61–62; newspapers and trade journals as sources of information for, on trade conditions, 62; labour arrayed against itself, 62–63; the value of reading, 63–64, 66, 67–68; education for the masses of the people, 64, 70; lack of education has prevented the recognition of labour, 65–66; the acquirement of useful knowledge, 66–67; study and observation give ability to render the best service and open the way to promotion, 68–69; better knowledge on the part of workmen of economic laws would do much to obviate their troubles with employers, 70; importance of amusements, 70–71; the unsuccessful man has only himself to blame, 72; hours of labour, regulation of, 72–73; advantages of the workman of the present day over his predecessors, 73; labour divided into two great armies—the agricultural and the industrial, 85; the two diverse forces in operation—in the former further distribution of land, in the latter concentration of business in the hands of the few, 85, 86–87; the lowering of prices of manufactured articles made possible by this concentration, 86–87; benefits that come from investment by the workmen of a corporation in its shares, 96–97; its share of the profits of industry never so large, 113; the partnership of labour with capital and business ability in industry, 241–243; see also Capital.
Lackawanna Iron and Steel Works, 199, 200.
Land, the wider distribution of ownership of, 85.
Latin Union of Europe, the, 32.
Laws of the economic world remain unchanged through all vicissitudes, 129.
Lawyers, 182–183.
Lehigh University, 189.
"Levant silver thalers," 32.
Lincoln, Abraham, 123.
Liquor, the excessive use of, a bar to business success, 3, 98.
Living, cost of, at its low point, 73; comparative cost of, in the United States and Great Britain, 207–219; the tariff and, 215–216.
London, the financial centre of the world, 34.
Lorain, Ohio, 199.
Lowell, James Russell, on the value of Shakespeare, 64.

McCargo, David, Superintendent of the Alleghany Valley Railroad, 1.
McKinley Bill, the, 17, 51, 215, 284.
Macbeth, 137.

Machinery, the age of, 267, 270.

Macmillan's Magazine, 223, footnote.

"Making money" by government a delusion, 26–27.

Manchester (England) ship canal, the, 139.

Manchester School of English Radicals, the doctrines of, discussed and combatted, 263–273; their view of the destiny of nations and of Great Britain in particular, 265–266; their claim for the monopoly of manufacturing by Great Britain successfully challenged by other nations, 267–273; their work not to be belittled or forgotten, 272.

Manning, Secretary Daniel, attitude on the silver question, 52–53.

Manufactured articles, exports of, from the United States, 216–217.

Manufacturing, indebtedness of, to improvements and inventions suggested by workmen, 68, 97; startling fall in prices of manufactured articles, 86; the cheapening process made possible only by concentration of manufacturing in huge corporations and immense establishments, 86–87; rapid increase of capital of manufacturing and commercial concerns, 87; the spread of, among the nations, 267–273.

Mark Twain, 153.

Marriage, the desirableness of, 2, 248; a serious business, 109–110.

Marshall, Alfred, 265.

Maryland Steel Company, the, 200.

Mechanics, the advantage of scientific training for, 92–93.

Mechanics, value of a knowledge of, in business, 65.

Mellon, Judge, of Pittsburg, 20.

Mesaba Iron Mines, the, 273.

Mexico, continuance of the coinage of silver by, 38; development of a capacity for manufacturing in, 149; growth of manufacturing in, 268.

Midas, 9.

Middle class workers, the savings of, the basis of the safety and progress of our country, 79.

Mill, John Stuart, 145, 264.

Millionnaires, their services to society, 114–116; the number of, 116–117.

Mills Bill, the, 51.

Milton, 64.

Money, the A B C of: barter, or the exchange of one commodity for another, 18–20; the use of some staple commodity, as wheat or tobacco, as a medium of exchange, thus serving as "money," 20–21; whatever is used as "money" must have a stable value in itself and be limited in supply, 21–22; the adoption of certain metals for use as money as complying with these requirements, 21–22; the introduction of coinage of metals into "money" by government in response to the demand for it, to prevent cheating in the amount of metal, 22–23; the device of milling the edge of coins to prevent swindling, 23; the interest of the farmer and labourer in the maintenance of the fixity of value of money, 23–24, 29; the reason for the use of base metals in coins of the smaller denominations, 24–25; "token" money, 25, 32; "debasing" the coinage, 25–26, 38, 40, 41–42, 43; the delusion that a government can "make" money, 26–27; "greenbacks," 27; the use of cheques and drafts in lieu of money and the proportion of business done in this way in the

United States, 27–29; the clamour for "more money" in times of financial stress when the real remedy is restoration of confidence, 29–30; the "silver question," 30–54; *see also* Gold *and* Silver question.

Monongahela River, the, 224.

Monopoly, the impossibility of maintaining, 141.

Moreland, Mr., City Attorney of Pittsburg, 2.

Morris, Richard, 185.

Murraysville, Pa., natural gas in the region of, 226–229, 237.

Napoleon, 254.

Natural gas, *see* Gas, natural.

New York Central Railroad, its formation from thirteen short lines, 111, 131; number of stockholders, 112; its profits incite the building of the West Shore Railroad, 138.

New York City, as a shipping point for steel, 200, 201.

New York *Evening Post,* 193; attitude on the silver question, 51.

New York *Journal,* the, 241, footnote.

New York *Sun,* the, 106, 107, 119.

New York *Tribune,* the, 85, footnote.

Newspapers, as sources of information on trade conditions, 62.

Nickel, its use in coins of the smaller denominations, 24–25.

Nineteenth Century, the, 263, footnote.

North American Review, the, 17, footnote, 129, footnote.

North Star, the, 22.

Norway, placed on the gold basis, 32.

"Obey orders if you break owners," falsity of the axiom, 8–9.

Ohio River, the, water transport on, 201.

Oil and gas wells of western Pennsylvania, 224–238; the famous oil well of Storey Farm and its returns to its developers, 224–225; quantity and value of the oil produced by the region, 225–226; the natural gas wells, 226–238; *see also* Gas, natural.

Oil Creek, Pennsylvania, 226.

Park Brothers & Co., early steel manufacturers, 194.

Partnerships more successful than corporations, 94–95, 171–172.

Patent office in Washington, models of useless inventions in, 69.

Patriotism of race, the, 152, 153.

Peace and prosperity of nations, the need of measures for the promotion of, 150–152.

Pennsylvania, use of wheat in, as a medium of exchange, 20; early State assistance to the manufacture of steel, 193; percentage of steel manufactured in, 193; the coal fields of western, 223–224; the natural oil and gas wells of western, 224–238.

Pennsylvania Railroad, the, 65, 138, 223–224, 247, 249, 250; many stockholders of, 112; earnings of, 132.

Pensions, decline in government expenditure for, 277.

Petroleum, the early recognition of its importance by a few able business men, 132; *see also* Oil.

Philadelphia, as a shipping point for steel, 201.

Philippines, the, 152.

Phipps, Henry, 63.

Pitcairn, Robert, Superintendent of the Pennsylvania Railroad, 1–2.

Pitt, William, 121.

Pittsburg, 1, 199, 223, 226, 227, 228,

230, 232, 233, 236, 237, 238, 247, 249; workmen well paid at, 59; beginnings of the steel industry in, 194.

Polytechnic and scientific school, fruits of the, in the manufacturing field, 91–92.

Poor boy, the one who has the greatest chance of success in the business world, 13, 93, 105–108; the great inventions, discoveries and accomplishments have sprung from the ranks of the poor, 71–72; some of the men who have risen from poverty to power and wealth, 88–90.

Population, centre of, in the United States, 210.

Potter, Mr., of the Homestead Steel Works, 92.

Pratt, Charles, of Brooklyn, 120.

Pratt, Enoch, of Baltimore, 120.

Prestige, the value of, in business, 173.

Production, restriction of, and its results, 136, 137.

Professional man, career of, compared to that of the business man, 183–185.

Protection, the two kinds of, British and American, 145, 146; the protective tariff of the United States and its results, 146–150, 155; in the British colonies, 148; the only sound defence of a protective duty, 264; see also Tariff.

Railroads, policy of Great Britain regarding, 139; American people enjoy the cheapest railway transportation in the world, 140; railroads, past and present, 247–254; old-time railroading, 249–250; comparative speed of trains past and present, 250–251; the straight line in the future construction of railroads, 251; progress in the care and treatment of employes, 251–253; temperance of railroad employes, 253; the road to promotion clear, 254.

Railway pools and combinations, 138–140.

Reading, the value of, 63–64, 66, 67–68.

Real estate, the creation of fortunes by rise in the value of, 111.

Reciprocity, 287.

Rent, comparative rates of, in the United States and Great Britain, 211.

Respectability and purity of life essential to business success, 2–3.

Riches, the handicap of young men born to, 13, 105–108; see also Wealth.

Romans, "debasing" of their coinage by, 26.

Rosebery, Lord, 263.

Russia, practically closes her mints to silver, 32; no millionnaires in, 116; as a factor in the steel industry, 202; growth of manufacturing in, 268, 273.

Sage, Henry W., 116.

Salt Trust, the, 132.

Satisfactions, the highest reward in life, 57.

Savages, the absence of thrift among, 77, 78.

Savings, see Thrift.

Schoenhof, Mr., tariff-reform writer, quoted on clothing and dry goods costs, 214.

Schwab, Charles M., 92, 257.

Scotland, "debasing" of the coinage of, in past times, 26.

Scott, Thomas A., 247, 248, 250.

Scott, Sir Walter, 68.

Seneca oil, "the great Indian remedy," 225.

Serfdom, 73.

Service to mankind the noblest aspiration in life, 124, 125.

Shakespeare, 64, 71.

Sherman, Gen. William T., 123.

Siam, "cowries" or shell money of, 22.

Siemens-Martin open-hearth furnace in steel manufacture, 197–198.

Silks, comparative amounts of domestic production and imports in the United States, 213.

Silver, limits to size of coins of, 24; discovery of new deposits and improvements in machinery greatly increase its production, 31; varying values of, 31.

Silver question, the, 30–54; the more advanced nations formerly on a gold basis, the less advanced on a silver basis, and both equally well served under former conditions, 30–31; the value of silver in gold as fixed under the old order, 31; the equilibrium upset and the "silver question" raised by reason of the greatly increased production of silver and consequent lowering of its value as compared to gold, 31–32; financial confusion and disaster in countries on a silver basis and disturbances in those on a gold basis, 31–32; the moves of European nations to escape from the silver danger and rid themselves of the metal, 32–33; the United States the only more important nation to continue the coinage of silver, 33; failure of conferences for the fixing of a new gold value of silver because of the uncertainty of the future supply and consequently its value, 33; Great Britain's attitude towards silver, 33–35; silver legislation in the United States from 1878 onwards and its results, 35–54; the disgrace of a debased coinage, 26, 38, 40, 43; a double monetary standard impossible, 41; unlimited silver coinage would drive gold out of circulation, 41–42; danger of panic and financial revolution, 43; free coinage of silver proposed, 43; free coinage would result in the draining of the United States of gold by foreign countries, 43–44, 46; other ills that would follow upon free coinage, 45–46; arguments of the advocates of silver and the reply to them, 46–50; our prosperity under the gold standard, 50–51; opinions of trustworthy men on the free-silver-coinage idea, 51–53; government cannot permanently give to silver a higher value than it has intrinsically, 53; advice to the people regarding silver, 53; silver the tool of speculators, 54.

Singer, Nimick & Co., early steel manufacturers, 194.

Slavery, 37.

Smith, Adam, 130, 145–146, 147.

Sorghum, 286.

South American republics, adoption of the silver standard by, 30; troubled by fall in the value of silver, 31.

Spain, "debasing" of the coinage of, 26.

Specialist, this the age of the, 67.

Specialization the order of the day, 161.

Speculation, the dangers of, to the young business man, 4–5, 98–99; the counterfeit of business, 175.

Standard Oil Company, the, 132–134.

Steam engine, Watt's inception of the idea, 110.

Steamship and train, revolution in business created by, 264–265.

Steamships and docking facilities needed by the United States, 258–259.

Steel, and protection, 146; can be best produced in America, 146; steel manufacture in the United States in the nineteenth century, 193–204; first production of crucible steel in the United States, 194; the successful struggle with foreign steel, 194; the Bessemer process and lowered cost of steel, 195–196; the Siemens-Martin open-hearth furnace, 197–198; the age of Bessemer steel, 198; possible manufacture of steel in the South, 198–199; distribution of manufacture of, in the United States, and shipping points, 199–201; export of, 202–203; commanding position of the United States in the production of, 202–204; cost of, less in the United States than Great Britain, 214; use of natural gas as fuel in the production of, 233; comparison of the iron and steel industry at home and abroad, 257–260; consolidation of iron and steel interests, 259–260.

Steel rail manufacture, an illustration from, of the difficulty of adjusting wages to selling prices and the cost of materials, 60–61.

Steel-rail Trust, the, 132, 136.

Storey Farm, on Oil Creek, Pennsylvania, famous oil well at, 224–225.

Success, *see* Business success.

Sugar, and protection, 146–147, 148.

Sugar Trust, the, 137.

Swank, "Iron in All Ages," by, 193.

Sweden, placed on the gold basis, 32.

Switzerland, closes her mints to silver, 32; silk manufacture in, 258.

Syndicate, passing out of use of the term, 129.

Tarentum, Pa., natural gas in the region of, 229.

Tariff, the, and the cost of living, 215–216; what to do with the tariff, 277–292; luxuries should be taxed rather than necessities, 278–284; tariff for revenue, not protection, 278; higher taxes would not seriously lessen the use of luxuries, 280–281; the Wilson Bill, 281, 282–283, 284, 290; raw materials, 284; works of art, 284–285; raw materials for export manufacture, 285–286; raw sugar, molasses, etc., 286; reciprocity, 287; treatment of Canadian products, 287–288; tariff revision once in ten years sufficient, except in case of emergency, 288, 291; the attitude in which revision should be approached and facts to be considered, 288–290; summary of tariff recommendations, 290–291; *see also* Protection.

Technical schools, 66–67.

Temper, as a business qualification, 11.

Thackeray, 68.

Thomas, Sidney Gilchrist, 196.

Thomson, Edgar, 65, 249.

Thrift, saving money and the careful investment of it, 9–10; the higher aim of saving, 10; importance of saving, 59, 109, 249; the habit of, one of the greatest differences between the savage and the civilized man, 77; the small savings of millions of people, combined in bank deposits, furnishes the capital for great enterprises, 77–78; thrift the source of the material advantages of civilization, 78; it is a duty and at the same time the condition of personal independence, 78–79; savings of middle class workers the basis of safety and progress, 79; small savings sufficient, 79; great wealth not usually the result of savings in the ordinary sense of that word, 79–80; the duty to contribute to the general good of the community, 80.

Tobacco, use of, as a medium of exchange, in lieu of money, 20, 21.

"Token money," 25, 32; limited as legal tender, 25.

Trade, Anglo-American, 145–155.

Trade, the vanished prejudice against, 185–188.

Trade journals, as sources of information on business conditions, 62.

Travelling, cost of, less in the United States than in Great Britain, 208.

Travers, William R., 170.

Troy, N. Y., steel works at, 200.

Trusts, the genesis and development of, 129–132; their methods of operation and the question as to whether they are a danger to the nation, 134–136; free competition, its effects on, 135–136, 137, 140–141; how the trusts encompass their own defeat, 136, 137; railway pools and combinations, 138–140; their efforts to defeat economic laws in vain, 140–142; "Presidents' Agreements," 141–142.

Truthfulness, essential to business success, 2.

Ulysses, 64.

Union College, Schenectady, 105, footnote.

Union Iron Mills, the, 233.

United States, the "debasing" of the silver coinage, 26; bonds issued during the Civil War sold below par though afterwards redeemed at face value, 27; proportion of the business of, handled through bank cheques and drafts, 28; the only nation to continue the coinage of silver, 33; the only possible rival of Great Britain in finance, 34; silver legislation from 1878 onwards and its results, 35–54; the disgrace of a "debased" coinage, 26, 38, 40, 43; the country's gold supply would be driven out of circulation or drained by foreign countries under unlimited coinage of silver, 41–42, 43–44, 46; free coinage of silver proposed, 43; other ills that would follow free coinage, 45–46; arguments of the advocates of silver and the reply to them, 46–50; has more circulating medium than any European country except France, 48; prosperity of, under the gold standard, 50–51; the republic will survive the silver controversy, 53–54; millionnaires in, 117; has the cheapest railway transportation in the world, 140; trade relations with Great Britain, 145–155; protection and its results, 145, 146–150, 155; the desirableness of brotherly relations with Great Britain, 151, 152–155; prospect of the reuniting of the entire English-speaking race, 154–155; commanding position in the steel industry, 202–204; the cost of living in, compared with Great Britain, 207–219; centre of population of, 210; exports of manufactured articles, 216–217; higher wages and living conditions of American workingmen, 218–219; comparison of the iron and steel industry at home and abroad, 257–260; need of steamships and large docks, 258–259; leads in electrical appliances and machine tools, 271; government revenues and expenditures in 1895 and 1901, 277; the Golden Age of the Republic, 292.

Vanderbilt, Commodore, 111.
Villiers, Charles P., English politician, 264, 272.
Virginia, use of tobacco in, as a medium of exchange, 20.

Wage-earner, the, his interest in the maintenance of the fixity of value of money, 23–24; what the results of free coinage of silver would be to, 50; higher wages and living conditions of the American workman as compared to Great Britain, 218–219; see also Labour.
Wages, difficulty of keeping them adjusted to selling prices and cost of materials, 60–61; a sliding scale of, to meet these conditions, 61–62, 73; of English workingmen, 209.
Walker, Mr., of the Illinois Steel Co., 92.
Washington, George, 123, 185.
Washington, Pa., natural gas in the region of, 230.
Water power, use of, for generating electricity, 273.
Watered stocks, 129, 138.
Wealth, the true use for, 10; usually the result of enterprise and exceptional ability for organization, not of saving in the ordinary sense of that word, 79–80; the hoarding of wealth, 79,

80; riches to be regarded as a sacred trust to be administered for the good of others, 80, 120–121; how wealth is created and distributed, 110 ff.; is being more and more distributed among the many, 113–114; millionnaires and their services to society, 114–116; the number of millionnaires, 116–117; the duty of rich men in the use and distribution of their wealth, 118–121; the willing it to children a curse as a rule, 118–119; some ill results of gifts by will to public institutions, 119–120; the only noble use of surplus wealth, 120–121.
Welland Canal, the, 200.
West Shore Railroad, the, 138.
Wheat, use of, as a medium of exchange, in lieu of money, 20, 21.
Wheeling, West Virginia, 199.
Wilson Bill, the, 281, 282–283, 284, 285.
Windom, Secretary William, quoted on the results of the free coinage of silver, 46; his attitude on the silver question, 52–53.
Wire-rod Trust, the, 132.
Woollen goods, domestic production and imports in the United States compared, 212–213.
Workingmen, see Labour.

Yale University, 189.
Youghiogheny River, the, 224.
Young men, four classes of, and their aspirations in life, 121–125.
Youth's Companion, the, 77, footnote.